AF477788

Foreign Policy of India

West Asia and North Africa (WANA)

Foreign Policy of India

West Asia and North Africa (WANA)

Edited by

Faisal Ahmed
Associate Professor and Chairman,
International Business Area,
FORE School of Management, New Delhi

and

Suresh Kumar
Professor and Head,
Department of African Studies,
University of Delhi, Delhi

New Century Publications
New Delhi, India

Ｎｅｗ Ｃｅｎｔｕｒｙ Ｐｕｂｌｉｃａｔｉｏｎｓ
4800/24, Bharat Ram Road,
Ansari Road, Daryaganj,
New Delhi - 110 002 (India)

Tel.: 011-2324 7798, 4358 7398, 6539 6605
Fax: 011-4101 7798
E-mail: indiatax@vsnl.com • info@newcenturypublications.com
www.newcenturypublications.com

Editorial office:
LG–7, Aakarshan Bhawan,
4754-57/23, Ansari Road, Daryaganj,
New Delhi – 110 002

Tel.: 011-4356 0919

First Published: **2016**

ISBN: **978-81-7708-406-1**

Published by New Century Publications and printed at Salasar Imaging Systems, New Delhi.

Designs: Patch Creative Unit, New Delhi.

PRINTED IN INDIA

About the Book

West Asia and North Africa (WANA) region is socially vibrant, economically promising and geo-politically volatile. From the 1973 oil crisis to the Arab Spring and from the African Peer Review Mechanism (APRM) to the Islamic States of Iraq and the Levant (ISIL) crisis, the region has seen it all.

India's engagement with the region has been historically evolving. India shares strong cultural ties with the countries of the region. The trade and diplomatic relations between India and WANA countries are also witnessing an evolving trend. The Persian Gulf states have already been termed as our *extended neighbourhood*, while most of the African countries are becoming preferred destinations for Indian investments. In fact, India and WANA countries are mutually indispensable for each other in terms of natural resources, sea routes, maritime security, geo-economic co-operation, potential markets and participation in global value chains.

Given this backdrop, the present volume contains 11 well-researched papers, authored by experts in the field of India's foreign policy.

About the Editors

Dr. Faisal Ahmed is presently Associate Professor and Chairman of International Business Area at FORE School of Management, New Delhi. He has also taught at Indian Institute of Foreign Trade (IIFT), New Delhi as a visiting faculty.

He has been consultant to the United Nations Economic and Social Commission for Western Asia (UNESCWA) and also to The Associated Chambers of Commerce and Industry of India (ASSOCHAM). He has also led projects supported by the Ministry of Commerce and Industry and Ministry of External Affairs, Government of India. He has travelled extensively in India and abroad on academic assignments.

Dr. Ahmed has written several research papers, chapters in edited books and monographs. His articles have appeared in *The Financial Express*, *Business Standard* and *The Economic Times*.

Dr. Suresh Kumar is currently Professor and Head and Director (2015-18), Department of African Studies, University of Delhi, Delhi. He has travelled widely in East Asia, Europe, South America and Africa on research and teaching assignments. He is an active member of the Africa Committee of Confederation of Indian Industry (CII) and an executive member of Indo-Africa Chamber of Commerce in India (IACCI).

Dr. Kumar has published 125 articles in different books, journals and newspapers.

Contents

Contributors

Faisal Ahmed	Associate Professor and Chairman, International Business Area, FORE School of Management, New Delhi.
M. Absar Alam	Senior Fellow, Asian Institute of Transport Development (AITD), New Delhi.
Suresh Kumar	Professor and Head, Department of African Studies, University of Delhi, Delhi.
Paramjit	Department of Economics, Delhi School of Economics (DSE), University of Delhi, Delhi.
Rashmi Kapoor	Assistant Professor, Department of African Studies, University of Delhi, Delhi.
Prahlad Bairwa	Assistant Professor, Department of Political Science, Motilal Nehru College (Evening), University of Delhi, Delhi.
Halilu Babaji	Lecturer in the Department of General Studies, Federal Polytechnic, Bauchi, Nigeria.
Gajendra Singh	Assistant Professor, Department of History, Satyawati College, University of Delhi, Delhi.
Juhi Bhatnagar	Department of African Studies, University of Delhi, Delhi.
Alokka Dutta	Associate Professor, Department of Political Science, Bhagini Nivedita College, University of Delhi, Delhi.
Mahjabin Banu	Researcher on Expatriate Management and International Labour Migration Issues.

Harendra Kumar   Area Chairperson of Economics and International Business, Amity International Business School, Amity University, Noida.

Tanvi Tripathi   Department of African Studies, University of Delhi, Delhi.

Jaikhlong Basumatary   Centre for West Asian Studies, Jawaharlal Nehru University (JNU), New Delhi.

Vibha Gupta   Assistant Professor, Department of Commerce, Lakshmi Bai College, University of Delhi, Delhi.

Rachna Madaan   Ansal University, Gurgaon.

Jitender Bhandari   Associate Professor and Area Chair of Economics and International Business, Ansal University, Gurgaon.

P.S. Bisht   Professor, Department of Economics, Kumaun University, Nainital.

Christopher Zambakari   Peace Fellow and Doctor of Law and Policy, Rotary Centre for International Studies in Peace and Conflict Resolution, School of Political Science and International Studies, The University of Queensland, Brisbane, Australia.

Introduction

By

Faisal Ahmed and Suresh Kumar

West Asia and North Africa (WANA) region is socially vibrant, economically promising and geopolitically volatile. From the 1973 oil crisis to the Arab Spring and from the African Peer Review Mechanism (APRM) to the Islamic States of Iraq and the Levant (ISIL) crisis, the region has seen it all. The Arab Spring has reiterated the vast experiences of Indian democratic set up and accommodated it in their constitutions accordingly.

India's engagement with the region has been historically evolving. India shares a strong civilization and cultural ties with the countries of the region. The trade and diplomatic relations between India and WANA countries are also witnessing an evolving trend. The Persian Gulf states have already been termed as our *extended neighbourhood*, while most of the African countries are becoming preferred destinations for Indian investments. In fact, India and WANA countries are mutually indispensable for each other in terms of natural resources, sea routes, maritime security, geo-economic co-operation, potential markets and participation in global value chains.

WANA supplies more than 60 percent of India's oil and natural gas requirements. Saudi Arabia and Iraq are largest suppliers of oil to India. Egypt, Libya and Algeria are other important oil suppliers. Morocco, a major source of phosphate, caters to 85 percent of India's requirements.

There is a diaspora connect too. More than 7 million Indians live and work in the region and constitute all segments of labour, viz. unskilled, semi-skilled and skilled. India receives annual remittances of more than US$ 30 billion (i.e. almost half of the total remittances received by India) from this region.

The history of India and WANA has been shaped by the amalgamation of a rich culture and shared values. Indian culture carries the essence of the civilisation and cultural values of the

Arab, Persia and Turkey. India enjoys a vibrant and an indispensable relationship with each of them, and with the region at large. India and Arab cultures have been enriched by a prolific and mutually beneficial exchange of goods, services, people and ideas over the centuries. Similarly, Indian and North African relations were created and enriched in the writings of Ibn Batuta, a Moroccan traveller who voyaged to India in the 14th century. India and Egypt enjoy their historical ties right from the days of King Ashoka.

Basil Davidson rightly pointed out, "What the Phoenician-Berber connection had achieved in north-western Africa, the traders and mariners of Greek-ruled Egypt, southern Arabia, East Africa and India largely repeated the same in the last centuries before the Christian era. By then, the steady winds of the western half of the Indian Ocean, blowing back and forth between West India and East Africa in regular seasonal variation, were used by sailors who had learned how to trim their sails..." (Basil Davidson, 1966, "Africa in History: Themes and Outlines", revised edition, 1995, New York).

Geopolitically, India and WANA have been connected through land and sea routes right from the days of early history. Post-1990, the region has played a pivotal role in globalisation, particularly in the Indian sub-continent. It is noteworthy that 40 percent of world's hydrocarbon reserves, often referred to as a 'strategic good', come under the WANA region. This serves as both—an economic as well as a geopolitical pivot.

Given this backdrop and with an urge to contribute to the discourses on India and WANA, the present volume comprises of 11 well-researched papers, contributed by experts in the field.

Faisal Ahmed and M. Absar Alam in their paper, *India's Economic Engagement with the Maghreb,* explore the new paradigms under which India's economic relations with Maghreb may be shaped. They argue that the economic engagement between India and Maghreb is limited to mineral resources and hence other important areas for economic engagement need to be articulated. The authors have also used two different methods of statistical analysis to support their analysis of potential sectors for enhancing mutual cooperation.

Suresh Kumar, Paramjit, Rashmi Kapoor and Prahlad Bairwa in their paper, *India-Morocco Trade and Investment Opportunities,* explain India's trade and investment opportunities with Morocco in the changed international market economy, where one enjoys the investment and business freedom environment. According to the authors, normal procedures for conducting business have become streamlined in Morocco and foreign investment is generally welcome in different sectors. They suggest that the investment regime needs more transparency to spur dynamic growth.

In their paper, *Arab Spring: Arms Movement and Terrorism in Sub-Saharan Africa,* Halilu Babaji, Suresh Kumar, Gajendra Singh and Juhi Bhatnagar point out that Arab Spring has created political uncertainties in the entire North Africa, the Sahel and the Sub-Saharan Africa. The authors argue that this has benefited a good number of militia groups, thereby boosting both arms movement and terrorist groups. They further argue that the Arab awakening has unleashed unforeseen consequences on the Sub-Saharan Africa, following an inflow of weapons.

Alokka Dutta in her paper, *Revisiting India-West Asia Relations,* explains that the friendly and beneficial relations with the countries of West Asia have remained a key component of India's foreign policy on account of geopolitical, economic and strategic interests. It is in India's economic and strategic interest to maintain a positive relationship with all the West Asian countries. The author discusses various factors which are vital in explaining India's interests in West Asia.

In the paper, *Expatriation from India to UAE: Role of Recruitment Consultancies,* Mahjabin Banu maintains that India is a leading labour-sending country and receives a huge quantum of remittances. The author examines the process of expatriation from India to the United Arab Emirates with focus on the modes of recruitment and the role of overseas recruitment consultants. The study focuses on the modus operandi of overseas recruitment consultancies by interviewing consultants working with these consultancies in Delhi through a field study.

Harendra Kumar in his paper, *Changing Geo-political Situation in WANA and Policy Implications for India,* argues that the situation has become increasingly complicated in West Asia and North Africa because of continuous conflicts and unrest. He argues that the current crises in Iraq, Israel-Palestine, Libya, Syria and Egypt have continued to challenge the traditional alliances and actors in the region. The author further maintains that in the emerging order, there will be greater devolution of powers to the regional actors. The author has also elaborated on the cross-cutting issues in the region besides discussing India's strategic role therein.

Another paper on the theme of migration is titled *Indian Migrant Workers in the WANA Region* and is authored by Tanvi Tripathi. The author reflects upon the substantive engagement of Indians in the WANA region. The presence of Indian diaspora is highest in the Gulf region and negligible in other parts. The author highlights the understated yet massive contribution of Indian migrant workers to both India and the host countries and outlines specific conditions and problems faced by these workers.

Jaikhlong Basumatary in the paper, *Deterrence in Israeli Counter-Terrorism,* explains that since the establishment of the state of Israel, it has dealt with waves of terrorist activities on its borders. Consequently, Israel has adopted various counter-terrorism strategies to fend of terrorist attacks from its soil and to its citizens elsewhere. The author argues that, for Israel, terrorism is an extension of war and counter-terrorism is often and naturally discussed as a part of the 'war paradigm'. The author further maintains that Israel's exposure to terrorism is long-standing and intensive, and as a result there has been the doctrine of pre-emption and prompt retaliation against the terrorists to deter them from future attacks.

The paper, *India-Senegal Trade Relations,* by Paramjit, Suresh Kumar and Vibha Gupta explains and examines post-1990 financial sector reforms in Senegal. The authors argue that the scope and pace of reforms in Senegal were based on liberalization and balance sheet restructuring. They maintain that the human development in Senegal needs political assurance.

The paper titled, *Outward FDI from India to WANA Region*, by Rachna Madaan, Jitender Bhandari and P.S. Bisht examines the motives and types of OFDI and assesses its global trends and perspectives. The authors also trace the evolution of OFDI policy of India and FDI flows into Africa. The authors also outline the opportunities and success factors for Indian businesses in Africa.

Christopher Zambakari in his paper, *South Sudan and the East African Community (EAC)*, analyses the development challenges of the South Sudan which celebrated its second anniversary of Independence on July 9, 2013. The emergence of a new state in Africa with the secession of South Sudan from Sudan marked the most important development in the post-colonial period since South Africa transitioned to a democracy in 1994. This study seeks to make a contribution to the ongoing debate on nation and state building, economic development and the East African Community's attempt to build a monetary union followed by a political federation.

We take this opportunity to place on record our deep gratitude to all the contributors to this volume for their scholarly research papers and co-operation. The volume, it is hoped, would contribute immensely to the existing body of literature on the subject.

New Delhi   **Faisal Ahmed**
                                                     Suresh Kumar

1

India's Economic Engagement with the Maghreb

Faisal Ahmed and M. Absar Alam

Introduction

The Maghreb, comprising of the Arab countries in North Africa, is a region situated along the southern shore of the Mediterranean Sea. The region primarily consists of countries like Morocco, Algeria, Tunisia, Libya and Mauritania. These countries are the western most located Arab nations and, therefore, collectively referred to as Maghreb. Historically, for the Arabs, Maghreb has been the gateway to Europe in the western side of the Mediterranean Sea. During their respective colonial periods, these countries were mostly under French colonial regimes that significantly impacted the trade routes and pattern of their trade and commerce with the outside world. The natural course of trade of Maghreb, therefore, gradually changed from West Asian countries to Europe. Notably, during the pre-colonial period, Maghreb had been trading with West Asian countries. This change in trade pattern and structure is still evident.

The colonial era also had other significant impact on the Maghreb's geo-economic diplomacy as a whole. The Arabs of Maghreb were western colonies and therefore, they fought with Arabs under Ottoman Empire during World War I. Maghreb was among the region that suffered highly during the World War I. This subsequently caused gradual movement towards independence. During the post-colonial period in Asia and Africa, Maghreb also stood against their colonial masters. Maghreb countries, along with other colonies entered into the

Non-Aligned Movement (NAM). This movement brought countries of Maghreb and India together at various international forums. As a result, India's relations, particularly diplomatic engagements with the Maghreb, have been evolutionary in nature. It was duly shaped with the idea of NAM. India's external as well as trade relations with Maghreb, have traditionally been cordial and progressive.

There are two important periods in which India's economic and geopolitical relations with Maghreb may be examined. The first period starts with India's first prime minister, Jawaharlal Nehru's call for non-alignment at the global level and mixed economic system at the national level. These two factors progressively engaged India with the Maghreb. However, particularly during the early 1990s, India's economic and diplomatic policies experienced a shift towards the Western bloc through economic instruments like liberalisation and globalisation. This was the second period that still continues. The present period of economic reforms and economic liberalisation in India is the extension of the second period which also had considerable impact on its engagement with Maghreb significantly.

The process of economic liberalisation is a ubiquitous phenomenon in the world, which spreads from Asia to Africa and from Africa to Latin America. In such a scenario, bilateral relations with countries are based on two major factors i.e. economic and geographical. These two factors have been shaping India's international engagement as well. In this scenario, India's relations with Maghreb will also be experiencing such transformations.

Another factor that will design India's future engagement with Maghreb is the political transformation in Maghreb countries. The event of mass level agitation demanding democracy in Maghreb has critical importance in designing Maghreb's economic relations with the rest of the world. As the largest democracy in the world, India's engagement with these transition economies in the world not only strengthens the cause of democratic values but also the democratic institutions therein. As these countries transform, their economic policies will also experience transition creating opportunities for deeper economic engagements. In fact, Maghreb is likely to play a pivotal role in India's urge for market diversification.

Presently, the economic engagement between India and countries of Maghreb is based on bilateral initiatives and there is no formal trade agreement between India and Maghreb as a bloc. This is possibly also because of a formal framework for regional economic cooperation within the Maghreb region i.e. the Arab Maghreb Union is largely inactive owing to disagreements between Morocco and Algeria on various issues including the issue of Western Sahara. However, India has also maintained good relations with the League of Arab States, which constitutes the Maghreb countries. More recently, the limited economic engagement between India and Maghreb is further affected by conflicts in Libya.

Despite such challenges, the trade between India and North Africa (which includes Maghreb as well as Egypt) has been flourishing. India's imports from North Africa grew at a rate of 42.7 percent per annum during the period 2005-2011, from US$ 863 million in 2005 to US$ 7.2 billion in 2011. North Africa in fact, accounted for over 18 percent of imports from Africa to India. This statistics also includes Egypt. As per the recent trends, Egypt, Algeria and Morocco have seen a high positive growth in exports to India. [1]

Maghreb is an important region endowed with mineral resources and has been critical in meeting India's mineral requirements. This region is endowed with phosphate, crude oil, natural gas and chemicals. Morocco is the only non-oil exporting country in the region with a relatively diversified export basket, albeit concentrated in chemicals, fertilisers and phosphates. All other countries in the region are suppliers of crude oil and natural gas. India is one of the major markets for phosphate and its derivatives. Other main items that India imports from Maghreb are metallic ores and metal scrap, semi-finished products and inorganic chemicals.

India's economic engagement with Maghreb has a multi-dimensional approach. India has traditionally been engaged with Maghreb bilaterally as well as multilaterally such as under the framework of the World Trade Organization (WTO). In addition, India's broad engagement with Africa has also been shaping its economic engagement with the Maghreb. The top six African countries account for 90 percent of the total exports from Africa to India. Algeria and Morocco fall under these top six African countries. [2]

With the above background, this chapter tries to explore the new paradigms under which India's economic relations with Maghreb may be shaped and also examines such factors. Economic engagement between India and Maghreb is limited to mineral resources. This chapter examines some other important areas for economic engagement of India with the Maghreb. The chapter begins its discussion with the current state of politics in the region. This discussion is followed by the present macroeconomic situation and the pattern of trade diversification in Maghreb followed by the analysis of bilateral trade between India and the Maghreb.

Present Political and Governance Scenario

Since the advent of Arab Spring and North Atlantic Treaty Organisation (NATO)'s unilateral war against Gaddafi regime in Libya, the region has mixed experience of both political and economic stability. A major country which connects Maghreb with Arabs and East, i.e. Egypt has also been in political turmoil. The impact of political instability is evident upon the economic indicators of the region. Macroeconomic fundamentals of Maghreb have not been attractive for emerging markets. Most of the countries are still not providing economic and political security to investors leading to unsafe business environment. Maghreb's business environment has been deteriorating.

There is always hope amidst conflicts. The example is

Tunisia and Algeria. Presidential elections have been held recently in Algeria and Tunisia. These two countries elected their new presidents. Preferably, these two countries elected liberal democratic ideologues. The agenda will be both political and economic reforms, as any further political instability will create difficult conditions for regional economic growth in North Africa in general and the Maghreb in particular.

A stable North Africa will also have profound and significant impact on Western Africa. Several West African countries (bound together by the regional congregation called ECOWAS) [3] and Maghreb, share common borders. A stable Maghreb with flourishing democratic institutions has the potential to help achieve stability in countries of West Africa such as Mali, Nigeria and Chad and would also benefit the process of pan-African integration. [4] In addition, stabilized Maghreb has direct impact on the economic prosperity of developing and poor countries of Middle East and North African regions.

Corruption is one of the key issues when a country's political situation is not stable. A corrupt institution leads to an increase in the number of rent-seeking economies. This also hinders economic activities in many ways. This is still evident in some of the countries of the region wherein increasing activities of rent-seeking economies have been taking place. Table 1.1 presents the current ranking of Maghreb countries over corruption perception index and scores for last three year period.

Table 1.1: Score and Rank of Maghreb Countries on Corruption Perception Index

Country	Score			Rank
	2012	2013	2014	2014
Algeria	34	36	36	100
Libya	18	15	21	166
Morocco	39	37	37	80
Mauritania	30	30	31	124
Tunisia	40	41	41	79

Source: Transparency International, 2014.

In 2014, scores were getting higher as compared to previous years, suggesting some improvements taking place in these countries. These scores are measured out of 100 wherein 0 is the worst and 100 is the best score. The country which has the least corruption is Denmark, getting a score of 92 out of 100. India also has a limited performance on account of corruption ranked 85th out of 175 countries in 2014. Doing business in Maghreb becomes tough due to these factors.

Doing Business in the Maghreb

Political instability causes obstacles to business and commerce. Doing business is complicated and risky in the Maghreb region. The World Bank suggests that an overall ranking of doing business in Maghreb is not favourable and it has declined for each of these countries. In case of Algeria, there is an improvement in getting electricity. In case of Morocco, three indicators of doing business have shown an overall improvement in 2015 against 2014. These indicators include construction permits, registering property and trading across the border. Amidst conflicts, Tunisia and Libya are yet to set changes on the parameters set out in 'Doing Business Report' co-published by the World Bank and its constituent International Finance Corporation. The improvement in business environment is still limited in Maghreb. Table 1.2 shows the ranking of Maghreb countries on various indicators of doing business.

The indicators are quite evident from Table 1.2. Overall, doing business is ranked under 'Ease of Doing Business'. Except Tunisia and Morocco, all other countries in the Maghreb are worst performers on 'Ease of Doing Business'. Only Mauritania has ranked 77th and 66th while dealing with construction permit and registering property respectively. The higher the level of rank on account of other indicators particularly those related to 'trading across border', the further it indicates the restrictive regimes related to trade and trade facilitation. The Table further outlines that it is hard to do business in countries like Algeria,

Mauritania and Tunisia.

Table 1.2: Ranking of Maghreb Countries Regards Indicators of 'Doing Business 2014' (Among 189 Countries)

Economy	Ease of Doing Business Rank	Starting a Business	Dealing with Construction Permits	Getting Electricity
Tunisia	60	100	85	38
Morocco	71	54	54	91
Algeria	154	141	127	147
Mauritania	176	164	77	169
Libya	188	144	189	65

Contd...

Economy	Registering Property	Resolving Insolvency	Getting Credit	Protecting Minority Investors
Tunisia	71	54	116	78
Morocco	115	113	104	122
Algeria	157	97	171	132
Mauritania	66	189	171	166
Libya	189	189	185	188

Contd...

Economy	Paying Taxes	Trading Across Borders	Enforcing Contracts
Tunisia	82	50	78
Morocco	66	31	81
Algeria	176	131	120
Mauritania	187	151	86
Libya	157	139	126

Source: Doing Business Report, 2014, The World Bank.

The country-wise reforms and reformation in policies and infrastructure related to doing business indicates that Algeria has made improvements in infrastructure at Algiers port in 2014.

Earlier in 2013, Algeria had improved the regime of 'access to credit' through the elimination of minimum threshold for loans. [5] On account of 'trading across border', Morocco has reduced the number of documents required for the trade procedure in 2014.

Earlier in 2013, Morocco reduced registration fees for 'starting a business' and also encouraged using electronic medium for paying taxes. Mauritania has also improved on account of 'starting a business' and 'access to credit' in 2014. The country created a one-stop shop and eliminated the publication requirement and the fee to obtain a tax identification number.

Similarly, it improved its credit information system by lowering the minimum threshold for loans which was to be included in the registry's database. [6]

Tunisia on the other hand, made 'trading across border' more complicated owing to deteriorating port infrastructure. However, the country has made tax paying less costly to tax payers by reducing corporate income tax rates. Of course, this indicates that there is a need for radical changes in economic policies in these countries. This can only be achieved through a stable government which can initiate policies and expedite the economic reforms process which is likely to be the future.

Macroeconomic Performance

As per the World Economic Outlook published by the International Monetary Fund (IMF), economic performance of Maghreb has deteriorated from the 2005 and 2006 levels. The average GDP performance was 6 percent in 2005 and 6.6 percent in 2006 in the region.

This economic progress, as a result of repeated conflicts in the region, declined to a negative growth rate of more than 10 percent in 2011, which is gradually recovering following the aftermath of Arab Spring. IMF projects that the average annual growth in GDP of Maghreb countries is likely to be about 7 percent in 2014 and more than 7.5 percent in 2016. A positive sign in economic indicators is likely to be a catalyst for trade and investment opportunities in the region with the rest of the world.

Table 1.3 indicates major macroeconomic indicators of the Maghreb. The Table indicates projections from 2014. The projections for 2015 and 2016 have been updated which indicates that in the near future, Maghreb is going to offer more business, subject to political stability. Maghreb as a whole has, therefore, great potential to attract investments and also business, particularly for trade in goods.

Table 1.3: Macroeconomic Indicators of Maghreb (Average of Growth of 5 Countries)

(in percent)

Indicators	2005	2006	2007	2008	2009	2010
GDP Growth	6.0	6.6	3.9	3.7	1.5	3.8
Maghreb Share in World GDP (PPP based)	1.1	1.1	1.1	1.1	1.1	1.1
Export Growth (Goods)	4.1	9.9	6.3	0.3	-9.0	8.8
Import Growth (Goods)	7.0	0.8	17.1	12.9	7.0	1.4

Contd...

Indicators	2011	2012	2013	2014	2015	2016
GDP Growth	-10.4	24.2	0.5	-0.6	6.8	7.7
Maghreb Share in World GDP (PPP based)	1.0	1.0	1.0	1.0	1.0	1.0
Export Growth (Goods)	-13.2	47.8	-5.5	-8.4	10.2	15.1
Import Growth (Goods)	-6.5	34.7	11.0	2.0	6.5	5.6

Source: World Economic Outlook, IMF.

Table 1.3 indicates the macroeconomic performance as well as international trade performance of goods for Maghreb region. This data includes the following countries, namely Algeria, Libya, Morocco, Tunisia and Mauritania in Maghreb. The data clearly depicts that the region had been growing at a growth rate of more than 6 percent annually during 2005 and 2007 and that it suddenly declined in 2007 and later became negative in 2011. This remained the same in 2014, although it recovered from the turmoil in 2012. IMF projects the GDP growth rate of Maghreb for 2015 at 6.8 percent. This would eventually enhance the international trading position of the region. The trend of export and import of goods has also been fluctuating in the region. Instability in political situation contributed to this fluctuation.

In addition to the performance of GDP and trade, it would be important to examine the private sector participation in Maghreb countries. Only one indicator has been selected to examine the role of private sector in the economy. Domestic credit to private sector as a percent of GDP is presented in Table 1.4. This indicator varies greatly between the countries. On the one hand, Morocco and Tunisia have more than 70 percent of GDP as credit to the private sector; this is limited in case of Algeria, Libya and Mauritania. This also suggests that financial sector openness in these countries is limited. Restrictions are imposed on foreign currency purchases. [7] A large number of commercial banks are state-owned. Commercial lending to private sector, therefore, is subject to financial reforms. In the next section, the reforms agenda would be discussed to assess the economic competence of the region.

Table 1.4: Domestic Credit to Private Sector

(percent of GDP)

Country	1990	2000	2005	2010	2011	2012	2013
Algeria	56.14	5.95	11.85	15.19	13.76	14.33	16.45
Libya	30.36	23.06	7.67	9.30	19.61	10.52	13.90
Mauritania	35.37	N A	28.37	27.67	25.87	29.21	N A
Morocco	14.34	50.73	46.02	68.54	71.86	73.31	70.07
Tunisia	55.08	53.40	55.52	65.14	72.54	72.09	71.93

Source: World Development Indicators, The World Bank.

Economic Competence Factors in Maghreb

New governments in the region after the Arab Spring have mainly focused on economic reforms in order to boost economic recovery of the region. This in totality, would bring economic competence in the region. However, the programmes and policies for structural changes in economic sectors need to be examined carefully. Considering the call for economic transformation in Tunisia and Algeria, there are several factors which would transform the region as a whole.

The first factor is economic recovery of the region. The region is going to open the doors of greater opportunities as a market, for developing world like India and China. This suggests that the market of Maghreb has been expanding. Domestic consumption is likely to increase in the event of an increase in overall income of the countries. In 2008, the average final consumption expenditure in Maghreb was 61 percent of the GDP for all the five countries. The recent data indicates an increase of 10 percent in this indicator (excluding Libya). In 2013, the average of financial consumption expenditure as percentage of GDP of Algeria, Morocco, Mauritania and Tunisia was 70 percent. [8] The disposable income of the population in Maghreb has already been increasing and is likely to surge further.

The second important factor which is likely to shape economic engagement of the region with the rest of the world is its traditional mineral endowments. At present, crude oil is an attractive sector for investment in the region. These investments are particularly from Europe. In the past, foreign investment inflows increased from US$ 3 billion per year during the early 2000s to US$ 12.3 billion in only one year i.e. 2008. In the year 2008, foreign direct investment (FDI) was recorded to be 3 percent of the GDP in Maghreb which was lower than the other emerging market economies. This share further went down to less than 2 percent of the GDP with US$ 6.5 billion FDI flows in 2011. [9] The expected reforms in the regulation of mineral extractions will further attract investment flows in the Maghreb region in the future.

The investments are mostly inflowing from Europe which accounted for 80 percent of foreign investment inflows in Tunisia and 60 percent in Morocco. [10] The expansion of market in the Maghreb will attract investments from other countries as well. Since the European Union (EU) has bilateral agreements with countries like Morocco, Algeria and Tunisia, it becomes easy for them to make direct investments in these countries. The expansion of the economy would therefore, need expansion of bilateral trade and investment agreements of this region with the global South in order to take advantage of the changing economic dynamics at the multilateral level.

The third important factor is the locational advantage of the Maghreb. It is situated next to the world's largest common market i.e. the EU. It enjoys its colonial lineages with the EU. Its population is young, educated and striving for better economic life. Thus, the market with young population located near EU has many reasons to be engaged with. In 2013, the population of 0-14 year age group accounted for 30 percent of the total population of the Maghreb, as against the global average of 26 percent.

The fourth factor is the gradual globalisation of the region. Morocco, Tunisia and Mauritania are WTO members. Algeria and Libya have observer status and a significant progress has been made in case of Algeria towards acceding to the WTO membership. As a whole, Maghreb is moving towards multilateralism and progressing to adopt liberal regimes in its economic structure. The gradual shift towards liberal economic policy will attract significant reforms agenda leading to the creation of a market with abundant natural resources. Algeria, Tunisia and Morocco have free trade agreements (FTAs) in goods with the EU.

With a relatively small market size, countries in the Maghreb are showing greater trade openness over the period of time. Maghreb countries seem to be open to trade as all the countries have a higher share of trade in their GDPs. This is because of the export dependence of these countries. Almost all the countries, except Algeria, have more than 80 percent share of trade in the GDP. The share of services in GDP is still low and hovered around 17.12 percent in 2013. [11] The share of imports of goods and services in Maghreb was more than 50 percent in 2013. Maghreb's share of non-oil exports in GDP remains lower than other regions. The gradual inclusion of Maghreb in and its increasing participation in the multilateral trading system would create opportunities for diversification of its trade basket.

Finally, it is the service sector of Maghreb countries which offers the region a major opportunity for economic engagement with the rest of the world. In Maghreb, the services sector is playing a vital role in the economy. In case of Algeria, the sector contributed more than 38 percent to GDP and was placed next to the industrial sector which contributed 52 percent to the GDP. In case of Libya, the sector contributed more than 38 percent to the GDP (as of 2013) and more than 49 percent to the GDP in Morocco. In case of Tunisia, this sector emerged as the top contributor to GDP; whereas, in Mauritania, 48 percent contribution to GDP was from the services sector in 2012. [12] The economic structure thus entails that most of the Maghreb countries are likely to offer services sector as an important area for both trade and investments. On the other hand, industrial sector is the main activity in the Maghreb region (except that for Mauritania). These two sectors are likely to support the economic progress of the region.

In terms of social indices, as per the Human Development Report, 2013 published by the United Nations Development Programme (UNDP), among the Maghreb countries, Libya is the highest ranked nation with 64th position and with a human development index (HDI) of 0.769. Libya is followed by Algeria which is ranked 93rd. Algeria's HDI is 0.626. Similarly, Tunisia also had a HDI of 0.722 and was ranked 94th among the 186 countries. On the other hand, Morocco and Mauritania were ranked 130th and 155th respectively with their respective HDIs of 0.591 and 0.467. The per capita income is high in Maghreb, but it has not translated well into its social sector development. [13]

North Africa's growing population of 170 million,

accounting for more than 15 percent of the African total, and its total GDP of US$ 550 billion (over one-third of the African total), makes it an attractive consumer export market for India.

Thus, with the above economic opportunities offered by the Maghreb, it seems that there are potential opportunities for both intra-regional and inter-regional economic engagements of Maghreb. The commercial relationship between countries of Maghreb needs to be deepened to achieve a high level of intra-regional trade. On the other hand, an analysis further indicates that the total trade of Maghreb would expand by another US$ 4 billion to US$ 5 billion (3 to 4.5 percent) if the EU and the United States were to separately establish FTAs with the Maghreb countries and by nearly US$ 9 billion (approximately 8 percent) if both were to do so. [14]

Trade Diversification and Concentration in Maghreb
The concentration of exports to fewer commodities from Maghreb remains high as compared to other regional groupings in the world. This can be understood by the fact that the average number of products exported by Maghreb countries in 2004 was 100 which was half the number of products exported by other regions. Since then, attempts have been made to diversify trade. This will enhance the possibilities for Maghreb to increase its trade basket with more number of products being exported. The export basket of Maghreb consisted of 252 products in 2011 as against 260 for the NAFTA countries. This indicates that trade diversification has been followed by Maghreb at a rapid pace which is, for all the good reasons, is an important agenda. While analysing country-wise diversification of export basket, each country has been performing differently.

Table 1.5 brings out trade diversification and concentration indices of both exports and imports in Maghreb countries as per the UNCTAD. A comparative analysis is shown for the period 1995 and 2013. Over the period of almost 20 years, concentration of exports has increased in Algeria, Libya and Tunisia.

Table 1.5: Market Concentration and Diversification Index

Country	Exports			Imports		
	1995			1995		
	Number of Products	CI	DI	Number of Products	CI	DI
Algeria	99	0.52	0.83	231	0.08	0.45
Libya	77	0.76	0.82	225	0.06	0.39
Mauritania	38	0.53	0.83	184	0.09	0.48
Morocco	197	0.17	0.73	237	0.13	0.44
Tunisia	193	0.21	0.68	242	0.08	0.40
Country	2013			2013		
	Number of Products	CI	DI	Number of Products	CI	DI
Algeria	95	0.54	0.74	237	0.09	0.45
Libya	129	0.80	0.79	249	0.09	0.44
Mauritania	78	0.48	0.83	218	0.16	0.56
Morocco	237	0.16	0.67	250	0.11	0.32
Tunisia	218	0.54	0.74	244	0.08	0.37

CI = Concentration Index; DI = Diversification Index
Source: UNCTAD.

On the other hand, diversification of exports reduced in these countries. Similarly, in case of imports, diversification index has been increasing in these countries. In order to achieve further diversification in trade basket of Maghreb, particularly exports, countries are likely to explore new policies. Until now, these countries are having limited free trade agreements with other nations and regions.

Countries in the Maghreb are diversified in their respective natural resources. This difference in the natural endowments presents a major opportunity for these countries to cooperate with each other. This also presents a base for diversification of their trade baskets as well as trade markets. The differences in natural resources also define different export potential of these countries. On the one hand, Libya and Algeria are the two countries depending on oil exports while on the other hand, Morocco and Tunisia are able to export more of manufacturing products.

Trade in Maghreb has been experiencing limited growth owing to restrictive regime in terms of applied tariff levels (World Bank, 2010). [15] Mauritania, Morocco and Tunisia are members of the WTO. [16] The simple average most favoured nation (MFN) applied rates [17] in these countries on agricultural products were: 15.5 percent in Tunisia (year 2012) and 40.7 percent in Morocco (year 2012). [18] High level protectionism in Maghreb resulted in lowering of competitiveness on those products which are used as inputs for final production. At present, Algeria, Tunisia and Morocco have been aiming at diversifying domestic sectors in order to stabilise their respective economy by adopting economic reforms agenda.

An important development in case of Algeria is its changing direction of imports. China has replaced France as the largest source of imports for Algeria in 2013. China accounted for 12 percent of Algeria's total imports in 2013 from the level of 2 percent in 2001; whereas, France dropped to 11 percent in 2013 from the level of 24 percent share in Algeria's imports in 2001. However, such changes in case of other countries are limited.

Dynamics of India's Trade with the Maghreb

India's present economic engagement with Maghreb has primarily been bilateral. India's recent exports to Maghreb have been increasing over the period of time. During 2005 and 2010 (5-year time period), the total exports from India to Maghreb increased more than two-folds. This increase has continued even during 2010 and 2013. In the year 2011, the annual growth rate reduced to about 2 percent but during the two subsequent years, India's exports to Maghreb rebounded and experienced a growth of 26.7 percent in 2012 and 17.5 percent in 2013 over their respective previous years.

Imports from Maghreb countries to India fluctuated during the same period. The total imports from Maghreb decreased from US$ 4,055 million in 2012 to US$ 2953 million in 2013. This decrease was more than 27 percent when compared with the previous years.

The commodity-wise analysis of India's trade with these countries indicates that more than 97 percent of India's imports from Algeria were mineral products during the last few years. Algeria's exports to India were concentrated to petroleum oil and gas. There is a diversified export pattern from India to Algeria but limited to commodities like automobiles and parts, pharmaceuticals, cereals, chemicals, etc. India's imports from Libya are also limited to mineral products, particularly crude oil. In the recent years, the share of these products decreased to 78 percent from more than 95 percent during 2013, yet Libya has been an important source of crude oil for India. In case of Mauritania, negligible imports have been reported with concentration on commodities like ores and slag, iron and steel and aluminium products, etc. India exports cotton, pharmaceuticals and cereals, etc. to Mauritania.

Morocco has been an exporter of inorganic chemicals and minerals resources like phosphates, calcium, aluminium, etc. These products accounted for more than 95 percent of India's total imports from Morocco in 2014. On the other hand, India's exports have well been diversified, spreading across sectors like machinery, automobiles, cotton, iron and steel and chemicals including pharmaceuticals, etc. Similar is the case of Tunisia, where India's imports from the country is limited to mineral resources like phosphates and phosphoric acids, accounting for more than 80 percent of imports from Tunisia in 2014. The exports from India to Tunisia is diversified among various products such as automobiles, cotton, plastics, tea and coffee, electronic products, chemicals including pharmaceuticals, etc. Considering Maghreb as a whole, India's trade basket with the region need to be further diversified.

Analysis of Key Sectors

In this section, two indices revealed comparative advantage (RCA) index and intra-industry trade (IIT) index have been calculated by the authors; and based on that the potential sectors of India's bilateral trade with the Maghreb have been identified. To simplify the analysis, Maghreb as a whole is taken. The RCA index which is a ratio of two shares i.e. percentage share of a commodity exports in a country's total exports and percentage share of the same commodity's export in world's total export in a given year. Mathematically, it is expressed as in equation (1):

$$RCA_{ij} = (X_{ij}/X_{wj})/(X_i/X_w) \tag{1}$$

Where, X_{ij} = i_{th} country's export of commodity j; X_{wj} = world exports of commodity j; X_i = total exports of country i; and, X_w = total world exports.

An RCA index value of more than 1 reveals that the country has a comparative advantage. The data for calculation of RCA has been taken from Trade Map database of International Trade Centre, Geneva. This ratio translates into comparative advantage of a country in exporting a commodity at the global level. As per the RCA statistics and calculations for 2013, India and the Maghreb have a potential to complement each other in trade. India has a higher RCA index in commodities like vegetables, cotton, carpets, coffee, tea, spices, textile products, silk and edible oils, meat and pharmaceuticals, etc. On the other hand, Maghreb has higher RCA indices in sectors like fertilisers, minerals, sulphur, chemicals, crude oil, etc.

Trade has multiple dimensions. The examination of top sectors of trade between India and Maghreb indicates that the Maghreb exports to India concentrates on commodities like crude oil, non-crude oil and petroleum gases, and inorganic chemicals such as phosphates used in fertilizers, etc. These products account for more than 95 percent of exports from Maghreb to India. In case of India's export to Maghreb, automobiles, machineries, electronic and electrical equipments, petroleum products (finished), meat, organic chemicals like pharmaceuticals and vegetables account for more than 60 percent of India's total exports to Maghreb.

As of now, India is able to diversify its exports with Maghreb, whereas Maghreb is still not able to diversify its export basket with India. Even in case of commodities being exported from Maghreb to India, potential is still to be utilised. For example, India imports phosphates from Maghreb which only meets 23 percent of the total demand in India. The rest of the demand is filled from other parts of the world. Similar is the case of phosphoric acid. 51 percent of the total imports in India are met from Maghreb. Calcium phosphates are other products in this category which only meet 13 percent of the total demand in India. In these items, Maghreb has the potential to meet further demand in India. Considering further diversification of exports from Maghreb, India is a large market for primary products produced in Maghreb such as dates, grapes, etc. Copper is another product which has the potential to tap markets in India for Maghreb.

Further, intra-industry trade (IIT) index has been calculated. The use of this index has been important to understand the direction of intra-firm trade between countries. There are several approaches to do this analysis. However, we have used Grubel-Llyod index for our purpose. [19] Using this analysis, the paper identifies the sectors in which intra-industry trade is happening in countries in Maghreb and India. Considering Maghreb as a whole, the IIT index suggests that there are limited sectors in which intra-industry trade is happening both in Maghreb and in India. Based on Grubel-Llyod index, five important sectors are identified and placed in Table 1.6 with their respective IIT index for India and the Maghreb. Among the five major sectors, manufacturing of plating material and electrical and electronic items are important. The formula for the calculation of the index is presented in equation (2):

$$GL_i = \frac{(X_i + M_i) - |X_i - M_i|}{X_i + M_i} = 1 - \frac{|X_i - M_i|}{X_i + M_i} \quad ; 0 \leq GL_i \leq 1 \tag{2}$$

Where X_i denotes the export from the world, M_i the import from the world, of good i.

The index varies from 0 to 1. If the index is 1, there is a perfect intra-industry trade. Trade between India and Algeria is limited. There is limited bilateral trade of India with Algeria Morocco and Mauritania, etc. Therefore, there is limited scope of intra-industry trade between countries of Maghreb and India. However, there exists potential in inter-industry trade.

Table 1.6: Intra-Industry Trade (IIT) Index of India and Maghreb with Major Sectors

HS Code	Sector	IIT of Maghreb	IIT of India
07	Vegetables and certain roots and tubers	0.85	0.76
46	Manufactures of plating material, basket work, etc.	0.74	0.93
85	Electrical and electronic equipment	0.74	0.55
88	Aircraft, spacecraft and parts thereof	0.67	0.76
71	Pearls, precious stones, metals, coins, etc.	0.66	0.79

Source: Authors' calculations based on data from ITC, Geneva.

Investment and Services Trade

Investments and trade in services are other areas of India's economic engagement with the Maghreb. Presently, India's investment in Maghreb countries is on a rising trajectory. The investment flows increased from US$ 28.5 million in 2008 to US$ 108 million in 2013. A consistent investment has been made in Libya and Morocco. Of the total investment in Libya during 2008-2013, the maximum investment has been made in the manufacturing sector which accounted for 99 percent. These investments have been made in oil and gas sectors. In case of Morocco, manufacturing accounted for more than 92 percent of investment by Indian enterprises. Of this investment during the period, major investment has been made in the beverages industry (Table 1.7).

Table 1.7: India's Investment in Maghreb Countries

(US$ million)

Country	2008	2009	2010	2011	2012	2013
Algeria	0.0	0.0	0.0	2.0	0.0	0.0
Libya	24.5	12.9	52.5	3.5	0.6	27.4
Mauritania	1.5	0.2	0.0	0.0	3.8	0.7
Morocco	2.5	1.1	0.0	38.0	4.9	5.8
Tunisia	0.0	0.0	0.0	0.0	0.0	108.2
Total	28.5	14.1	52.5	43.5	9.2	142.1

Source: Monthly OFDI from India, Reserve Bank of India.

With limited investment in Maghreb region, India is also engaged in trade in services. It directly exports human capital for various sectors such as construction, health and education. In case of Algeria, 2,500 Indians were working mostly in remote areas of Algeria. [20] In Libya, at the outset of uprising, an estimated 18,000 Indians were working. Morocco and Mauritania had limited presence of the Indian community ranging between 200-300 Indians in each of the country. In case of Tunisia, the case is almost the same. Market access to services sector is limited in Maghreb countries. Financial integration with the global market is still due. In view of the limitations of trade in services, the opportunities are still to be utilized.

In Algeria, imports are now largely sourced from China. China accounted for 12 percent of imports in Algeria and France accounted for 11.4 percent in 2013. In addition, Algeria has bilateral investment agreements with US, China and the EU. Chinese are also making huge investments in Algeria. It also exports services through human capital working in Algeria. [21] New sectors are progressively being opened in services for FDI. These sectors are ICT and financial sector.

The northern part of the country attracted 67 percent of the total investment during 2002-2012. The transport sector attracts the maximum investment.

In case of Libya, the recent conflicts in Libya have been a major deterrent to economic reforms. Establishment of the Privatisation and Investment Bank in 2009 has catalysed the trade and investment in the country. During the post-Gaddafi period, Libya is undergoing economic reconstruction. The oil sector in the country is the traditional sector for investment and trade. In addition, sectors like renewable energy, transportation and tourism are likely to emerge as attractive sectors in the country. India's traditional bilateral relations with Libya will be an added advantage to help flourish its economic engagement in the future.

In Morocco, the National Pact for Industrial Emergence (2009-15) is underway which aims at reviving the industrial growth. Reforms are underway which favour private sector. New industries like aeronautics and automobiles are now the leading contributors towards economic growth of the country. Morocco is planning to open more and more sectors for foreign investments.

These sectors also include services sectors like information and communication technology (ICT) and financial services. India needs to explore opportunities for investments in sectors like energy, ICT and logistics.

In Mauritania and Tunisia, India's engagement is limited. The economic reform in Mauritania is still slow. A strong call has been made to carry out radical reforms in Mauritania's economic structure, particularly in the areas of food, transportation, health and education. India's experience in these sectors would enable India to benefit from opportunities in Mauritania. The country is experiencing higher rate of growth but it has a limited diversity in its economic activities. Tunisia is also experiencing economic reforms. Tunisia will now enter into a transition phase with reforms agenda on the anvil. This will lead to creation of more opportunities for investment and trade. India's policies towards North Africa would therefore, need a progressive approach to get engaged with these transforming economies, possessing huge potential for cooperation.

Conclusions and the Way Ahead

The potential of India's trade engagement with the Maghreb depends upon two main factors pertinent to trade and investment. The first is the confluence of supply and demand, and the second is trade and investment related measures undertaken by the Maghreb countries. India has no formal trade agreements with any of the Maghreb countries. In order to enhance trade potential with Maghreb, trade agreement can be a way forward. Based on bilateral trade analysis, we have already identified several sectors where trade potential may further be explored.

India's policy towards Africa will be incomplete without its aggressive engagement in the Maghreb. Maghreb is gradually moving towards a democratic system of governance. India's engagement in services sector, particularly education, health and other services, will further strengthen the opportunities for India's investment in sectors like oil, infrastructure and would support the development of small and medium enterprises.

It is, however, important to note that the future trade and investment potential between India and Maghreb countries remains apprehensive owing to the political instability and absence of globally integrated value chain in the region. The enhanced participation of the Maghreb countries in the global value chain shall help enhance their international trading position also. This will, in turn, create further avenues for enhanced cooperation at bilateral, regional and multilateral levels for the Maghreb countries.

Endnotes

1. "India-Africa: South-South Trade and Investment for Development", WTO and CII Publication, 2013, available at:

http://wv/w.wto.org/english/tratop_e/devel_e/a4t_e/global_revie
w13prog_e/india_africa_report.pdf.

2.   Ibid.

3.   ECOWAS stands for Economic Cooperation of West African States. It comprises of fifteen countries of West Africa and was established on 28th May, 1975 through the Treaty of Lagos. ECOWAS aims to promote economic integration among West African countries.

4.   The process of pan-African integration can be attributed to the Organization of African Unity (1963), Lagos Plan of Action (1982) and the Abuja Treaty (1991). Though, the genesis of the idea of pan-Africanism has its roots in institutions prior to the Lagos Plan such as the Monrovia Declaration. The African Union was created in the year 2002 in Durban to replace the OAU.

5.   World Bank and IFC, "Doing Business, 2013".

6.   Ibid.

7.   Amor Tahari, Patricia Brenner, Erik De Vrijer, Marina Moretti, Abdelhak Senhadji, Gabriel Sensenbrenner, and Juan Solé (May 2007), "Financial Sector Reforms and Prospects for Financial Integration in Maghreb Countries", IMF Working Paper, WP/07/125.

8.   World Bank, "World Development Indicators".

9.   UNCTAD, "World Investment Report, 2012".

10. UNCTAD, "World Investment Report, 2012".

11. This is based on the World Bank database.

12. "Economic and Social Conditions in North Africa: The Industrialisation for a Sustainable and Inclusive Development in North Africa", 29th Meeting of the ICE, Rabat, Morocco, 4th-6th March, 2014, available at:
http://www.uneca.org/sites/default/files/publications/ice_2014-_survey_english_final.pdf.

13. "Human Development Report, 2013", UNDP.

14. "Maghreb Region and Global Integration: A Dream to be Fulfilled", Peterson Institute for International Economics, October 2008, available at:
http://www.piie.com/publications/briefs/maghreb.pdf.

15. "Economic Integration in the Maghreb: World Bank Middle East and North African Region", The World Bank, 2010, available at:
http://siteresources.worldbank.org/INTMENA/Resources/Maghr

ebpub.pdf.

16. As per the WTO, Morocco is a founding member of WTO since 1st January, 1995. It joined GATT on 17th June, 1987. Mauritania is a WTO member since 31st May, 1995, while it joined GATT on 30th September, 1963. Tunisia is a member since 29th March, 1995, while it joined GATT on 29th August, 1990.

17. MFN is an instrument of the WTO 'Principle of Non-Discrimination'. The MFN principle implies that a country cannot discriminate among its trading partners. If a country grants any of its trading partners a special favour such as a lower customs duty for one of their products, then it has to do the same for all other WTO members. However, trade agreements like FTAs etc. are an exception to the MFN principle.

18. WTO Tariff Profiles 2014.

19. Grubel, Herbert G. and Lloyd, Peter J. (1971), "The Empirical Measurement of Intra-Industry Trade", *Economic Record*, Vol. 47, No. 4, pp. 494-517.

20. "India-Algeria Relations", Ministry of External Affairs, Government of India, December 2014, available at: http://www.mea.gov.in/Portal/ForeignRelation/Algeria_Dec201 4.pdf.

21. "Chinese Investment and Employment Creation in Algeria and Egypt", Economic Brief, African development Bank, 2012, available at: http://www.afdb.org/fileadmin/uploads/afdb/Documents/Publica tions/Brochure percent20China percent20Anglais.pdf.

2

India-Morocco Trade and Investment Opportunities

Suresh Kumar, Paramjit, Rashmi Kapoor and
Prahlad Bairwa

Introduction

The unrestricted economic plunder of European colonialism motivated them finally for the Scramble of Africa in 1879 and divided the social matrix under the policy of divide and rule. The speech of HM King Mohammed VI of Morocco to 69th Session of United Nations General Assembly on 26th September, 2014 also emphasized, "colonialism caused severe damage to colonized countries. For many years, it hindered their development process, exploited their resources as well as the energies of their sons and daughters, brought about profound change in the customs and cultures of the peoples concerned and sowed the seeds not only of division between members of the same community, but also of conflict and discord between neighbouring states" (General Assembly, 2014). Prior to colonial business expedition, a parallel between Europe, India and Africa is an eye-opener (Table 2.1). The statistics of population and GDP of these years (1000-1820) explains the outline of change in India, Africa and Europe. The population and income magnitude attracts the attention of European myth of supremacy. In the year 1000, India and Africa taken together, accounted for 40.2 percent of world population and 39.1 percent of world income as compared to European population of 12 percent and 11.1 percent of world income.

Table 2.1: Distribution of Population and Income in the World Economy: 1000-1820

Population and GDP (in percent)					
1000		1500		1600	
India	28.1	27.8	25.1	24.4	24.3	22.4
Africa	12.1	11.3	10.6	7.8	9.9	7.0
Europe	12.0	11.1	16.2	20.5	16.3	22.6
Other World	47.8	49.8	48.1	47.3	49.5	48.0
Total	100	100	100	100	100	100

Contd...

Population and GDP (in percent)			
1700		1820	
India	27.3	24.5	20.1	16.1
Africa	10.1	6.9	7.1	4.5
Europe	16.6	24.9	16.3	26.5
Other World	46.0	43.7	56.5	52.9
Total	100	100	100	100

Note: Europe includes Western and Eastern Europe.
Other world includes USA, Canada, Australia, New Zealand, former USSR and Japan.
Source: http://www.ggdc.net/maddison/content.shtml, accessed on December 26, 2013.

Africa had minerals richest in the world but surviving in the worst condition with very low standard of living, with a wide difference between their cultural and economic attainment in comparison to Europe led to the cruel pattern of barbarity of de-forestation, which continued for 400 years without any obstacle.

The *Economic Crisis of Europe* led to the division of Africa and became an important instrument of their foreign policies and diplomacy.

The divide and rule doctrine concluded that even today, the neo-colonialism has given way to 'new tactics' which are Western development model in character and leading to further scramble in Africa. It is observed that the relations of the European powers are influenced more and more by the considerations of territorial commercial rivalry outside Europe and particularly in Africa. "What applies to the West should not be used as the sole criterion for determining the efficiency of other development models; nor should one make comparisons between countries—however similar their circumstances may be—even when these countries belong to the same geographical area. Accordingly, the first call I should like to make from this rostrum regards the need to respect the characteristic values and principles of each country as it builds its own development model. This is particularly true for developing countries, which are still suffering from the consequences of colonialism", observed HM King Mohammed VI in his speech (General Assembly, 2014).

Morocco prioritizes South-South cooperation. The King took the initiative to cancel the debt of very poor African countries. This decision was only the beginning of a long-term economic strategy to get back to the suitable position it occupied in the African diplomatic landscape. To reinforce its economic leverage in the area, Morocco is settling human and social development projects. The private sector participation is also a relevant asset of its policy. Several Moroccan public or private companies have established themselves in sub-Saharan Africa to invest in sectors that could foster some countries' growth, for example 'banking sector (such as *Attijari wafabank* is present in Senegal and Mali), finance sector with Deposit and Management Bank (CDG) and the group Chaabi in Ivory Coast, Mali, and Guinea and even telecommunication sector (Maroc Télécom) that owns communication companies in Senegal, Mali and Burkina Faso' (African Bulletin, 2014).

The Moroccan main phosphate company OCP uses all of its knowledge and experience in agri-food industry to favour food security in the area. The exportation of its renewable energy model is also very important, as it is a decisive innovation that will influence positively on the countries suffering from frequent power and water cuts. Similarly, Prime Minister of India Narendra Modi, in his speech to 69th Session of UN General Assembly, United Nations on 28th September 2014, vehemently said, "India is a country that constitutes one-sixth of humanity; a nation experiencing economic and social transformation on a scale rarely seen in history. It is this timeless current of thought that gives India an unwavering belief in multilateralism. An extraordinary vision and a clear recognition of our shared destiny brought us together to build this institution for advancing peace and security, the rights of every human being and economic development for all.

We have achieved much in the past six decades in our mission in ending wars, preventing conflict, maintaining peace, feeding the hungry, striving to save our planet and creating opportunities for children" (General Assembly, 2014).

The central theme of the UNO for the year 2014 focusing on the sustainable development post-2015 as part of the development agenda is the main focus of this paper.

In interpretation of different development models, which stress on European-centric approach, is summed up in a way that the conditions in the pre-first world which led to the scramble can re-grow if one cannot check the effects of neo-colonialism.

Post-1990 Africa needs a serious orientation to strengthen inclusive development, accountability towards people and avoid the colonial pattern of education. "As you know, sustainable development is not something which can be achieved through decisions and ready-made prescriptions. Nor is there a single model in this area. Each country follows a path of its own, having taken into consideration its historical development, cultural heritage, human and natural resources, specific political circumstances, as well as its economic choices and the obstacles and challenges facing it. Aware of these critical challenges, I have sought to set up a distinctive development model rooted in the culture and in the specific national values of the Moroccan people—a model which also takes into accounts the need for positive interaction with international principles and objectives in this area", opined HM King Mohammed VI in his speech (General Assembly, 2014).

The similar opinion was echoed by Prime Minister Modi,

"Democracy is trying to find a voice in West Asia and North Africa. There is a new stir for stability and progress in Africa. India desires a peaceful and stable environment for its development. A nation's destiny is linked to its neighbourhood. That is why my Government has placed the highest priority on advancing friendship and cooperation with her neighbours" (General Assembly, 2014).

The mid-1990s UN calculations established the fact that the 358 richest individuals in the world controlled economic assets equal to the combined annual incomes of poor countries with 45 percent of the world's population (UNDP, 1996). The poverty curtain dividing North and South need to be balanced only through South-South systematic dialogue and promoting inclusiveness in decision-making.

Demographically, Africa's median age at present is 20 years, which is the strongest pillar of human resource and hence needs better education and employment opportunities in their respective countries. South-South cooperation is desirable for an examination to link human development, economic growth and poverty reduction.

An industrial system of multinational production exists along with a global market for finance capital and a new social and economic reality for all of us, rich or poor. HM King Mohammed VI further said, "Africa does not need humanitarian aid as much as it needs mutually beneficial partnerships. I also stress that Africa needed to turn the page on the past and overcome its political, economic and social problems that it needed to rely on its own resources to achieve its development. This is an outstanding model of South-South cooperation which reflects our capacity as African countries to develop the continent by relying on ourselves and investing in the natural resources of our countries" (General Assembly, 2014). This parameter can play in furthering and enhancing mutual respect for the sovereignty of states, their territorial integrity, culture, customs and political stability, which will lead to self-reliant development and guide towards sustainable development.

Even Prime Minister Modi asserted on this issue and said, "Technology has made things possible; the cost of providing it has reduced. Each country must of course take its own national measures; each government must fulfil its responsibility to support growth and development. At the same time, we also require a genuine international partnership. At one level, it means a better coordination of policy so that our efforts becomes mutually supportive, not mutually damaging. In India, the most important aspects of my development agenda are precisely to focus on these issues. The eradication of poverty must remain at the core of the post-2015 development agenda and command our fullest attention. Technology has made many things possible. We need imagination and commitment. India is prepared to share its technology and capabilities, just as we have announced a free satellite for the SAARC countries" (General Assembly, 2014).

The process of democratization began in Africa since 1990s to promote democratic governance elected through the process of free and fair national elections. There are differing interpretations and discourses on democratic governance in Africa that has led to challenges, problems and prospects. The globalization caused the social forces representing democratic champions and agency in Africa to reconfigure the political landscape in Africa. Morocco's Constitution of 2011 is the initiative towards democratization and participatory governance showing the way for democratic governance in Africa. Everywhere in Africa, governments are launching development agendas as a strategy for their self-reliance movement. It has become an indispensable tool in the fight against underdevelopment in Africa. It provides unprecedented opportunity to meet people's vital development goals such as poverty reduction, basic healthcare education and working for sustainable and human development.

African governments' national development programme cannot function in isolation. The idea of today's investment by democratic governments will nourish a debt free Africa and strengthen economic development as tomorrow's prosperity. African politics cannot ignore international relations to build up national development and this partnership is a way towards sustainable development. Modi said, "we must seek a more habitable and sustainable world. We should be honest in shouldering our responsibilities in meeting the challenges. The world had agreed on a beautiful balance of collective action-common but differentiated responsibilities. That should form the basis of continued action. This also means that the developed countries must fulfil their commitments for funding and technology transfer" (General Assembly, 2014).

It is the time to integrate regionally to build common market, barrier-free trade and political and economic integration to seek global benefits and contribute to greater economic growth. It develops the increased inter-state and intra-state trade having greater share of foreign capital ultimately producing higher per capita incomes to minimize the cross-border threats. "As the world grows more acutely and being aware of the cross-border threats posed by the lack of sustainable human development, and as we realize that ours is ultimately a common destiny, I am sure there will be a global awakening regarding the need to work for a more secure, more equitable and more humane world", remarked HM King Mohammed VI in his speech (General Assembly, 2014).

Regional cooperation and integration among African states has resulted in diversification of exports to less developing regions, thereby strengthening the South-South cooperation.

Development Agenda for Morocco

The Sub-Saharan economies having international support for infrastructure investment have set higher growth rates today, as compared to 2011 with prudent use of macroeconomic policies to speed up the recovery from the crisis-induced slowdown. Maintaining macroeconomic balance is a priority for the Moroccan public authorities. Various structural actions and reforms have been undertaken to commit the country to strong, stable and durable growth. 'The economy of Maghreb relies on Europe as a source of tourism, remittances and FDI flow' (Background Note, 2012: 52).

Morocco being a global exporter, focuses its development activities on manufacturing products. Morocco had welcomed the post-1990 globalization and has followed a policy of privatization of certain economic sectors, which used to be in the hands of the government earlier. Morocco is just 14 kilometres away from European coast and at the crossroads of the main trade routes linking America, Africa, Europe and the Middle East and has truly become the region's exporting hub.

Different places of Morocco such as Marrakech, Rabat, Casablanca and others directly connect to Europe via the regular daily train and ferry services. 'The transport infrastructure appears to be well developed across North Africa, which has reached levels that are at par with those found in Southeast Asia. The three North African economies tend to perform better in terms of availability of transport infrastructure (with a score of 5.1 out of 7), while the quality of infrastructure is still insufficient (a score of 3.8). Although Morocco and Egypt are well connected to global maritime routes (16th and 17th, respectively, on the trans-shipment connectivity index), port quality in Algeria is poor, ranked at 113th, (The Africa Competitiveness Report, 2013).

Table 2.2 shares the information about the different stages of development of African economies and suggests reviewing the factor-driven economies and having basic step towards improving productivity and competitiveness. The step towards building sound institutions and macroeconomic policies, adequate infrastructure and the skill development of the workforce will lead towards the next stages. Morocco and six other African economies mark their presence in the second stage representing the efficiency-driven stage of the GCI having higher education and market efficiencies (goods, labour, financial) prominently.

Morocco has become a major player in the African economic

affairs and is the 5th largest African economy by GDP (PPP) today. The World Economic Forum placed Morocco as the 2nd most competitive economy in North Africa after Tunisia. Moroccan government has a coherent strategy in place since the early 2000s to achieve its medium-term vision and has made a good start on structural changes. "To date, the African Development Bank has committed a total of € 8.6 billion in Morocco, equivalent to 96.3 billion dirham. The Bank's current active operations portfolio in the country is about € 2 billion, equivalent to 22.4 billion dirham. The portfolio is dominated by the infrastructure sector—including transport, energy and water and sanitation—and governance' (ADB, 2011).

Table 2.2 Global Competitive Index and Morocco

Stage	African Countries	Important Areas for Competitiveness
Stage-1 (Factor Driven) GDP per Capita <USD 2,000	Benin, Burkina Faso, Burundi, Cameroon, Chad, Côte d'Ivoire, Ethiopia, Gambia, Ghana, Guinea, Kenya, Lesotho, Liberia, Madagascar, Malawi, Mali, Mauritania, Mozambique, Nigeria, Rwanda, Senegal, Sierra Leone, Tanzania, Uganda, Zambia, Zimbabwe	Basic requirements (60 percent), efficiency enhancers (35 percent), and innovation factors (5 percent)
Stage-2 (Efficiency Driven) GDP per Capita >USD 3,000 to 5,000	Cape Verde, Mauritius, **Morocco**, Namibia, South Africa, Swaziland	Basic requirements (40 percent), efficiency enhancers (50 percent), and innovation factors (10 percent)
Stage-3 (Innovation Driven) GDP per Capita >USD 17,000	Germany, Republic of Korea, Norway, Spain, United Kingdom, United States	Basic requirements (20 percent), efficiency enhancers (50 percent), and innovation factors (30 percent)

Source: World Economic Forum, 2012.

International Finance Corporation (IFC) of The World Bank Group focuses on increasing access to finance by supporting the development of local financial institutions, particularly those that concentrate their lending on small and medium enterprises. With an unemployment rate of almost 14 percent in urban areas, the Moroccan government realizes the importance of creating jobs to reduce poverty in its labour-abundant country. Morocco is also working with IFC on projects to create a corporate governance code and identify public-private partnership opportunities.

The IFC kept around US$ 150 million for mobilization in cross-border and financial sector investments during the fiscal year 2012 and its portfolio for Morocco, it allotted US$ 200 million that included:

- 'A US$ 8.3 million partial credit guarantee for Morocco's third-largest microfinance institution, FONDEP, to facilitate access to finance for local micro, small and medium enterprises.
- US$ 3 million to Kasbah Resources Limited in fiscal year 2011 and US$ 2 million in fiscal year 2010 to build a successful exploration and mining company that will focus its exploration in a frontier region of the country.
- Over US$ 8 million in the Argan Infrastructure Fund in fiscal year 2010 that will make investments in infrastructure projects' (IFC, 2012).

The period of 2009-15 National Pact for Industrial Emergence [Pacte national d'émergence industrielle, (PNEI)] is the result of strategic choices made at the start of the 2000 to encourage the emergence of new centres of growth, competitiveness and jobs. Morocco has focused on encouraging niche industries for export and on international promotion of emerging services to businesses. As a result, relocation of services, the automotive sector and transport and logistics are all thriving. "Morocco enjoys one of the most highly developed infrastructures in Africa. The country is served by a network of 57,847 kilometres (35,946 miles) of primary and secondary roads, of which 30,254 kilometres (18,800 miles) are paved. With growing number of licensed automobiles, the road system, especially in urban areas, has become highly congested. Plans are currently underway to modernize the country's railway system, which plays an important role in the transport of phosphates and its derivatives. Having a strong infrastructure is crucial for the country and to turn the country into a platform of investments and exports to the European Union and the United States" (Documents, 2015).

Moroccan King visited Mali, Guinea Conakry (Capital of Guinea), Cote d'Ivoire and Gabon. This visit combined effectively, conventional goals aimed at strengthening established historical relations and the values of solidarity and South-South cooperation with a significant reference to the latest version of the concepts of post-MDGs (Millennium Development Goals), especially the concept of sustainable security versus sustainable development as an associated mechanism for the progress of the continent. He emphasized in his speech in Cote d'Ivoire, "In the past, diplomacy served to consolidate political ties. Today, it is the economic dimension which predominates. It is a crucial component of diplomatic relations" (Speech, 2014). In recent years, Morocco has been placed in the economically developed countries with greater cooperation in the fields of banking, telecommunications, housing, commerce and industry. It also offers its expertise in infrastructure, public health, roads and education. It also takes a great interest in national education by offering fellowships to students belonging to different African countries.

Morocco is a transport hub for trade between North Africa and Europe. However, much improvement is required to compete on an international scale. Hence, the road, rail, airport and port sectors will be key priority areas for infrastructure expansion. Morocco had welcomed the post-1990 globalization and has followed a policy of privatization of certain economic sectors which used to be in the hands of the government earlier. Different places of Morocco such as Marrakech, Rabat, Casablanca and other directly connect to

Europe via the regular daily train and ferry services.

Investment Opportunities in Morocco

Having a strong infrastructure is fundamental to the development of any country. It makes it easier for local investors to create businesses and factories that drives growth and creates jobs. Moreover, having a concrete infrastructure attracts foreign investors and international organizations to bring their expertise, which also creates jobs. The major resources of the Moroccan economy are agriculture, phosphates, tourism, fish and seafood and outsourcing in manufacturing cars, aircrafts and textile industry. Handicrafts are an important industry and craft products are exported throughout the world. Morocco has three quarters of known reserves on the planet and is a prominent exporter of phosphates in the world, having total exports of US$ 20.17 billion. The major partners include Spain (20.1 percent), France (11.2 percent), India (6.7 percent), Brazil (4.8 percent), Italy (4.7 percent) and U.S. (3.9 percent). Morocco has benefited from the globalization in the manufacturing sector.

Infrastructure Sector

The infrastructure sector deals with different varieties of sub-sectors as per the need. It includes cement, construction, iron and steel, real estate, general machinery, machine tools, technology, turnkey projects, drilling equipment, earthmoving equipment, minerals, hotels, resorts, shopping malls, food courts, amusement parks, automobiles (bus, cars, trucks), bicycles, auto parts and ancillaries, railway construction and rehabilitation, construction and rehabilitation of power stations to develop rural electrification, energy transmission and distribution, rehabilitation of existing facilities and addition of new infrastructure to supply potable water, sewage drainage and treatment, building hospitals and setting up of health system, manufacturing of pharmaceutical products, diagnostic and medical services and diagnostic centres, pharmaceutical industries, mineral water and other liquid food hygiene, cement production, paper and technical maintenance, building radio and TV stations and digitalization of the terrestrial television transmission network.

Mutual Connectivity of Road, Railway, Sea and Air: Building infrastructure such as roads and highways will have a positive impact on commerce and trade; it will connect some of the most isolated villages with other parts of the country. It will also reduce road accident rates, and make access to schools and hospitals easier for thousands of people who are still suffering because of the lack of basic infrastructure. 'The African Development Bank (AfDB) Group and the Government of Morocco signed six loan and grant agreements amounting to € 303 million (3.4 billion dirham) in 2011. The agreements included a €300 million (3.4 billion dirham) investment loan to the national railway company—Office National des Chemins de Fer (ONCF)—to finance a major upgrade of the Tangier-Marrakech rail link (ADB, 2011). Morocco has 70th rank in the world having more than 2,000 kilometres of railway network. It connects most of the urban regions throughout the country.

The Tangiers Marrakech Railroad project has the potential of connecting the country to its North African neighbours. When completed in 2016, it is expected to significantly boost rail travel, with an improvement in rail traffic fluidity and increased frequency of shuttle, mainline, and freight trains; increased population mobility in the project area; and creation of direct and indirect jobs during the project implementation and operational phases.

The ONCF project is part of an ongoing national development strategy in the transport sector, which includes upgrading and modernizing infrastructure and transport services to increase Morocco's economic competitiveness. The project is being implemented from 2011 to 2016 and aims to strengthen the rail infrastructure to meet the growing annual passenger and goods traffic on the Tangier-Marrakesh axis.

Annual passenger traffic on the line is expected to increase from 16 million in 2010 to nearly 23.5 million from 2016.

"Morocco has 70 airports, 11 of which are major and quite modern, and efforts are underway to modernize all of them. The largest of them, an international airport just south of Casablanca, offers flights to several destinations in Europe, the United States, Canada, the Middle East and Africa. It is serviced by more than 50 airlines that bring in most of the country's tourists" (Documents, 2015). In the recent few years, the Moroccan government launched different projects to upgrade, maintain, or expand the country's infrastructure such as building Tangier-Med port, expanding the international airport of Casablanca, connecting Casablanca and Tangier with high-speed rail, building new highways, etc. Almost all data indicators show that Morocco has a long way to go to upgrade, maintain, and expand its basic infrastructure, including roads, ports, bridges, airports, schools and universities, hospitals, sports facilities, access to water and electricity, access to fast internet, and research and development facilities.

"Rabat has 24 ports, which handles 98 percent of the Morocco's foreign trade. The port of Casablanca is a world-class port and the second largest in Africa. In addition to goods, Morocco's ports also service tourist ferries to and from Spain and France. A € 678,000 (7.6-million dirham) grant was allotted to the National Ports Agency (PNA) to conduct an analytical and development study on the reinforcement and renovation of several ports in the country, notably Nador, Safi, Al Hoceima, Tangier, Casablanca and Agadir" (Documents, 2015).

Electrical Power Generation: The electricity generation is under the charge of the state-owned Office National de L'électricité (National Office of Electricity, ONE). "Despite the recent discovery of modest amounts of oil reserves in Morocco, most electricity is produced from imported fuels, mainly from Saudi Arabia. Morocco's total power capacity is estimated at 13.16 billion kilowatts, 124 million of which is imported, mainly from Spain. Power shortages are common.

The government is planning to build additional power plants and boost electric capacity to meet the increasing demand of industrial projects and extend electric services to currently un-served rural areas. About 80 percent of Morocco's rural areas are not electrified having an estimated 12 million rural inhabitants" (Documents, 2015). The World Bank agreed to provide US$ 297 million in financial assistance to Morocco for the development of one of the world's largest solar power plants in November 2011. The loan will support the first phase of the solar power plant, which is due to have a capacity of 500 MW.

The Ouarzazate concentrated solar power plant is part of the country's solar power programme, worth US$ 9 billion, and holds significant importance for Morocco. "Africa Development Bank (AfDB) will provide a US$ 800 million loan to the Moroccan government. The loan will be used to finance the development of the country's renewable energy sector. This will include the construction of a solar power plant at Ouarzazate, which will eventually generate 500 MW of electricity. Termed as the largest CSP in the world, it is to include an investment of € 1.04 billion (US$ 1.3 billion), which will also be funded by six other agencies, including the World Bank and the European Investment Bank. In addition, the amount provided by AfDB will also be used to increase the country's wind power capacity by 1,070 MW and would help in providing electricity to 79,436 homes. This will be undertaken as part of the Moroccan Integrated Wind/Hydro and Rural Electrification Programme. The project requires a total investment of US$ 2.16 billion, with completion due for 2017" (ADB, 2011).

Morocco intends to generate 42 percent of its electricity from renewable sources by 2020. Also, on September 24, 2012, the consortium led by ACWA Power International received a contract worth nearly US$ 1 billion to construct a solar power plant in Morocco. The consortium also includes Aries Ingeniería y Sistemas and TSK Electrónicay Electricidad.

"Telecommunications services in Morocco are thoroughly modern and have greatly improved since the mid-1990s. Most telephone service are provided by the state-owned Maroc Telecom and Meditel, the country's two largest telephone companies. The country had 1,455,853 phone lines at the end of 1999. Mobile service is also available. In 1999, Morocco had 27 internet service providers" (Documents, 2015).

Investments in renewable energy projects will enable 42 percent of the country's energy to be generated through solar, wind and hydro power by 2020, and will propel Morocco to become one of the first in the world to export green energy. In fact, the nation aims to meet 17 percent of Europe's energy demand by 2050 through its Desert solar power plant. With projects such as these, Morocco will soon lead renewable energy generation in Africa. Since these ambitious plans require large-scale funding, the government relies on private and donor organisations for financing. Public-private partnerships will therefore, be a common trend.

Construction Industry: The Moroccan construction industry is estimated to have experienced real growth of around 7.4 percent in 2011, with the sector recovering from the period of relatively subdued growth seen in 2009 and 2010. Underpinned by a healthy pipeline of infrastructure projects, multilateral financing and a robust economic growth outlook, one may expect the sector to continue on this strong growth trajectory over the medium to long-term. The research has pencilled in real growth of 7 percent year-on-year (y-o-y) for Morocco's construction industry in 2013 and a real industry average growth rate of 7.4 percent per annum is expected between 2013 and 2020.

Overall, the government is the primary driver for infrastructure development in Morocco and all projects are prioritized within each sector so that none are neglected. Further, the country has invested US$ 7.61 billion in renewable energy, and leads the integration of green technology with infrastructure in Africa. HM King Mohammed VI on the occasion of the throne day in 2013 underlined, "The government has found not only a positive and constructive legacy, but also concrete achievements in the economic and social spheres. I am eager to show the same will power and determination to achieve further progress and development" (Royal Speech, 2013).

FDI in Morocco and India

Multilateral Investment Guarantee Agency (MIGA) and the Foreign Investment Advisory Service (FIAS) promote the implementation, deregulation and promotion of foreign direct investment in Africa. A few officials from Morocco have been successful in attracting foreign investors and were invited to the workshop to share their experiences (Backmann, 1996:19 and 117). Morocco consumes far less time and it enjoyed a comparative advantage. Corporate taxes on export industries are generally investor friendly and a vigorous FDI promotion programs have been launched in Morocco with a zero tax rate. Morocco is ranked 36th in the export commodities with a revealed comparative advantage in the global average.

Africa has proven oil reserves of around 117 billion barrels which is close to 10 percent of total world reserves. Morocco is one of the countries having main oil refineries. New opportunities are also emerging in the iron ore sector. It is estimated that at a capital cost of more than US$ 50 billion, mining projects worth 500 mtpa have been planned in Africa over the next eight years and Morocco is one of them (Table 2.3).

Morocco's chemical sector is still small in comparison to the global market, though current trends suggest that its contribution to global production of chemicals will continue to grow. Morocco has one of the largest chemical industries in the continent and is willing to grow. Petrochemical commodities, polymers and fertilizers are the main products. India has capacity in the investment of pharmaceuticals production and is willing to invest in oil and gas, which are key drivers for the chemicals industry. A key focus for the sector is the production of agricultural chemicals and the Indian investors include public sector companies like

ONGC, OVL, etc. along with the private sector, who are willing to play a vital role.

Table 2.3: Iron Ore Production by African Countries, 1995-2008

Iron Ore Production by African Countries (mt.)				
Year	1995	2000	2005	2008
South Africa	19.80	21.57	24.90	30.80
Mauritania	7.00	7.50	7.00	7.10
Algeria	1.10	0.82	0.80	1.00
Egypt	1.12	1.90	0.90	1.00
Tunisia	0.11	0.10	0.10	0.10
Zimbabwe	0.16	0.22	0.20	0.02
Nigeria	0.062	0.009	0.02	0.02
Morocco	0.032	0.004	0.004	0.005

Source: Morgan, J.P., 22nd November, 2010, 'This is Africa', CAZENOVE, Thomson Research.

India's leading fertilizer manufacturer Tata Chemicals Limited (TCL) is investing over ₹ 1,300 crore to buy a 5-10 percent stake in an upcoming urea plant in Africa. The plant which is being built by Oram International, a Singapore based agri-food processing company in collaboration with the Republic of Gabon is expected to have a manufacturing capacity of around 2,200 metric tonnes of ammonia and 3,850 metric tonnes of urea per day (Tataafrica, 2014). TCL already has a significant presence in Morocco and chemical project is also in line with their focus to partner in the growth and development of Africa.

India's leading tractor manufacturer Mahindra & Mahindra (M&M) plans to set up AN assembly plant in Morocco. The auto giant already has satellite plants in Gambia, Chad, Mali, Ghana and Nigeria for manufacturing farm equipment. These facilities will now be used to assemble three-wheelers, light commercial vehicles and utility vehicles to drive volumes in a fast-growing economy in Africa with rising disposable incomes. M&M currently has a presence in 24 out of the 53

African countries and is amongst the few in the world to have set up tractor assembly facilities in Africa. M&M plans to increase penetration in Africa by also bringing in their three-wheelers, LCVs and Bolero in the market (PEI, 2011).

Marketing strategies are increasingly focusing away from coastal and safari tourism (although these destinations still remain the mainstay of tourism in many countries) and developing special interest in cultural and ecotourism and adventure-based holidays. Joint regional marketing is also on the rise as more regional trading blocs harmonize. Even though a number of countries are actively utilizing the internet, the use of electronic marketing technologies largely depends on Internet access and penetration rates in different countries. The World Trade Organization (WTO) forecast for international tourist arrivals to Africa indicates that there will be 77.3 million visitors in 2020. This represents an annual growth rate of 5.5 percent over the decade, which is above the global growth rate of 4.1 percent (UNCTAD, 2008: 27).

The "Tourism 2020 Vision" also says long-haul travel in Africa will grow at a slower rate than intra-regional travel, with the result that by 2020, there will be almost twice as many intra-regional arrivals recorded from long-haul source markets. On the individual inbound country forecasts for the main tourist destinations within Africa, South Africa will increase its dominance as the continent's principal destination accounting for almost 40 percent of all international tourist arrivals in 2020—over 30 million. Morocco will be the next most important, accounting for close to 9 million arrivals by 2020.

India and Morocco have a great cultural heritage, diverse natural vistas, incomparable bio-diversity and a rich variety of cuisines, art, textiles and adventure locales. Ibn Battuta of Morocco spent almost ten years in India during Mohammad Tughlaq's period, which is a link to re-investigate the rich cultural history of India and Morocco. However, what both lack is a tourism infrastructure that adequately addresses the needs of the well-heeled, value-added tourist visitor. There is an acute paucity of goods, safe budget hotels, good airport facilities in tourist centres, comfortable bus routes and in many cases, physical safety of visitors. Issues like access to good health facilities at short notice, ATM machines, safe but cheap food etc., also compound problems for both the countries. Morocco has done tremendously well in terms of building infrastructure. In the case of India too, some states have done better than others, like Rajasthan, Goa and Himachal Pradesh, while others lag behind. There has been a surge in investments in the hospitality and tourism industry in India fed not just by the demand from foreign, but also the domestic tourists. India's large middle-class is increasingly a big source of tourism revenue, not just in India, but globally.

Both Indian and Moroccan policy-makers need to realize the importance of tourism. There is a direct link between tourism and ecological preservation, as well as the preservation of culture and arts. There is a huge scope that India and Morocco can do together to nurture their tourism sectors. Some specific measures that need to be sustained and be initiated with reference to tourism are:

- Opening up investment in hospitality sector. Identifying areas where Indian private sector can invest in Morocco.
- An Indo-African Tourism Business Council that helps African countries including Morocco and especially the lesser known destinations, showcase their attractions to the Indian middle-class market.
- The Tourism Business Council can also serve as a resource to exchange ideas on the best practices of tourism management and learn from the mistakes and successes of each other.
- India can provide help in development of English language skills for workers in the hospitality sector.
- Work in conjunction with the Tourism Business Council to develop low-cost training modules in hospitality management, ecological tourism and adventure tourism.

- Developing low-cost airline connections between India and Morocco.
- Help governments promote the shared heritage of India and Morocco to attract visitors.
- Jointly develop effective research and data collection to understand the needs of the global tourism sector that is often under-represented in policy making.

As regards India's imports from Africa, Morocco has its rational share of India's total imports from Africa during 2012-13, reflecting significant imports of chemicals from the country (Table 2.4). According to data from the Ministry of Commerce, no clear trend emerges from the data as the year 2008-2009 and 2011-2012 are very significant as they show almost doubling of Indian imports from Morocco. The international financial depression of 2008-2009 had influenced the India-Morocco trade and its effect is clearly visible in the following years. It was revived again in the year 2011-2012 with almost a 100 percent growth.

Table 2.4 India's Import from Morocco (value in US$ million)

Year	Import	Percent Share	Percent Growth
2007-08	499.40	0.1984	1.92
2008-09	948.15	0.3122	89.86
2009-10	861.51	0.2987	-9.14
2010-11	839.64	0.2271	-2.54
2011-12	1,658.45	0.3389	97.52
2012-13	1,309.03	0.2667	-21.07
2013-14	879.18	0.1953	-32.84
2014-15 (April-June)	224.08	0.1981	

Source: Department of Commerce, Export Import Data Bank, Ministry of Commerce & Industry, Government of India.
http://commerce.nic.in/eidb/Default.asp

Role of India in Morocco's Development

The historical ties between post-Independent India and

Morocco strengthened right from the days of Jawaharlal Nehru, the first Prime Minister of India as he met HM Hassan II and discussed the common issues of colonialism. The French agreed to leave the de-facto transfer of power to the Government of India on the former French Colony of Pondicherry, in India on 1st November, 1954. The French had decided to abandon its colonies in India but they insisted on the formality of a reference under Article 27 of the then French Constitution which required popular consultation before transfer of power. They were very keen on this as to avoid repercussions in other colonies like Algiers, Morocco and Tunisia. The ties were further strengthened by Mrs. Indira Gandhi during her Prime Ministership when she met HE Hassan II (Morocco in Focus, 2013:10-11). Our trade with the region witnessed a steady growth. Work continued apace on the Indian joint venture in Morocco and this project came up in 1999. India's relations with Morocco witnessed qualitative enhancement when Prime Minister Shri Atal Behari Vajpayee visited Morocco on 13th-14th February, 1999. He had a meeting with Prime Minister Abderrahmane El Youssoufi and King Hassan II.

The King honoured the Prime Minister by conferring on him the "Grand Cordon of the Alawy Wissam". During the Prime Minister's visit, bilateral investment protection agreement, tourism co- operation agreement and agreement between Press Trust of India (PTI) and Maghreb Arab Presse (MAP) for mutual professional co-operation were signed. Foreign Minister of Morocco Abdellatif Filali called on Prime Minister Shri Atal Behari Vajpayee on the margins of the NAM Summit in Durban in August 1998 and Minister of External Affairs (then Deputy Chairman of Planning Commission) Shri Jaswant Singh met Morocco's Prime Minister Abderrahmane El Youssoufi in New York on the sidelines of the Special Session of the UN on Narcotics and Drugs held in New York from 8th-10th June, 1998 (Indian Delegation Meetings, 2014).

India has been one of the major markets for Moroccan

phosphates (90 percent of total import) and its derivatives. Along with it, India imports metallic ores, metal scrap, semi-finished products and inorganic chemicals. India's major items of export to Morocco are cotton yarn, synthetic fibre, transport equipment, pharmaceuticals, agricultural implements, chemicals, spices and manufactured metals. The balance of trade is in favour of Morocco because of imports of phosphates for making agriculture fertilizers. 'The quantum of bilateral trade, which was USD 1.15 billion in 2010-11, reached USD 1.7 billion in 2012-13 (including India's exports to Morocco at USD 426.38 million and India's imports from Morocco at USD 1300.35 million)' (Morocco in Focus, 2013: 24).

India's imports from Africa are predominantly crude petroleum, gold and inorganic chemical products, reflecting India's high demand for energy resources. India is the world's fifth largest consumer of energy, and this is expected to double over the next 20 years in the face of the country's expanding economy and growing population. However, India's petroleum reserves have been stagnant at less than 0.5 percent of the world total, which helps to explain in large part, the country's high dependence on imported oil. To diversify its sources of energy and become less reliant on one global region (currently 75 percent of India's oil is imported from the Middle East), India is increasingly engaging with African oil producing countries including Morocco.

However, geological abundance of resources does not automatically translate into a strong primary sector. Morocco's natural resource exports are less diversified than those of other regions. Despite the heavy concentration of raw commodities in Moroccan exports, the range of such commodities in which Morocco has a comparative advantage is limited compared to other regions. India is willing to provide all paraphernalia under science and technology schemes and move ahead with the transfer of technology under oil and gas refinery, mining and other sectors.

FICCI and Casablanca Chamber of Commerce agreement

pursues the Indian textiles, ICT, packaging machinery, agricultural implements, tractors, spices, automobiles tyres and consumer products apart from phosphate trade. This agreement attracts Indian companies such as Tata Motors, Escorts, KEC International, Jindal Power and Steel, Apollo International, WAPCOS and State Bank of India. All these enterprises focus upon the PPP model supported by African Development Bank, Exim Bank of India and Department of Economic Affairs, Government of India.

Similarly, as per the MEA, the Minister of State in the Ministry of External Affairs Shri E. Ahamed visited Morocco from 14th-17th June, 2012. During the visit, he had discussions on bilateral and international issues with the political leadership of Morocco including Prime Minister Abdelilah Benkirane, Foreign Minister Saad Eddine Otmani, Minister-Delegate to the Foreign Minister Youssef Amrani, Minister of Industry, Trade and New Technologies Abdelkader Amara, and Minister of National Education Mohamed El Ouaafa. Mr. Nasser Bourita, Secretary General of the Moroccan Ministry of Foreign Affairs and Cooperation paid an official visit to India on 2nd-3rd, April 2012 and held talks with Foreign Secretary and called on the External Affairs Minister.

Bilateral relations between the two countries and cooperation in international forums were discussed during the visit. An 18-member National Defence College (NDC) delegation visited Morocco from 13th-18th May, 2012 as part of Foreign Countries' Study Tour of the 52nd NDC Course (Annual Report, 2014: 55). Along with it, the policy initiative announced in the Annual Supplement to FTP on 5th June, 2012 highlights that '7 new markets have been added to the Special Focus Market Scheme (Special FMS). These countries are Belize, Chile, El Salvador, Guatemala, Honduras, Morocco, and Uruguay' (The External Sector and India's Foreign Trade Policy, 2009-14: 41).

Today, India-Africa partnership has touched 5.8 percent of African global trade. The third India-Africa Forum Summit is scheduled held on December 6, 2014 at New Delhi had new enthusiasm and more participation from more African countries. At present, India is the number one trading partner of Morocco in Asia and the third largest in the world and the idea of South-South cooperation will be effectively supported by African continent including Morocco (Table 2.5).

Table 2.5: India-Morocco Joint Ventures

S. No.	Name of the Indian Company	Location in the Country
1.	IMACID, joint venture of fertilizer, November 1999	Jort Lasfar, 150 km. south of Casablanca, Morocco
2.	M/s Chambal Chemicals & Fertilizers Ltd. (Birla Group) and Office Cherifien des Phosphates (OCP), Morocco	South of Casablanca, Morocco
3.	Tata Chemicals Ltd. 2005 and Office Cherifien des Phosphates (OCP), Morocco	South of Casablanca, Morocco
4.	Moroccan Phosphate Organisation (OCP) and Paradip Phosphates Ltd.	India
5.	Tata Motors Plant for manufacturing bus bodies	Casablanca
6.	Ranbaxy and Afric-Phar for manufacturing plant for medicines and commercial production and distribution of finished products	Casablanca
7.	PepsiCo India, beverage maker's entire franchise bottling operation	Morocco
8.	Tata Consultancy Services (TCS) to establish offshore delivery centre and a project to impart national training and e-governance in 2007	Casablanca
9.	FICCI and Casablanca Chamber of Commerce signed a cooperation agreement, 8th October, 2010	Casablanca and Delhi offices

Source: Morocco in Focus, 2013: 24-25.

Suggestions and Conclusion

Morocco has already been taking steps to integrate with the global economy. It is also performing well in terms of investment freedom and business freedom. The country is also open to foreign investment in many sectors. The following recommendations, thus, need a consideration:

1. The Moroccan government needs to pursue steps to improve the investment climate by ensuring more access

to finance, strengthening small and medium enterprises and supporting infrastructure development.

2. There is a need to strengthen the general Confederation of Moroccan Enterprises, Moroccan Female Entrepreneurs Association (AFEM) and other commerce bodies for mediation and arbitration on promoting judicial mediation to help foreign investors and companies resolve legal disputes quickly and amicably.

3. The government should mitigate credit risk and expand its lending operations to micro, small and medium enterprises. Al-Amana, a leading microfinance institution needs to improve its credit operations and follow a sustained growth path, helping the microfinance industry to grow and improve.

4. The government should reinforce the *Institute Moroccan des Administrateurs* to become a leading director-training institution and corporate governance advocate in Morocco, promoting corporate governance practices and allowing board members of private sector companies to fulfil their responsibilities with efficiency, integrity and transparency.

5. Morocco's infrastructure sector is a part of the Environmental Growth Partnership Service program and related research services. Since these ambitious plans require large-scale funding, the government relies on private and donor organisations for financing. Public-private-partnerships should therefore be given priority.

6. Lastly, in the case of North Africa, transparency of border administration appears to be the most important factor, limiting trade in goods in the three North African countries assessed—Algeria, Egypt, and Morocco. These countries could also benefit from open access to domestic and foreign markets. These improvements are necessary for countries to fully participate in global value chains, which account for a significant and rising share of trade flows, and to advance towards a higher degree of regional integration. More trade integration within the region would

also contribute to higher food security across the continent.

References

ADB, 2011, http://allafrica.com/stories/201103180520.html, accessed on October 6, 2014.

African Bulletin, 17th February 2014, http://www.african-bulletin.com/7570-king-mohammeds-tour-in-africa-with-new-patterns-for-post-mdgs-development-implementations-in-the-continent.html, accessed on October 6, 2014.

Annual Report, 2012-2013, Ministry of External Affairs, 2014, Policy Planning and Research Division, Ministry of External Affairs, Government of India, New Delhi.

Backmann, Heinz, 1996, "Implementing Deregulation and Promoting Foreign Direct Investment in Africa", The World Bank/IFC/MIGA, Washington, D.C.

Documents, 2015, http://documents.wfp.org/stellent/groups/public/documents/ena/wfp192811.pdf, and http://www.nationsencyclopedia.com/economies/Africa/Morocco-Infrastructure-Power-and-Communications.html, accessed on April 1, 2015.

"External Sector and India's Foreign Trade Policy (FTP) 2009-14", Frost and Sullivan, 2013, http://www.frost.com/sublib/display-report.do?id=M869-01-00-00-00, accessed on October 7, 2014.

General Assembly, 2014, http://www.un.org/en/index.shtml, accessed on October 6, 2014.

IFC, 2012, http://www.w-t-w.org/en/wp-content/uploads/2013/08/Doing-Business-in-Morocco.pdf, accessed on October 6, 2014.

Indian Delegation Meetings, 2014, http://eoi.gov.in/eoisearch/MyPrint.php?1571?000/0017, accessed on October 7, 2014.

"Morocco in Focus", 2013, Embassy of the Kingdom of Morocco, New Delhi.

PEI/ICA, 2011, "Infrastructure Investor Africa: An Intelligence Report", http://www.icafrica.org/fileadmin/documents/2011/Ica_investor_report.pdf, accessed on August 31, 2014.

"Royal Speech", 2013, http://www.map.ma/en/activites-royales/full-text-royal-speech-delivered-tuesday-occasion-throne-day, accessed on October 7, 2014.

"Speech", 2014, http://www.map.ma/en/activites-royales/hm-king-chairs-abidjan-opening-ceremony-moroccan-ivorian-economic-forum-and-gives, accessed on October 6, 2014.

The Africa Competitiveness Report, 2013.

"Annual Report, 2012-2013", The External Sector and India's Foreign Trade Policy (FTP) 2009-14, 2013, Department of Commerce, Ministry of Commerce and Industry, Government of India.

UNCTAD, 2008, "World Investment Report", TNCs and the Infrastructural Challenge, United Nations, New York.

3

Arab Spring: Arms Movement and Terrorism in Sub-Saharan Africa

Halilu Babaji, Suresh Kumar, Gajendra Singh and Juhi Bhatnagar

---

Introduction

Post-1990 period initiates the new era of democratic system ensuring the mass participation and multi-party system throughout the world. Arab spring is the result of world-wide recognition to the democratic system and their accountability towards the people. This mass movement forced members of West Africa and North African (WANA) countries to restructure their constitution and decentralise the political system. Arab Spring led to the formation of people's elected government and their participation in the decision-making bodies. Egypt, Morocco, Tunisia, Nigeria, Senegal and other have modified their constitutions and have respected the democratic system. Wherever Arab Spring was not implemented in the true spirit, it led to political uncertainties in the entire North Africa, the Sahel and the Sub-Saharan Africa. This has benefited a good number of militia groups thereby boosting both arms movement and the thriving of religious terrorist groups, which are largely responsible for the longstanding threat to the security and stability of the states.

The Arab awakening has unleashed unforeseen consequences on the Sub-Saharan Africa, following an inflow of weapons and armed fighters who are motivated by weak governance, insecurity and poverty. The social, economic and political environments make it a fertile breeding ground for the penetration and development of terrorist groups in Sub-Saharan Africa.

The democratic structure and terrorism cannot walk side by side as both have different conception of implementation of their theories. The Arab Spring came to raise the people's voice, who suffered unemployment, hunger, deteriorating health condition and social security. The Arab Spring with the idea of people's elected government having multi-party system cannot be linked with terrorism. But unfortunately, the local terrorist groups supported by international terrorism either in the name or excuse of religion or in the name of no welfare policies for the people, are trying to convert the slogan of Arab Spring in their own favour.

The situation in Sub-Saharan Africa is frightening because the region is the most backward in terms of development and most vulnerable as far as peace, security and stability are concerned. Looking at Africa's map from every angle, north to south and east to west, there is hardly a state untouched by violence armed conflict. The North Africa's unrest stretches from the frozen conflict in Western Sahara to the post-civil war violence in Libya, and the post-Arab Spring instability in Tunisia and Egypt. Throughout the conflict belt in Sub-Saharan Africa, especially Somalia, Mali, the Central African Republic, Chad and Sudan to North-eastern parts of Nigeria and Northern Cameroun, armed conflicts have driven the whole of population to a life of fear, disease and unremitting poverty (Small Arms Survey, 2013).

The awakening and the political and social structure of some Arab countries in North Africa for the past three years have witnessed unprecedented demonstrations and changes in their political life. Arab awakening or spring is a peaceful and non-violent wave of demonstrations and protests occurring in the Arab world. Arab spring remained invisible and the old conflict resurfaced through the mobilisation of floating populations wishing to participate in the process of emancipation and to fight against military rule and autocratic regimes. The other cause of reactivation of frozen conflicts has to do with the role and influence of the Libyan leader in the Sahara (Laurence, 2012).

Arab Spring sparked dramatic changes throughout North Africa, particularly Tunisia, Libya, Egypt and to a lesser extent in Morocco and Algeria. Popular movements have brought a range of avowedly Islamist political parties to power, replacing the largely secular former regimes (Moha, 2014: 1). The year 2011 brought an end to decades of political stagnation in North African countries, raised citizen's expectations, and brought about new political dynamics. Citizen's demands focused on constitutional amendments, empowering parliament, strengthening local government, holding free elections, setting up independent national commissions and easing restrictions on political and civic participation.

In the late 1980s, ill-advised socio-economic measures, bureaucratic misconduct, corruption, and cultural and identity problems combined, provoked a popular demand for a change in Egypt, Libya, Algeria, Morocco and Tunisia. Instead of revising their policies and implementing major political and economic reforms, the authoritarian regimes hampered democratic change. The recent uprisings in the North Africa have been abrupt and unexpected. Various countries in North Africa face important underpinning challenges, particularly the strength of political Islamist movements, violence, both state-sponsored and from opposition movements, corruption, regime stability, social and economic crises, the issue of minority and the prospects of promoting growth and a greater regional integration (Moha, 2014: 2). Thus, North African countries still face a host of political, social and economic challenges. The specifics vary from country to country, often widely, but there are common premises.

The escalation of protest in Tunisia started when a college graduate, who was selling fruits at a roadside after police confiscation of his wares, doused himself with petrol and set himself on fire on 17th December which brought together various groups dissatisfied with existing system to protest. Such protest let to the ousting of the long time President Ben Ali in January 2011 and his exile to Saudi Arabia. The protests constituted the most dramatic wave of social and political unrest in Tunisia, resulting in scores of deaths and injuries, most of which were the result of action by police and security forces against the demonstrators (Davies, 2011).

The year 2011 was full of movements, the revolutions, the riots and the uprisings across the entire globe and the power of the protesters manifested most clearly in the Arab world. The uprising in the Arab world was a defining period for the region and for the rest of the world (Chathan, 2011: 2). The Arab Spring protests have shared techniques of civil resistance in sustained campaigns involving strikes, demonstrations, civil disobedience, defection, rebellion, revolution, riots, self-immolations, marches, rallies, as well as the use of social media to organise, communicate and raise awareness in the face of state attempts at repression and internet censorship, online activism, protest camps, uprising and urban warfare. These campaigns met violent responses from authorities as well as from pro-government militias and counter-demonstrators.

The movements and or uprising spam a large expanse of land comprising of about twenty countries. However, generalisations will not take into full consideration depending upon the cultural variation and the peculiarities of each country.

Background of Arab Spring

The Arab Spring uprising is a democratic revolutionary wave of demonstration and a series of protests occurring in the North Africa (Tunisia, Egypt and Libya) and other Arab world, which began with unrest in Tunisia in late 2010. The Arab Spring has brought down regimes in some Arab countries, sparked mass violence in others, while some governments managed to delay the trouble with a mix of repression, promise of reforms and state largesse. The Arab awakening involved both violent and non-violent movements. The catalysts for the revolts in Northern Africa have also been the concentration of wealth in the hands of autocrats (authoritarian leaders in power) in power for decades. The major slogan of the demonstrators in the Arab world has been *Ash-sha'b yurid isqat an-nizam* (the people want to bring down the regime), (Abulof, 2011).

The Arab Spring was quickly termed as 'revolution' that refers to the attempts by subordinate groups to transform the social foundations of political powers. Tunisia, Egypt and Libya have experienced successful displacement of the regime, but yet to be politically stable. Hence, the Arab Spring and uprising as a concept covers a wide range of changes in an existing structure that changed the history of the Arab countries.

There have been various angles from which the Arab Spring has been attempted to be looked at, mostly through the theories of democratization, social movement theories, revolutionist theories, mobilization and social media theories. However, a new paradigm within the study of social movements has not been given enough attention and as the above mentioned quote highlights, it is even more interesting to explore the depth of these movements and understand why they could create such a change in the political and social sphere.

The Egyptian social movement was not one single movement, but it includes many small players into the fold. The Arab Spring that took place in a number of Arab states led by Tunisia, Egypt, Libya and Yemen have special features, causes and consequences that differ much from the nature of civil wars, regional wars and wars between nations as well as armed and unarmed conflicts.

Arab Spring and its Implementation in WANA

The success and failure of Arab Spring is categorised in different phases. The first took place in the North African countries of Tunisia, Egypt, Libya and Morocco. The second phase involved the rise of sectarianism in the region. And the third, the Jihadist movement in the region and its trajectory throughout the Arab Spring. In this aspect, Arab Spring is a witness of new social movement with new goals and methods, the movement stands out from other rebellions movements, rather it argues and protests for the recognition of the basic human rights, freedom, justice and equality for all in the society.

In the aftermath of Arab Spring, many hope that the authoritarian regime in the North African states would be swept away from power and new democratic governments would replace them. Yet the transition from old authoritarian rule to a new democratic order has not been smooth. Tunisia, Egypt and Libya have all seen a sharp rise in political instability, security problems, social unrest, and above all a growing presence of Islamist militants.

The uprising in Tunisia and Egypt reached a high level of success and had many common grounds. When the Tunisian President Ben Ali was ousted by protests and political contestation, it was for the first time that an Arab Head of State was removed by a popular uprising rather than military coup. Meanwhile in Egypt, the Arab awakening exploded in liberation square in Cairo where Egyptians looked for a post-Mubarak era and that this would present an unprecedented opportunity to reshape the political landscape (Chathan House: 2011).

The Tunisian state was among the most progressive in the Arab world. Tunisia has the Arab world's best education system, a large middle class and very robust civil society rooted in a strong labour movement (Jason, 2012: 314). While in Libya, the popular movement failed as a result of weak and fragmented society. The revolution resorted to the traditional tribal and regional divisions for security and support. Even the military was divided and not a cohesive institution (Lisa, 2011: 2).

Morocco avoided much of the Arab Spring violence because the Islamist Justice and Development Party (PJD) has been a recognised opposition party for years. The old government has remained in power, and the Islamists have succeeded as well. The PJD pursued a measured approach as to how it will push the king for reforms. It did not cause instability or invite a harsh response from the regime. It is not clear how much power the king was initially willing to concede, but the king and his advisers may have realized that their reforms had to be deep if they wanted to avoid developments in neighbouring countries where both governments were completely toppled.

Clashes also were reported among different armed groups in Libya. In addition, government officials and security forces were frequently targeted. The violence continues as the battle over the country governance, balance of power among competing groups, and control of Libya's oil fields intensifies (Yonah, 2014: 6). However in 2012, numerous political, religious and tribal militias emerged in the power vacuum contesting the new Libyan government. These militias are being enabled by small arms as well as sophisticated weapons looted from Gaddafi's armouries during and after the revolution.

Movement of Arms in Sub-Saharan Africa

The rapid movement of arms and ammunitions across the Sub-Saharan Africa has a long-lasting effect on human security. These movements are responsible for the majority of battle-related conflicts and deaths—an estimated 60-90 percent of all direct conflict victims are killed with firearms. Large numbers of men, women, older people and children die indirectly from the effects of armed conflict on the economy, ruined health and security infrastructure, disease and famine. Many people are made refugees or are internally displaced, injured or abused.

These weapons are frequently moved and recycled from country to country, and their ownership is transferred among fighters, security forces and war profiteers. However, in Sub-Saharan Africa, movement of arms is motivated by weak governance, insecurity and poverty. They have been used in intra- and inter-communal feuds, local wars, armed insurrections, armed rebel activities and terrorism, thereby causing a general state of fear among various communities in the region.

The war in Libya has made weapons flow in great numbers to North Africa as well as the Sahel and West Africa. This movement of arms in Sub-Saharan Africa has a long standing threat to the security and stability of the region and the situation has worsened since the fall of Gaddafi, the former Libyan leader (Hazelton, 2011).

The proliferation of heavy arms combined with the porosity of borders has introduced a new threat for Libya as well as the entire African region. The numerous arsenals without surveillance, accessible to all sorts of racketeers, smugglers and mercenaries, harbour a rich diversity of arms: Kalashnikov assault rifles, rockets, mines, shells, RPG-7 surface-to-air-missiles—of which Libya has a stock of 20,000 units—and Russian SA-24 missiles, among the latest generation aerial missiles capable of shooting down fighter jets.

These arsenals have also benefited some of the rebel factions who recognise neither the authority nor the legitimacy of the National Transitional Council (NTC) and make it a counterpart in order to challenge the government and weigh upon it political choices. Moreover, many heavily armed Gaddafi loyalists, together with their children, have taken refuge in neighbouring countries. The presence of the former regime members in Algeria, Niger and Chad remains a challenge for the region.

Large quantities of weapons and ammunition have been smuggled out of Libya. Algeria, Mali, Mauritania and Niger are the frontline countries affected by this outflow. Unsecured weapon storage facilities that were previously guarded by the Libyan government are the main source of the outflow. The movement of these weapons (which include rocket-propelled grenades, anti-aircraft artillery, ammunition and possibly surface-to-air missiles) across state borders by former fighters who were either members of the Libyan army or mercenaries participating in the Libyan conflict, has led to the proliferation of arms, to the benefit of arms traffickers and terrorist and other groups operating in the region. The large amount of arms that are missing or unaccounted for are a cause for concern in the Sub-Saharan Africa.

Map Showing Firearms Flow in West Africa

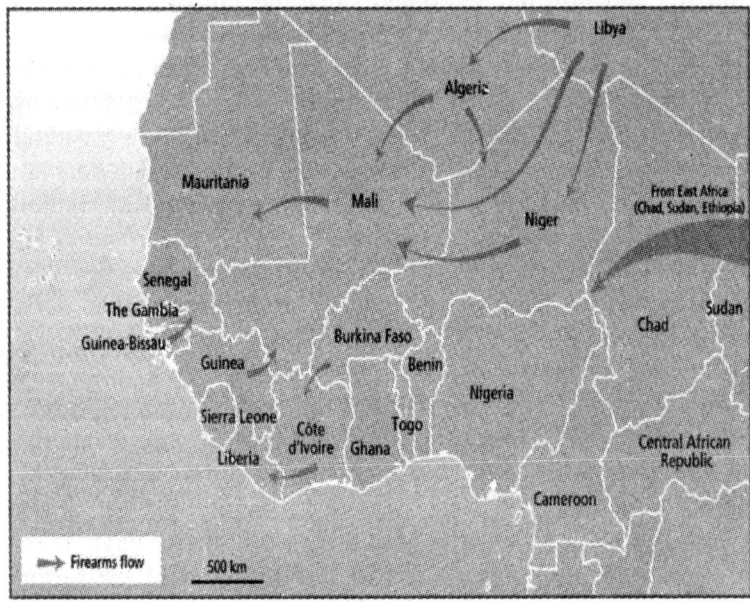

Source: www.unodc.orgtoctawestafrica/westafricatocfirearms; accessed on 29th October, 2014.

The movement of illicit weapons has been prevalent and widespread within Sub-Saharan Africa where achievement of stability and peace remain illusive and a farfetched reality for most African countries. The Libyan crisis in particular has unleashed unforeseen consequences on the West African Sahel states, Mali, Niger, Nigeria and Mauritania. Following an inflow of weapons, ammunition, and armed fighters from Libya's Islamic region into northern Mali by armed and Islamist groups in a battle for autonomy, Nigeria has also faced increasing violence by the armed group Boko Haram.

After the defeat of Gaddafi by the internationally-supported Libyan anti-Gaddafi forces, their aggression was transferred onto the Tuaregs for supporting Gaddafi's regime. This led to the dispersal of the group across the Sahel and Sub-Saharan Africa, particularly in Niger, Mali, Nigeria, Algeria and Morocco (Nathaniel, 2013). The dispersion provided the opportunity to transfer large catchments of arms and ammunitions across the Sahel and Sub-Saharan Africa. It also provided the opportunity for the Tuaregs, in Mali especially, to stockpile large quantity of arms in preparation for the secession plan.

According to Flood (2012: 3), 'the Tuaregs rebels return from Libya via Northern Niger with fresh stocks of weapons, ammunitions, fighting vehicles, and anti-aircraft weaponry, and they also accessed weapons stockpiled from previous outbreaks of political violence and raided arms depots abandoned by the retreating Malian troops...'. The availability of arms in Libya, with which the pro-Gaddafi Tuareg fighters escaped with, provided the impetus for renewed armed insurrection against the state in Mali and Nigeria by Asar Dine and the dreaded Boko Haram insurgents. Many other states in the Sahel and Sub-Saharan Africa are likely deposits of large catchments of arms and ammunitions circulating in the region, making these countries potential grounds for conflicts and instability.

Unfortunately, many of these states are not internally strong; in fact, most are very fragile. In other words, these states often do not have the capability to confront armed insurrection of non-state armed actors, because of the sophistication of their arms and the employment of guerrilla tactics in their fight against the state. This, in most cases, has propelled international intervention by Britain, USA, France and other African countries in Nigeria's confrontation with Boko Haram terrorist activities.

Again, in the development of domestic and transnational extremists groups, the proliferation of arms after the fall of Gaddafi's regime is a major factor. These arms were either bought at very low prices from criminal or terrorist networks in North and West Africa, or they are given freely as dividends of loyalty to a superior group like AQIM. Boko Haram's interaction with AQIM and other terrorist networks in West

Africa and the involvement of foreigners in Boko Haram's terrorist activities in Nigeria is certain. It is definite that the group receives weapons, training and possibly funding from some foreign elements.

By the early 1980s to late 2010, it was evident to many countries in the world that Gaddafi purchased vast arms (weapons) for the armed forces of Libya and funding of terrorist groups worldwide. And his regime made a massive investment in arms and recruiting of foreign (mostly African) mercenaries to boost the Libyan army.

Gaddafi was able to spend considerable sums sponsoring terrorist activities abroad primarily to Arab terrorists groups, but also to a variety of Central and West African groups as well. The arms and ammunitions moved freely around and within the Sub-Saharan Africa without any intervention by regional or national governments.

Arab Spring and the Rise of Terrorist Group in Sub-Saharan Africa

Terrorism has been in existence for many centuries, and is as old as humans. Terrorism can be seen as the purposeful act or the threat of the act of violence to create fear and/or compliant behaviour in a victim and/or audience of the act or threat (Stohl, 1988). The act of terrorism includes kidnapping, especially when employed on consistent basis, bomb attack, hijacking, arson, public execution, armed attack, hostage-barricade situations, and other serious threats to lives and property. Terrorism in the Sub-Saharan Africa and world at large is aimed at achieving the following purposes.

First, it is either organised by the "opposition" to discredit or/and overthrow a regime, or mobilised by state officials as a tool of political oppression. Second, it is aimed at giving a "minority" group a voice in a society. Stohl (1988) notes agreeably that the violence of the terrorist act is not intended simply to destroy but also to be heard. Third, terrorism is aimed at winning a specific concession through "coercive bargaining". It is assumed here that one conflict party might not accept the position of the other party except if some form of illegitimate force (violence) was employed.

However, terrorism can be national or transnational. It is national in situations where both the perpetrators and the victim's are located within the same state. In this case, the terrorist group works towards overthrowing a system of authority on the one hand and the transnational terrorism involves a group within one state, organising insurgency against groups or a government in another country on the other hand.

The major challenges facing the contemporary societies in Sub-Saharan Africa are two-fold. It stems from natural disasters to man-made threats which include crime, piracy, terrorism, ethnic and religious strife, and war. Since 9/11, a disturbing trend of security challenge with global reach is emerging in the Maghreb, Sahel, and Sub-Saharan Africa. It is brutally demonstrated by the escalation in violent attacks mounted by a broad range of lawless sub-national groups from Mali to Somalia and beyond (Yonah, 2014: 2).

Since the September 11, 2001 terrorist attacks on the World Trade Centre in New York and the Pentagon in Washington D.C., terrorism has now become a scourge. As sequence to the attacks, the US declared a war on terrorism on a global level. The first incident of terrorism in Sub-Saharan Africa occurred in September 1970 (Bailey, 1994), while the second major incidence was in 1976 at Entebbe, Uganda. This was the hijack of an Air France plane with some 250 passengers and a crew of 12 by the Popular Front for the Liberation of Palestine (PFLP). The Aircraft was forced to land in Benghazi, Libya. In all the cases reviewed above, Africans were simply victims of international terrorism.

With the growing terrorist activities in Sub-Saharan Africa and the withdrawal of coalition combat troops from Afghanistan, there is the possibility of Africa as a continent becoming the new front in the global terrorist activities (Mben et al., 2013). In

North-western Africa, there are significant threats from terrorist organisations. The present Islamic movements generate possibilities for extremists in the region. The region remains one of concern and faces recruitment possibilities by Al-Qaeda and like-minded terrorist organisations. As the group has links with disenfranchised Muslim youths in parts of Northern and Sub-Saharan Africa which for years have suffered corrupt governments and mass poverty, Al-Qaeda has endeavoured to exploit this situation of the Islamic youth and has mind washed them in the name of religion to die as martyrs.

It is of particular ominous concern to the region as well as to global interests that these political and social entities constitute formally or informally a holy alliance of like-minded movements as well as strange bedfellows operating in an arc of instability from the Atlantic to the Red Sea and elsewhere (Yonah, 2014: 3).

Table 3.1 lists the number of terrorist attacks in Maghreb during the year 2013 with Libya facing 143, Algeria 51, Tunisia 17 and Mali 16, indicating that the terrorist attacks in the Maghreb and Sahel increased at an alarming rate of 60 percent compared to the previous year, totalling 230 incidents in the region—the highest annual total in the region over the past twelve years. And since 9/11, terrorist attacks by AQIM and other extremists have increased by more than 600 percent from their low point (Yonah, 2014: 3).

**Table 3.1: Number of Terrorist Attacks in
Maghreb and Sahel since 9/11**

Country	Period	Number of Attacks
Algeria	2001-2013	1,285
Chad	2004-2010	58
Libya	2006-2013	152
Mauritania	2004-2011	27
Mali	2003-2013	70
Niger	2006-2013	40
Tunisia	2001-2013	21
Morocco	2003-2011	9

Source: Inter-University Centre for Terrorism Studies (ICTS), 2014.

In the name of change and labelling it as Arab Spring, the local terrorist groups allowed Al-Qaeda to consider repositioning itself in the African continent (Laurence, 2012). The collapse of the Libyan security forces and the setback to Al-Qaeda in Asia, were the two factors conducive to a new centrality for the Maghreb, the Sahel and West Africa via:

- A continental extension of jihadists through AQIM'S connections in the Sahel, Boko Haram in Nigeria and Al-shabaab in Somalia, especially consisting of operational collaboration, sharing training and tactics; and

- A strategic reshuffling of certain Al-Qaeda networks in the Maghreb and the Sahel to compensate for their weakening on the Asian front after the elimination of several of the organisation's leaders and recovering international visibility by seeking to participate in the upheavals underway. The transfer of Al-Qaeda's prominent figures to Libya demonstrates the will to exploit the advantages and opportunities offered by North Africa and the Sahel, and probably by West Africa as well.

The Arab Spring brought a lot of terrorist activities across the African continent. The consequent chaos and destabilization wrought in Libya and Egypt created a political vacuum that was filled by the forces of reaction, otherwise known as Sunni fundamentalism. The proliferation of this ideology in the name of the Arab Spring has been a disastrous development for the region, plunging it into an abyss of sectarian and communal conflict in Libya while growing in Africa and attracting more and more young Muslim men into its ranks across the world.

Increasingly, and in some cases at huge cost, Sunni fundamentalism and extremism is being resisted across the Arab world. It is this Sunni fundamentalism that gave rise to Boko Haram in Nigeria fighting to turn a secular state into a Muslim state and also telling Nigerians not to go to schools and get "Western Education". They have kidnapped hundreds, killed thousands and they now see themselves as demigods.

The abrupt end of authoritarian regimes in Tunisia, Egypt and Libya had renewed hopes of democratization but the terrorist groups took advantage of the fragility of states and expanded their operation in the Sahel and Sub-Saharan Africa. For instance, the porous boundaries and borders and fragile nature of the Sahelian states have allowed AQIM to link up with other terrorist groups such as the Movement for Unity of Jihad in West Africa (MUJWA) and Ansar Dine, while giving Boko Haram the opportunity to constantly transit from Nigeria through Niger to Mali, and link up with AQIM for financial and logistic support.

It is feared that Sub-Saharan Africa could become a safe heaven for the new variant of international terrorism. Poverty is one of the causes of terrorism and Sub-Saharan Africa is a poor continent and acts as a safe heaven. The proximity of Africa to the Arabian Peninsula and the lack of state capacity in Somalia are believed to be the main contributing factors to the vulnerability of Sub-Saharan Africa. The frustrations of day-to-day existence would lead to proliferation of domestic terrorism in many parts of the continent. The danger, however, is that domestic terrorists in African states can establish working relationship with their international peers if the quality of governance is not improved.

The United States 2011 Country Report on Terrorism indicated that 'Africa experienced 978 terrorist attacks in 2011, an 11.5 percent increase over 2010. This is attributable in large part to the more frequent attacks of the Nigeria-based terrorist group Boko Haram, which killed 1,132 people. Recently, the attack is estimated to be 3-4 times on daily basis and the number of casualties range from 1-100' (FATF Report, 2013).

Compounding the situation is the rising radicalisation and the southward migration of terrorists and extremists, particularly members of the Al-Qaeda in the Islamic Maghreb (AQIM), through the Sahel towards Mali, Mauritania and Niger. Indeed, there are indications that AQIM has operational bases in some West African countries and has forged tactical alliances with terrorist groups such as Boko Haram in Nigeria, the Movement for Oneness and Jihad in West Africa (MUJAO), the Movement of the Liberation of Azawad (MNLA), and Ansar Dine in Mali and Niger. These alliances have taken the form of AQIM's provision of training and logistical support to Boko Haram and other terrorist organisations. In addition, there is suspicion that Boko Haram has developed ties with the Somali militant group Al-shabaab.

More importantly, alliances and co-operation among Al-Qaeda, AQIM, and West African terrorist groups, and the alleged provision of support by certain West African politicians and public officials to terrorist and likeminded groups underpin the seriousness of the problem in the sub-region. Boko Haram has suspected relationships with AQIM and Al-shabaab, and the sophistication of its attacks in particular has raised concerns about the group's capacity to attack non-Nigerian targets in Nigeria and throughout Africa.

However, the Sub-Saharan Africa is vulnerable to terrorism and terrorist financing for a number of reasons:

- The region suffers from political instability.
- Ethnic and communal violence.
- Pervasive corruption.
- Widespread poverty.
- High rate of unemployment and underdevelopment among young people.
- Rise of religious radicalisation.
- Government impunity.
- Lack of effective capacity to monitor their borders among others.

The devastating effects of terrorism, including loss of life, destruction of property, insecurity, underdevelopment, and reputational damage, have attracted the attention of the authorities and national government in the Sub-Saharan region.

Libya was engaged in some activities interpreted by the western world as constituting international terrorism. Libya was accused of being involved in acts of terrorism in different parts of the world during the reign of Muammar Gaddafi. Gaddafi was accused in 1985 of sponsoring the assassination attempts of Libyan exiles in Greece, Germany, Cyprus, Austria and Italy. There were also a number of attacks on Libyan dissidents in the US. Gaddafi supported many radical groups in the Middle East, in form of training, safe haven, money and arms. There were also a number of terrorist organisations in Latin America such as Chile and Colombia that enjoyed the support of Libya (FBI Reports, 1988). This trend encourages national and domestic terrorism in Sub-Saharan Africa.

The Libyan crisis thus offers an unexpected opportunity for new destabilising intentions, as shown by the emergence of the Movement for Oneness and Jihad in West Africa (MOJWA), which has claimed authorship of kidnapping and suicide bombing by Boko Haram in Nigeria against the innocent citizens and religious leaders. In addition, there is a new front of instability instigated by the Libyan crisis and its regional repercussions that foreign intervention forces did not anticipate and has reopened old conflicts relegated to the history.

Security Implication of Arab Spring in Sub-Saharan Africa

The Arab democratic wave has potential security implications for Sub-Saharan Africa beyond the issue of regime change. North African nations have seen the culmination of various revolts in the Arab Spring movement, whereas in Sub-Saharan nations, frequent political dissatisfaction has often led to a permanent gridlock of ethno-political civil war. Given the gradual spread of Islam from Northern Africa to the Sub-Sahara Africa, it is not surprising that such new religious affiliation bears implications within the sphere of politics. Islamic principles of charity, unity and humility are what make it a prime cultivator for democratic uprising. As a larger democratic and egalitarian faith, autocratic or corrupt governments are more than ever subject to the scrutiny of the common man. Considering Africa's steady conversion, social instability, and increasing education rates, it is not improbable to suspect an impending revolution in the near future.

The political dynamics in North Africa have a number of security implications. The concept of security focuses on the protection of individual or collective actors from physical harm and from threats to other attributes of their existence, ranging from accustomed ways of life to prosperity and self-determination. Barry Buzan, cited in Jack (2010: 2), argued that "security" conveys the idea of freedom from danger, which can be articulated in its objective dimension as the reality of protection and in its subjective dimension as freedom of fear or, for lack of a better word, a sense of feeling secure'.

From late 2010, largely peaceful mass protests have spread from Tunisia to most part of Arab countries in North Africa and prompted considerable political change which resulted into a full fledged war in Libya after an attempt to repress protests by Gaddafi's loyalists and pro-government allies (Eberhard, 2013). A number of security challenges such as arms flow and trafficking, drugs, terrorist attacks by Al-Qaeda and kidnapping is now facing new threats associated with the instability born of Arab Spring, particularly in the area where the Sahara meets the Sahel.

The expansion of the area of instability to the whole of North Africa and the Sahel (and up to Western Africa) through the multiplication of flows and agents of the criminal industry, and the strengthening of local and international Jihadist networks have witnessed the reaffirmation of "ethnic" identities, and the re-emergence of territorial issues and demands for political representation and social justice.

Conclusion

The wake of Arab Spring presents an obvious wave of moment in history to rejoice over the end of authoritarian regimes in Tunisia, Egypt and Libya. The awakening has created situations of political uncertainties in the entire North Africa, the Sahel and the Sub-Saharan Africa as well. It has had and continues to have devastating consequences in the entire Sub-Saharan Africa. The achievement of stability and peace remain illusive and a farfetched reality in the current situation. The continued conflicts throughout the entire region together with the wake of Arab Spring, continues to threaten the entire security of the region and thereby impacting negatively on human security and related abuses.

Regional security cooperation in the entire WANA and Sub-Saharan Africa has been fragmented despite the grave implication of transnational crimes and terrorism. The potential role of various regional communities in WANA in easing instability in the region is worth exploring. Under the current political conditions— especially in Mali, Niger, Tindouf Camp of Algeria, Somalia and Mauritania among others—regional and international assistance will be a prerequisite to negate the threat of terrorism and manage the consequences of political and economic instability. Premised on this reality, most countries, however have acknowledge the need for initiatives and policies to arrest the problem of arms movement and terrorism and its negative effect in the entire WANA and Sub-Saharan Africa.

References

Abulof , U. (2011), "What is the Arab Third Estate?", *The Huffington Post,* www.huffingtonpost.com/unel-abulof/htm, accessed on 1st May, 2011.

Alfano, A. (2011), "A Personal Perspective on the Tunisian Revolution", in A. Mckay (ed.), The Arab Spring of Discontent: A Collection of E-International Relations.

Anderson, L. (2011), "Demystifying the Arab Spring", *Foreign Affairs*.

Baily, S.D. (1994), "The UN Security Council and Human Rights", London: The Macmillan Press.

Davies, W. (2010), "Tunisia: President Zine Al-Abidine Ben Ali Forced Out", BBC News, http/www.bbc.co.uk, accessed on 14th January, 2011.

FATF Report (2013), "Terrorist Financing in West Africa: Inter-Governmental Action Group Against Money Laundering in West Africa (GIABA)", October 2013, Ponty, Dakar, Senegal.

Federal Bureau of Investigation (FBI) (1988), "Terrorism at Home and Abroad: The US Government View", in Micheal Stohl (ed). The Politics of Terrorism, New York and Basel: Marcel Dekker, Inc.

Flood, H.D. (2012), "Between Islamisation and Secession: The Contest for Northern Mali", CTC Sentinel, Vol. 6, Issue 1.

Fotion, N. et al. (2007), "Terrorism: A New World Disorder", London: MPG Books.

Jack, M. (ed.) (2010), "New Security Threats and Crisis in Africa: Regional and International Perspectives", Palgrave Macmillan, US.

Jason, W.B. (2012), "Democratization and the Civil Society: Libya, Tunisia and the Arab Spring", *International Journal of Social Science and Humanity*, Vol. 2, No. 4, July.

Laurence, A.A. (2012), "Security Issues Emerging in the Maghreb and the Sahel after the Arab Spring", *Panorama*, Vol. 128, www.geopolisudeonconsult.com, accessed on 10th September, 2014.

Seth, Jones (2008), "The Rise of Afghanistan's Insurgency: State Failure and Jihad", *International Security*, Vol. 32, No. 4.

Seul, J.R. (1999), "Ours is the Way of God: Religion, Identity and Inter-group Conflict", *Journal of Peace Research*, 36(5).

Stohl, Micheal (1988), "National Interest and State Terrorism in International Affairs", in Stohl Micheal (ed.), The Politics of Terrorism, New York and Basel, Marcel Dekker Inc.

Nathaniel, D.D. (2013), "The Aftermath of the Arab Spring and its Implication for Peace and Development in the Sahel and Sub-Saharan Africa", *Journal of Strategic Review for South Africa*, Vol. 35, No. 2.

Mben, P.H. et al. (2013), "Gates of Hell: Mali Conflict Opens New Front in War of Terror" http//www.start.unid.edu/gtd, accessed on September 15, 2014.

Mckay, A. (2011), "Introductory Notes", in A. Mckay (ed.), The Arab Spring of Discontent: A Collection of E-International Relations.

Mike, Gonzalez and Houman Barekat (2013), "Arms and the People: Popular Movements and the Military from the Paris Commune to the Arab Spring", Pluto Press Archway, London.

Moha, E. (2014), "Contextualising Multiculturalism and Democracy in the North Africa", (ed.), Aftermath of the Arab Spring, Routledge Studies in Middle Eastern Politics, New York.

Pillar, P.R. (2011), "Alienation and Rebellion in the Arab World", *Mediterranean Quarterly*.

"US Strategy towards Sub-Saharan Africa", June 2012, The White House, Washington.

Wolf, A. (2013), "Tunisia: Signs of Domestic Radicalisation in Post-Revolution", *CTC Sentinel*, Vol. 6, Issue 1.

Yonah, A. (2014), "Terrorism in North Africa and the Sahel", Fifth Annual Report, Inter-University Centre for Terrorism Studies, (IUCTS), US.

Zenn, J. (2013), "Boko Haram's International Connection", *CTC Sentinel*, Vol. 6, Issue 1.

4

Revisiting India-West Asia Relations

Alokka Dutta

Introduction

West Asia has always been a crucial region for India primarily, though not exclusively, because of the fact that this region alone accounts for over fifty percent of the oil consumed by India. Also, because of its large Muslim population base, India has a direct stake in the peace and prosperity of the region. This is certainly a factor which can allow her a greater voice in the affairs of this region vis-à-vis the other emerging giant of Asia, namely China. The relations between India and West Asia, especially the Gulf countries, are not a recent phenomenon. They date back to many centuries. These relations have always been cordial, friendly and mutually beneficial. Since ancient times, India has had economic, cultural and political contacts with this region. This region has not only been strategically important to global powers such as the US and European countries, but also to India due to its geo-strategic location, adequate availability of energy resources, a home for a considerable number of Indians and a big source of remittances for India along with the emerging prospects in the field of education and health sector.

Not only this, centuries old interaction between India and the region and its pivotal role in the Muslim world makes West Asian countries, politically and diplomatically important for India. Many West Asian countries have always supported India at the international forums. The other equally important factor that should be taken into account is the socio-cultural affinity of Indian Muslims with two holy paces Mecca and Medina located in this region. Every year, more than a lakh Indian Muslims go there for pilgrimage. They work as the binding force between the regions. They carry the Indian culture and values with them and spread the same in the region. This reinforces the common brotherhood between India and the West Asia.

It is also true that India has always been supportive of the Arab cause, especially Palestinians since India's Independence. Great leaders like Mahatma Gandhi and Pandit Jawaharlal Nehru strongly supported the rights of the Arabs. They felt that the socio-economic and political problems of West Asian people were not different from those of the Indians. Both the leaders had the same view on the issue of Palestine and other West Asian nations. India had in fact, supported the cause of Palestine in every UN and other international forums. It has extended all possible material and moral support to the Palestinian people.

It is, however, witnessed since the early 1990s that India's West Asian policy began to shift from its earlier policy. It is now debated whether India's changing West Asian policy is in favour of India's national interest or not? This could be understood by considering some factors which are vital in explaining India's interest in West Asian countries.

Economic Factors

No doubt, political and diplomatic factors based on national interest, are important. But at the same time, economic interest is one of the most crucial factors that should be given priority, while formulating a foreign policy. Taking this factor into consideration, India is having good relations with the West Asian countries since ancient times. The trade relation between the two could be traced back to the early part of the 20th century. Geographical proximity and economic interdependence are perhaps the factors responsible for having this greater interaction between the two regions which leads to mutual benefits. There have been substantial commitments through investments by way of joint ventures from both the sides.

Many agreements were signed between India and the West Asian countries in order to promote trade and investment. It is noted that Indian imports from the region stood at more than US$ 3 billion, while exports stood at less than US$ 2 billion in 1991. These values increased to more than US$ 8 billion of imports and less than US$ 4.5 billion of exports to this region in 2000. [1] It is, thus, observed that bilateral trade got an impetus on account of economic liberalisation taking place in India and the West Asian countries. The total value of trade with this region was more than US$ 5 billion in 1991 and US$ 12 billion in 2000. [2] This is expected go up to US$ 130 billion by 2013-14 which was around US$ 100 billion in 2009-10.

It we look in terms of country-wise standings, Saudi Arabia is one of the most important trading partners of India in the Gulf region. It is the 14th largest market for India and accounts for 7 percent of total Indian exports. [3] On the other hand, India is the fifth largest market for Saudi Arabia, contributing about 4.5 percent of its total exports. Thus, on the trade front, India has to explore opportunities to add more items to its export basket. Currently, India's export to Saudi Arabia mainly consists of cereals, manmade filament, apparels and clothing and iron and steel. [4] The country has to focus more and more on value-added industrial products and services. It is moving steadily towards a free market economy with gradual decontrolling of many important sectors of the economy. The service sector that offers potential for greater employment opportunities has been identified as one of the major focal areas. It offers an excellent opportunity to Indian industry to forge partnership with its counterparts in the Kingdom to build strong and vibrant economic relations between the two countries.

UAE is another major trading partner of India in the Gulf region. It is, in fact, India's biggest market in this region. India's exports to the UAE are diversified and contain a large basket of goods. Thus, the significance of UAE for India is not only for imports but also for exports. This is so because

UAE has emerged as the top most trading partner in the region. The UAE alone represents 70 percent of India's exports to the GCC countries. [5] Exports to the UAE comprised of 6 percent of India's global exports. The major items of exports from India include gems and jewellery, textiles, metals, machinery and instruments, plastic and linoleum, tea, basmati rice, drugs, pharmaceuticals, primary chemicals and semi-finished iron and steel.

Apart from this, information and news exports are emerging as a new area. On the other hand, India's main imports from the UAE are petroleum crude and products, pearls, precious and semi-precious stones, gold, metaliferious ores and scrap, fertilisers and organic and inorganic chemicals. [6] There are many advantages to have good trading relations with the UAE, as it is the nearest destination and Dubai has emerged as a major trading centre and a gateway to entire Arab world. Almost 95 percent of trade to the GCC and 85 percent to the WANA region transits through Dubai. It is noted that many Indian companies are setting up their centres in Dubai and Sharjah and bidding for many ventures in the world market. Thus, we can say that UAE is an important trading partner of India. [7]

There is also a substantial trade movement to Qatar via Dubai. A number of consumer goods from India are available and popular in Qatar. There are good prospects for diversification and expansion due to the low level of customs duties in Qatar (4 percent), which is close to the proposed common GCC external tariff of 5 percent. India's export basket is fairly diversified and includes foodstuffs, spices, tea, coffee, textiles, readymade garments, jewellery, light engineering goods, basic chemicals, steel pipes, and consumer electronics. As the Qatar market is competitive and highly quality conscious, there is a room for expanding our exports further, in areas where we are globally competitive.

Ammonia, sulphur, ethylene and polyethylene and urea are the items which India imports from Qatar. India also has substantial dealings with the Qatar Fertiliser Company (QAFCO) and the Qatar Petrochemical Company (QAPCO). India has not been a major customer for Qatar crude oil and products. However, it is set to emerge as one of Qatar's most important customers for LNG. With the third largest gas reserves in the world, Qatar is poised to emerge as a significant international supplier of energy for many decades to come. The Government of Qatar has made large investments in the development of its two LNG projects and port at Ras Laifan. With its large, expanding and long-term requirements of natural gas, India is naturally keen to take advantage of the existence of a reliable and virtually inexhaustible source of natural gas situated so close to its own consuming centres. This is the biggest agreement of its type in the world and will significantly raise the economic and commercial profile of India in Qatar, and of Qatar in India. This will also make India the biggest buyer of natural gas from Qatar.

India and Bahrain enjoy a trouble free and close political relationship. They also have a mutually beneficial bilateral economic cooperation. Bahrain is a small country but an important one. Both these countries are very close to each other in many respects. India also exports a comparatively large amount of goods and services to Bahrain. Since most of Bahrain's needs are met through imports, there exists a good potential for enhanced exports from India. The Indian private sector could play a more active role in this area. Participation in exhibitions, bilateral business visits and consistency in quality and supply schedules can go a long way in promoting Indian exports. Keeping in view the policy of Bahrain Government to establish joint ventures, especially in the small and medium industries, [8] India can take a lead in this field in order to enhance its exports to Bahrain.

There are mainly five items of exports from India to Bahrain. These are textiles, wood, vegetables, meat and rice. Moreover, there are good prospects for export of Indian products, particularly agricultural products, sanitary fixtures, drugs and pharmaceuticals, plywood, ceramic tiles, power generation and transmission equipment, light engineering goods, leather products, textiles and related products.

There is a large number of NRI business communities in Bahrain, who are engaged primarily in trading activity. They have invested a good amount in their business establishments in Bahrain.

Our relations with Oman are historical. There is evidence of people-to-people contacts dating back to the seventh century. In olden days, there was constant sea trade between the two countries.

An Indo-Oman Treaty of Friendship, Navigation and Commerce was signed by Sultan Said and the President of India in 1953. [9] It was probably one of the first agreements to be signed between India and any Arab country. The umbrella agreement for cooperation in the hydrocarbon field was a breakthrough in exploiting the potential for economic cooperation with the Gulf States.

The economic content was further concretized with the signature of the Agreement on Economic, Trade and Technical Cooperation which aimed at strengthening cooperation in the economic, commercial, industrial, tourist and technical fields. There was also the setting up of a joint commission to meet annually to follow up and to review the developments.

The recognition of Oman's strategic significance was further highlighted by the demonstration of a new political will and new economic initiatives. India's need for energy sources particularly for the Southern Grid and the possibility of supply of gas through a submarine pipeline heightened the awareness on both sides of the existence of common strategic interests. This became explicit in Oman's proposal to develop a 'Strategic Trade Alliance'. It is interesting to note that Oman is the only country in the region where India had a surplus balance of trade. [10]

Of late, the cooperation between India and Kuwait has increased in the field of science and technology. A number of visits have taken place between the two countries especially between the two apex bodies in the field of science and technology viz., Kuwait Institute of Scientific Research (KISR) and Council of Scientific and Industrial Research (CSIR). A number of Indian scientists/researchers are with KISR and other such organizations to further cooperation for mutual benefits.

The trade relations between India and Iran continue to register growth. The new economic policies followed by both India and Iran, has provided new opportunities for economic cooperation. This is of course in the field of energy, oil and gas.

The other fields where cooperation is required are in the field of textile machinery, bio-technology, power generation, agro-processing. Apart from this, Iran could play a very important role in providing India with commercial linkages with the central Asian countries. They are emerging as big markets for Indian goods.

India and Iraq have traditionally been very close to each other. Iraq was one of the major sources of India's oil imports and was also good market for Indian goods. But after the Gulf crisis in 1990-91 and in 2001, its economic activities were badly disturbed. Iraq is fighting its own battle to get rid of foreign powers such as the US and the UK.

As far as the relation with Israel is concerned, it must be taken into consideration because of the national interest in mind. The previous NDA government was misled and adopted the policy which favoured Israel rather than Gulf countries. It is noted that as soon as the current regime came to power, it was realised by the government and there is a correction in its foreign policy towards the Gulf countries.

We further see that India's economic relations with Yemen showed positive signs after the first meeting of Indo-Yemen joint committee for cooperation in areas such as trade and investment, small-scale industry, telecommunication, hydrocarbons, civil aviation, construction, science and technology, health and education, etc.

It is evident that there is a flourishing mutually beneficial economic connection with the Gulf region for India. India's crude oil import from the Gulf is worth US$ 17 to US$ 18 billion annually and India's annual trade with Arab countries is about US$ 10 billion. Thus, it can be argued that Gulf countries are a vital destination not only for trade and investment but also for energy supply to India.

Energy Factor

The energy factor must be taken into account, while deciding the West Asian policy. This is so because the Gulf region is not only important to the Indian economy but also to the world economy. It is considered to be the integral part of the global economy because of its one-third share of world oil production. The Gulf has well over half of the world's proven oil reserves. Most of the supply required to meet growing world demand is expected to come from OPEC and the region. It is expected that production would rise to 60 mbd by 2020 from 28 mbd in 1998. Virtually all this increase would come from this region. [11] Thus, the Persian Gulf region remains the largest depository of oil reserves and a major source of hydrocarbons. OPEC estimates are that oil reserves are over one trillion barrels, which can meet the requirement for more than 40 years. This was all due to the new discoveries which added the net 415 billion barrels to the world reserves.

The global proven natural gas reserves have been put at around 15.9 trillion cubic meters which is a 38 percent increase over the 1988 estimates. Despite all this, one cannot ignore the global pace of energy consumption which is so high and this can upset the current supply of energy. It is also obvious that hydrocarbons are non-renewable source of energy. So, their life span is bound to be limited. But this is also true that the threat is not so imminent as far as the physical reserves are concerned. Definitely, it is going to continue for a longer period of time. It is also possible that by that time, there may be more new discoveries of oil and gas in this region.

Thus, the Gulf holds an indispensable position in terms of energy stock for most of the countries like India. The region holds 63 percent of total world oil reserves and 34 percent of the world proven natural gas.

Thus, it is now clear that Gulf is enormously important to India simply because it meets the bulk of our energy needs and houses a large number of Indians. India must adopt a policy which can promote mutual understanding the economic cooperation.

India has to play a proactive role in order to maintain its interest in the region. It is also clear that Gulf is strategically most important to India mainly due to its close proximity. Hence, importing oil from this region is economically most viable. [12] Thus, having a cordial, strong and good relation with West Asia is crucial for India.

According to the Vision Document, the share of oil and gas in the total energy will be 45 percent by the year 2025. India's oil consumption has exceeded 100 million tones of which 33 million tonnes are indigenous. The remaining 77 million tonnes come from other countries.

The demand for crude oil and petroleum products is expected to grow to 364 million tonnes by 2025. On the other hand, it is noted that domestic production has been stagnant. Indian oil reserves would dry up even if only 30 percent of its demand were met from domestic production. The demand is growing at the rate of 5.77 percent per annum.

To meet this growing demand, the five countries that provide bulk of our requirements include Saudi Arabia, UAE, Kuwait, Iran and Nigeria accounting for more than 75 percent of oil. This clearly indicates the importance of these countries as far as the case of India's imports is concerned.

It is also observed that Saudi Arabia is the leading country that accounts for nearly 20 percent of total imports. The GCC countries such as Saudi Arabia, UAE, Kuwait, Qatar and Bahrain account for more than 50 percent. The Persian Gulf which includes Iraq and Iran, constitutes around 60 percent of import. [13] Thus, India is presently importing 70 percent of hydrocarbon which is expected to grow in future, since the consumption of energy is rapidly increasing in India owing to development taking place in different sectors of the economy. It is evident that there is a dominance of the GCC countries in terms of oil supply to India.

Just like food and defence, energy security challenge is one of the most important concerns for India in the age of globalization and liberalization. Hence, it has been realized that it is now strategically important for India to have a strong economic linkage with the Gulf countries in order to overcome its energy security challenges.

This is so, because India still imports more than 60 percent of its oil from the Gulf countries and this percentage is expected to rise further. Presently, India ranks sixth in the world in terms of energy consumption. US, China, Russia, Japan and Germany are ranked before India in this respect. India is amongst a few countries which imports over 70 percent of its petroleum requirements from outside the country.

Moreover, it is important to note that out of the total petroleum imports, more than 60 percent comes from the Gulf region which constitutes six Gulf Cooperation Council countries including Bahrain, Kuwait, Qatar, Saudi Arabia, United Arab Emirates and two more countries, Iran and Iraq. These countries are crucial for oil importer like India and China which has also recently become a net importer of oil.

Hence, we can say that the Gulf region has immense significance for India not only for trade and energy but also for employment opportunities available in this region and the consequent inward remittances.

Employment Factor

The Gulf countries are not only important from trade and investment and oil and natural gas point of view, but they are equally crucial for India in terms of employment to Indians in their respective countries. It is reported that at least 5 million Indians are employed in this region. These expatriate Indians remit more than US$ 10 billion dollars to India every year. [14] Prior to mid-1970s, there were mainly Arabs such as Egyptians, Yemenis, Palestinians, Lebanese and Sudanese in this region. It was noted that the Gulf monarchies grew increasingly worried about the possible political repercussions in the 1970s. Palestinians were viewed as politically subversive and Yemenis were involved in various anti-regime activities. As a result, the Gulf countries started to opt for workers from South and Southeast Asia who were seen as less likely to get involved in host country politics.

After the oil boom of 1973, the Gulf countries recruited foreign workers from both Arab and Asian countries for construction and industrialization. Indians also benefited from it. These were about 2.5 lakh Indian expatriates in 1975. This number rose to over 1.5 million in 1991. In the year 1999, there were 3 million Indian nationals gainfully employed in the Gulf. The number of Indian workers in the Gulf reached over 3.6 million in 2004. Of this, Saudi Arabia alone had 1.5 millions Indians and UAE had 1 million Indians. Qatar and Bahrain had more than 1,00,000 Indians each. There were about 4.5 lakh Indian expatriates each in Kuwait and Oman.

It is also true that Saudi Arabia and the United Arab Emirates import the maximum number of Indian labour in their respective countries followed by other GCC countries. It is evident that there is a shortage of manpower in these countries which is fulfilled by surplus manpower countries like India. The Indian government is now changing its migration policy in order to promote manpower employment in these countries. This is important because the manpower contributes significantly in the development of 'country where they are employed as well the country from where they come. Hence, we can say that this expatriate Indian labour force is the real asset for India and for the host countries as well. This is so because both India and host countries are beneficiaries on account of the contribution made by these expatriates.

Moreover, it also noted that all the Gulf States have launched many developmental programmes and schemes for the overall development of their countries. They need highly qualified and trained personnel who can work in their developmental projects. Hence, they will have to rely on skilled expatriate workers. It is suggested hereby that the Indian government must act in this direction in order to enhance the prospects of Indian workers in this region. Since India has a vast reservoir of well trained technical manpower in all disciplines such as engineering, medical, management, computer sciences, etc., it is desirable that a large number of Indians may be able to find lucrative jobs abroad, especially in the Gulf. This can be made possible if we have strong and friendly relations with West Asian countries.

Social and Cultural Factors

Education and health which are in fact the crucial factors for human resource development are identified as major sectors for future cooperation between India and the Gulf countries. Many agreements were signed between the two sides to promote cooperation in the field of education and arts. Two important languages Arabic and Persian of this region have been taught in India for a long time. In the same way, Urdu and Hindustani are spoken and understood by the people in the Gulf region. Bollywood film stars are very popular in the Gulf. They frequently visit Dubai, Muscat and many other Gulf cities on their popular demand of the native population. This all clearly indicates the significance of common culture prevailing between the Gulf and India.

Not only this, there are over 60 Indian schools which have been established in the Gulf countries. All schools follow the CBSE pattern, except one which is affiliated to the KSB (Kerala State Board). The Indian Ambassador is the patron of all the Indian schools in the region. The control of the Indian schools is under the board of directors who are appointed by the ambassador from among permanent members of the Indian community. The board coordinates the functioning of management committees of all Indian schools.

There are more than 30 Indian schools in the UAE. They are doing well and are catering to the needs of Indian children. They are all well established and are serving the needs of the large Indian community residing in Kuwait and the Kuwaitis alike. It is noted that there are four major Indian schools such as Indian School, Muscat, Indian School, Al-Ghubia, Indian School, Wadi Kabir and Indian School, Dar Sait that are located in Muscat. Recently, an Indian School in Seeb, an adjacent township has started functioning. The oldest school is the Indian School, Muscat initially known as Arya Kelavani Mandal which was established on July 2, 1939. Hindu Maliajan Association took the responsibility of managing the school. Thus, the presence of 15 Indian schools in various parts of Oman indicates that Indian community attaches a great deal of importance to education for its coming generation. For higher and technical education, their wards generally come to India.

Moreover, Indian IT companies have been actively involved in setting up an IT park in Muscat and Knowledge Oasis in Muscat (KOM). Both the IT colleges have an Indian connection. One is in affiliation with the Manipal Academy of Higher Education while other is a joint venture with Birla Institute of Technology, Ranchi. [16]

Omani companies also have several joint ventures in India. Oman Computer Services International develops computer software at Bangalore. Shantha Bio-techniques, Hyderabad is one of India's most well known bio-technology company. Nisma Airocon International, Chennai manufactures heat pump for air conditioners. The Zubair Group has setup a furniture manufacturing unit in Tamil Nadu in collaboration with Balaji Group of Chennai. Bahwan Cybertech has an IT training company in Chennai and regularly sends trainees from

Oman to India. These trainees go back to Oman with great satisfaction.

Sultan Qaboos University in Muscat is the only university which is well-reputed and the most important institution of higher learning in Oman. It was found that many Omanis have studied in India and they still keep coming in large number to Indian universities and institutions of higher education, especially in technical subjects such as engineering, IT and medicine. Bangalore, Pune and Chennai are the major cities where they prefer to come for education. It is presently estimated that there are over 1,500 Omanis who are pursuing higher education in India. It was also found that every year a number of Omani officials come to India to acquire training in different fields under the ITEC Programme of the Government or India.

As far as the socio-cultural factor is concerned, it is witnessed that a large number Indian Muslims go to two holy places (Mecca and Madina) for pilgrimage every year on the occasion of Eid-Adha. This pilgrimage provides enough opportunities for cultural interaction between the Indians and the West Asian people. This cultural interaction strengthens our overall relations for our mutual benefit.

India and Egypt

For long, India has maintained close ties with such secular nationalist Arab states as Egypt, Algeria, Syria, Iraq and Libya. Among them, Egypt typifies the trend where traditionally close relations had declined in importance, as India has begun to pay attention to other power centres, especially the Gulf States. [17] Both India (which gained Independence in 1947) and Egypt (which established an independent government after the 1952 revolution) emerged on the world stage at the same time, fought the same number of wars, adopted nationalization as part of their economic policy, founded the NAM and remained closer to Moscow than to the US. But unlike India, Egypt drifted to being an authoritarian and repressive state. It also became a very close security partner of the US in the region and in the Arab-Israeli peace process, which did not make much progress.

In the 1990s, Indo-Egyptian ties were clouded by the Kashmir dispute, the destruction of the Babri Masjid, the BJP-led coalition government's policy towards Indian Muslims and growing Indo-Israeli military and strategic ties. All these led one Indian expert to conclude that 'with the NAM in disarray and with the Palestine issue losing its prominence in India's foreign policy agenda, there has been hardly any other significant political motive/issue either at the international or regional level to necessitate a high profile political *entente* between India and Egypt'. [18]

Nevertheless, India honoured Egyptian President Hosni Mubarak with the Jawaharlal Nehru Award for International Understanding for the year 1995, keeping in view the contribution of the Egyptian leader to the Arab-Israeli peace process. Mubarak delayed his visit to India to receive the prestigious award until 2009 due to the Arab countries' concern over India's growing ties with Israel, especially in the area of security. He may have also wanted to mediate over the Kashmir issue as he maintained close ties with Pakistan. In contrast to the cold political relations, economic ties have witnessed encouraging trends. The market-friendly policy followed by the two countries has contributed to diversifying and broadening the field of economic cooperation, allowing a much bigger role of the private sector since 1991.

India's response to the political unrest against the misrule of the Mubarak regime in early 2011 was cautious initially. The Ministry of External Affairs issued a statement on 30th January, 2011, merely noting that India was 'closely following with concern' the developments in Egypt. Perhaps the safety of some 3,200 Indians working (mostly in Cairo) in Egypt at that time was the prime reason for the restraint. Most of them were brought back safely. As the intensity of the protests grew in response to the brutal use of force by the government forces and in the midst of growing support from various quarters of the international community to the cause of the peaceful protesters, India too began to make suitable amends to its cautious approach. In particular, there was criticism within India regarding India's caution on internal developments in Egypt. Promptly, the Indian position turned positive. India acknowledged the Egyptian mass protests as an 'articulation of the aspirations of the Egyptian people for reform', while hoping that the political tension would be resolved in a peaceful manner, in the best interests of the people of Egypt.

Conclusion

Our interest in West Asia is manifold. We can now conclude by saying that there is a need to further strengthen our relations with West Asia, especially the Gulf countries. Now, the time has come to be interdependent so as to get maximum benefit in the process of development taking place on both sides. This is very much possible in the era of globalization and information technology. The economic and diplomatic potential of India is fully realised by the West Asian countries. They have no inhibition to expand their ties with India in any strategic field. Working together would make place them in a position to meet the challenges created by globalization. Hence, India needs to pursue a proactive economic policy towards the region.

India must act in such as way that it can be instrumental to promote stability in this region which is always beneficial for the region and India's energy security and manpower requirements. It would be a wise step to further develop economic, diplomatic and cultural relations with these countries. India must adopt a policy, which can promote to seek Indian manpower in the region so as to earn higher foreign exchange. An emphasis should also be given to diversify the relations beyond trade, energy and expatriates. It is also true that the influence of China and Pakistan is increasing in West Asia.

To compete with them, India has to play a proactive role in order to maintain its interest in the region. On the one hand, after a long period of time, these countries are hoping to become the shapers of their own destinies and on the other hand, there is resurgence of Taliban posing an imminent threat. Strong governance will be the need of the day and since this region is practically the neighbourhood of India, with Pakistan as a failing state, the role of India will become significant in the coming days. Her secular credentials, pro-Palestine stand, empathy towards the Kurdish community, experiences of viable democracy, her effective leadership in playing the role of a mediator and her contribution towards peacekeeping operations—all place India in an esteemed pedestal in the region.

Thus, we see that India now has a variety of interests in West Asia. These interests will only be best served if we adopt a pragmatic Indian policy based on existing reality. Despite challenges like religious extremism, maritime piracy, nuclear proliferation, US interference and democratic upheavals, it is surely possible for India to strive for beneficial and cordial ties with the countries of West Asia.

Endnotes

1. A.K. Ramakrishnan, "Mahatma Gandhi Rejected Zionism", released August 15, 2001, The Wisdom Fund, Arlington, VA, http://www.twf.org.

2. Bansidhar Pradhan, "Changing Dynamics of India's West Asian Policy", *International Studies*, Vol. 40, No. 1, 2004, p. 4.

3. Anisur Rahman, "Indo-Saudi Relations: A Need for Coming Closer", *Strategic Bulletin*, Vol. IV, No. 2 and 3, May-September 1999, p. 20.

4. Jaideep Singh and Tersest Schaffer, "Overview", *South Asia Monitor*, CSIS, Vol. 9, Issue 2, 2004.

5. Shivaji Sarkar, "Tapping Alternative Market", Special Gulf News, August 14, 2004.

6. Ibid.

7. Government of India, "Annual Report, 2000-2001", The Gulf, West Asia and North Africa, p. 38.

8. Indian Embassy (Bahrain), "Indo-Bahrain Relations", http://indianembassy-bah.com.

9. Embassy of India (Muscat), "Indo-Oman Relations", http://www.indemb-oman.org/india-oman-relation.html.

10. Muhammad Azhar, "Gulf Economies and Indo-Gulf Relations", Delhi, New Horizon Publishers, 1999.

11. Anisur Rahman, "Gulf: A Crucial Factor in India's Energy Requirements for Development", in S.N. Malakar (ed.), India's Energy Security and the Gulf, New Delhi, Academic Excellence, 2006, p. 28.

12. Ibid.

13. Girijesh Pant, "India's Energy Security: The Gulf Factor", Occasional Paper Series: CWAAS/SIS, JNU, GSP, 2002.

14. Anisur Rahman, "Indian Labour Migration to the Gulf: A Socio-Economic Analysis", New Delhi: Rajat Publications, 2001, p. 34.

15. *The Times of India*, New Delhi, Friday, November 18, 2005.

16. Embassy of India, (Muscat), "Indo-Oman Relations", http://indemb.oman.org/commercial-services-eco relations.html.

17. A.K. Pasha, "India and West Asia: Past and Future", in N.S. Sisodia and A.K. Behuria, (eds.), West Asia in Turmoil: Implications for Global Security, 2007, pp. 441-470.

18. P.R. Mudiam, "India and the Middle East", London: British Academic Press, 1994.

5

Expatriation from India to UAE: Role of Recruitment Agencies

Mahjabin Banu

Introduction

The process of expatriation is a complex phenomena and it varies from country to country. Expatriates are temporary workers who work in a foreign location under contracts for a limited duration. These work contracts may be renewed multiple times; thus prolonging the stay of expatriate workers in a foreign country. Though many studies also used the term 'migrants' and 'expatriates' interchangeably, this paper uses the term 'expatriates', considering the fact that migrant workers in Gulf countries are not entitled for permanent settlement. A survey, undertaken by HSBC called 'Expat Explorer 2013', also shows that expatriates in the GCC are among the most satisfied with the state of their local economies compared to individuals in other regions around the world. Four countries in the GCC, Oman (1st), Qatar (6th), UAE (9th) and Saudi Arabia (10th), are among the top 10 economies in terms of expat satisfaction. [1]

Moreover, GCC hosts 6 million Indians and globally, Indian diaspora accounts for 20 million (ILO-EU Asia Migration Project, 2010). [2] As per the World Bank, Indian is expected to receive US$ 71 billion in remittances in 2013, [3] the highest among the developing countries. [4] Discourses on Indian expatriates' favourite destinations shows that the six-member Gulf Cooperation Council (GCC) comprising of Bahrain, Kuwait, Oman, Qatar, United Arab Emirates (UAE) and Saudi Arabia, has been among the most preferred. Other than the GCC countries, Indian expatriates have been choosing neighbouring nations such as Sri Lanka, Bangladesh and Nepal. However, considering the case of Indian migration to Canada, an exception is also recognized owing to distant location.

There is also an impact on demographic structure of destination countries due to continuously increasing inflow of migrant workers. The presence of a large numbers of expatriates has outnumbered the national population in countries like UAE, where the national population has become a minority. Migration flows are characterized by a basic distinction between skilled labour, semi-skilled labour and unskilled labour. Khadria (2010), mentions that Indian migrant workers in the GCC countries belong to all three categories of labour *viz.* skilled professionals (e.g., doctors, nurses, engineers, architects, accountants and managers), semi-skilled workers (e.g., craftsmen, drivers, artisans and other technical workers), and unskilled labourers (e.g., those engaged in construction sites, farmlands, livestock ranches, shops and stores and households).

This paper also reveals that Indian white-collar workers and professionals comprise only about 30 percent of the Indian workers in these countries; the rest are semi-skilled and unskilled workers. In fact, UAE hosts all three categories of Indian migrants, and that too in large numbers. This distinction is highly relevant because the comparison on the basis of skills, positions them differently in the labour market in terms of their contribution and working conditions.

UAE is witnessing a high rate of growth as compared to other countries in the Arabian Gulf region. The gross domestic product (GDP) in the United Arab Emirates was worth US $ 360 billion in 2011. [5]

This has helped the country to attract expatriates from all over the world. Infrastructure and construction are going to assist this growth rate and sustain it further. UAE comprises of seven emirates, Abu Dhabi, Dubai, Sharjah, Ras-al-Khaimah, Al-Ain, Fujairah and Ajman. Dubai and Abu Dhabi are UAE's most vibrant emirates in terms of economy. Abu Dhabi is the emirate where majority of the country's oil reserves are concentrated. It is the capital city and the centre of political, cultural and business activities. Moreover, because of its continuous efforts in economic diversification, the country has been able to reduce the portion of gross domestic product (GDP) based on natural resources output, to 25 percent of the local GDP. [6] The country has become a modern state and has developed a state-of-the-art infrastructure which ensures a good quality of life.

Review of Literature

UAE is a transit point of international trade and a major entrepot (re-export) centre of the world. This rapid pace of infrastructural development and related developmental activities has in fact brought in a huge number of migrant workers to the country. Moreover, development of hydrocarbon infrastructure sector resulted in inflow of a large number of expatriates in UAE. The UAE's economy is the most liberal as well as transparent in the Arab world and is also closely linked to the free market factors. [7]

The UAE has one of the highest migrant to citizen ratios in the world with over 80 percent as migrants. Rahman (2010) identifies five phases of migration to the GCC: the first phase was the period prior to the 1970s oil boom, the second phase was post-1970 oil price hike, third phase was late 1970s and early 1980s, the fourth phase was late 1982 and the fifth phase was in 1990s. The expatriation of unskilled and semi-skilled segments was prominent after the oil boom in GCC which led to the increase in demand for both skilled and unskilled labour in the construction industry (Sasikumar and Hussain, 2008; Khadria, 2006).

As discussed earlier, Canada has been an exceptional case as a favourite destination for Indian expatriates. Attraction towards Canada has been for unskilled labourers. The institutional regime and policies of the Government of Canada has played a vital role. However, the case of UAE has been different. Movement of Indian expatriates to UAE increased further with the opening up of an absorbing global labour market since 2000, irrespective of the restrictive regimes therein. This has resulted in an increase in expatriates in high earning jobs.

Labour migration has played an important role and helped the countries of the Gulf to advance towards one of the most economically developed regions in the world, Dito (2008). He concludes that, if managed well, it can still play a decisive role in the development agenda of both receiving and sending countries and suggested to reduce their oil dependency for sustainable economic development and right based labour policy to overcome labour problems. Wikramsekara (2002) examines the trends and issues in Asian labour migration and challenges faced by countries and the trade union movement in protection of migrant workers. The study traces the main trends and features in Asian labour migration in the recent past, and identifies the most vulnerable groups of migrant workers who need priority attention. Khadria (2006) mentions that the labour migrants to the Gulf have been viewed as the main source of remittances, swelling India's foreign exchange reserves. Ray (2003) suggests improving relations between migrants and host communities, employers and recruitment agencies and governments and argues that contracted labourers are assumed to have been recruited by outsourcing agencies in their home countries. [8]

Sub-agents and labour brokers in the sending countries often have poor information about the contracts they arrange. [9] This disinformation leads to the various professional and living challenges which the expatriates face in the Gulf region.

A report titled "Return Migrant Entrepreneurs in India" under ILO-EU Asia Migration Project, focuses on those temporary migrants who return to India after completing their short-term employment contracts most of whom were employed in the Middle East and Southeast Asian countries (ILO). [10] Table 5.1 is a summary of those returned migrants who were interviewed as part of the case study. [11]

Table 5.1: Problems Faced by Indian Expatriates

Problems Mentioned by Migrants in the Country of Destination	No. of Mentions
Cheating or abuse by employers	8
Lack of help from embassy	4
Cheating by placement agents	4
Loneliness/cultural shock in destination	2
Health problems	2
Lack of insurance scheme for migrants in trouble	1
Helping stranded migrants	1
Visa/immigration and legal problems	1

Source: Authors compilation based on *ILO-EU Asia Migration Project*, ILO Sub-regional Office, New Delhi.

This study has a two-fold objective: (a) to examine the process of expatriation from India to the UAE, and (b) assessing the role of overseas recruitment consultancies in this process.

Though there exist various researches on India-GCC engagements in terms of economic and diaspora studies, yet there is negligible academic literature on the process of expatriation and the role of overseas recruitment consultants to the UAE.

Various researches, as mentioned in the review of literature, have identified and analysed the trends of migration to UAE and other GCC countries based on the skill set and the labour markets pull factors. [12]

This is because a major section of the workforce in the UAE constitutes of expatriates from different nationalities and varied cultural backgrounds. But, this study discusses the expatriation process which itself plays a significant role in diaspora studies and related policy interventions both by the home as well as the host countries.

This paper attempts to examine the process of expatriation from India to the UAE by conducting a field survey. The study is based on primary data, which includes field survey of six overseas recruitment consultancies based in New Delhi. The respondents are the employees of these consultancies and the sample size is 30. There exist a huge number of consultancies in Delhi, and most of them works with only 2 or 3 consultants working there. The researcher visited many consultancies with at least 5 consultants working there and got response from 30 consultants spread across six such consultants.

To fulfil the objective of the research, the researcher administered 20 questions to the consultants working in South Delhi areas. This survey was conducted during May-July 2013. Questions involved the basic recruitment process the consultant follows, such as how much they charge from candidate, mode of recruitment, who bears the cost of conduct of interview, in how many locations they schedule it and preferred location for that, what all facilities they provide to the candidate before and after expatriation, what they did for getting license and how much time it takes etc.

During the field study, it was found that the consultancies do not support the survey as they feel that some official from the Ministry has come for the investigation.

The researcher convinced that this is for academic purposes only and that the names will be kept confidential; even then some preferred not to fill the form in their own handwriting. Some of the consultancies did not gave chance to talk even after prior appointment and could not be included in the study.

Overseas Recruitment System and Expatriation Process

Understanding overseas recruitment system is a complex task, given the number of stakeholders involved in the process and the time associated with it. It, thus, requires an in-depth study.

Philippines has shown their well managed practice for temporary labour sending management practices. Philippines Overseas Employment Administration (POEA) shows government interventions in three areas: (a) linking participation to qualified employers, workers and recruitment and manning agencies, (b) creating rules and regulations to govern the recruitment process and set minimum standards of employment, and (c) maintaining a system of adjudication to ensure compliance (Migration Policy Institute).

There exist illegal recruitments by unauthorized placement agencies in India (MOIA-CDS Report, 2009). [13] This also affects employment in UAE and other Gulf countries by creating difficulties for the Government of India. It also poses serious problems for various stakeholders involved in the process, as these agencies are beyond the reach of the normal regulatory machinery.

The situation becomes more complex and troublesome when nexus is formed between the unauthorized (unlicensed) recruiting agents and the corrupt elements in the official regulative and law-enforcing agencies (MOIA-CDS Report, 2009).

To understand the whole process of recruitment and to get the actual insights to the actual picture of the process of expatriation, the researcher did field visit.

Based on the field study, it was found that generally there are three ways of recruitment as per the response of the consultants, which are as follows: (a) direct recruitment, i.e. directly by the employer (27 percent); (b) through recruitment agencies/consultancies (60 percent); and (c) other ways, i.e. through sub-agents (13 percent) or by any other means.

Direct Recruitment Drive by the Organization: It is conducted mostly by the company itself by giving advertisement in the print media directly from the company. Though it also includes recruitment through referral system, but does not involve any third party or a consultancy. Referral system means that employee who is already working with the organization tells about the vacancy to his known ones or relatives who are eligible for that particular job.

Recruitment by the Recruitment Agencies (RAs): Based on their types, they can be divided in two parts: (a)

Licensed: the Ministry of Overseas Indian Affairs (MOIA) keeps a list of 1,835 licensed agents; [14] and, (b) Unlicensed: there are several of unlicensed consultancies operating in the job market. They illegally recruit job candidates on the behalf of licensed recruiting agencies. [15] MOIA has also launched an awareness programme related to the fake employment activities operating through the sub-agents and has generated a toll free number, to know about the recruitment agencies through which they are getting opportunities to know if they are licensed or unlicensed. [16] It itself verifies that there still exist unlicensed recruitment agencies in the market.

The recruitments are further sub-divided as follows: (a) On company's payroll—in case of UAE, recruitments are done generally on company's payroll; and, (b) Third party payroll— in third party payroll candidates are not directly on companies payroll and their payroll is outsourced by another company. In such cases, a candidate does not get full salary for the first few months and the salary is deducted as commission by the third party. In some cases company later absorbs the candidate on their own payroll.

Recruiting Through Sub-agents: Sub-agents work with the consultancies and help them by providing manpower from remote rural areas. Sub-agents are, however, banned by MOIA. But during the field visit, it was found that most of the consultancies/recruitment agencies were working with sub-agents.

Sub-agents get money from consultancies and also charge from the prospective candidates depending upon how much a candidate can afford.

These sub-agents also threaten the candidates not to mention to the consultants, the fee charged by them. They go to the extent of saying that if the candidate reveals the truth to the consultancies, then the sub-agent will ruin his chances of being selected, explained one of the consultants during the field visit.

Generally, the workers are not aware of the licensed and

unlicensed process of recruitment by various recruitment agencies. Those who are deceived by the unlicensed recruitment agencies become more prone to financial and mental exploitation. Many a times, the agents at local level collaborate with travel agents and engage in illegal immigration which is another serious issue, which attracts policy attention. In such cases, protection to labourers is also limited and is not provided by both the home and the host country.

The process of recruitment in overseas organizations from India generally follows the process of direct advertisements or advertisements in collaboration with the authorized recruitment agencies in India. The advertisement for recruitment is also advertised on behalf of these agencies. Role of recruitment agencies/consultancies is not only limited to provide pool of talent but also to organize the whole recruitment drive such as hotel bookings for the company, delegation visiting to India for conducting interviews, hiring travel agents and managing the interview venue. They strive hard to do their best so that the project in hand converts into an annual event for them. The cost of hosting the overseas delegation is somewhere around ₹ 50,000 to ₹ 4 lakh and to compensate it, they charge from candidates as well, revealed a consultant after successive talks with him during the three months of field visit in New Delhi.

Requirement of large number of workforce for UAE and other Gulf countries results in large agglomeration of labour for the recruitment. Sometimes, these numbers are beyond the capacity of these agencies to handle it. Therefore, the big and authorized agencies/consultancies share their demand for talent acquisition with the sub-agents, who works at the grassroots to target the rural and sub-urban people. Most of these potential candidates are ready to pay between ₹ 50,000 to ₹ 1 lakh or even more for a job of ₹ 8,000 to ₹ 15,000 per month. This amount is paid as a recruitment charge. It is found during discussions with recruiters that occasionally, semi-skilled and unskilled labours have to sell their land to pay the amount. The

MOIA report also mentions that the working of recruitment agencies, both licensed and unlicensed, is a matter of serious concern as many cases of cheating and betrayal come to light frequently. [17]

The Minister for Overseas Indian Affairs, stated in the Parliament and to the media that "administrative apparatus itself has accentuated corruption as a result of the nexus formed between erring government officials and recruiting agencies, leading to increasing exploitation of the poor". [18] Also on the other hand, as Khowla Mattar, a senior specialist on worker's rights, said, "the culture of rights is weak in our societies; unless we enhance this culture at the regional level, migrant workers will continue to be exploited and their rights would be abused". [19]

Role of Overseas Recruitment Consultants

The Indian Council of Overseas Employment (ICOE) has set up three phases for a candidate seeking a job under India-Gulf migration process. [20] These phases include pre-departure phase, employment phase and the capacity building phase. The last phase means the return of the expatriates to his or her home country. The Indian government positively refers to this period as the capacity building phase. [21]

In case of unskilled India-UAE migrants, the UAE government has formulated policies to have a control over recruitment agencies to overcome the cases of labour abuse. The proper procedure for recruitment of an Indian wanting to work in the UAE is a due process to be followed by the recruitment agencies (MOIA, 2008). The process is designed in a way that when an overseas (in this case, the UAE) employer needs skilled, semi-skilled or unskilled manpower, it sends a demand letter to the recruitment agency (RA) or agencies through which it recruits. [22]

To curb the unreasonably high amount charged by the consultancy, MOIA has fixed the maximum amount a recruitment consultant can charge from a job-candidate, at

₹ 10,000 (approximately US$ 200). However, it is found that they charge ₹ 80,000 and even above in some cases, explains one of the candidate who already got selected by one of the 6 consultancies taken for study. [23] It was also found that as per the agreement, the employer has to pay a certain amount as commission to the recruiter, but it remains on paper and is actually not paid by the employer. [24] Consequently, recruitment agencies charge high fees from the candidates (revealed one of the consultants during the field study).

Consultancies say that they take charges for their services, —but they are already paid for that by the employer at UAE— apart from that if we add all the services charges, then also, it may range between ₹ 40,000 to ₹ 80,000. As in the case of UAE, the visa cost and visa processing is already borne by the employer. Also, 60 percent of consultants mention that the cost of conducting interviews at various locations in India and travel and lodging expenses of the employer during their India visit is borne by the consultants and it costs somewhere starting from ₹ 50,000 to ₹ 4 lakh, explained one of the consultants in informal talks during the field visit. 83 percent consultants revealed that they charge fee from the candidates.

With regard to the fee charged from the candidates, 64 percent replied that they charge up to ₹ 20,000 and 29 percent said they charge between ₹ 20,000 and ₹ 40,000 and 7 percent said they charge up to ₹ 80,000 in some cases. This contradicts the limits fixed by MOIA of ₹ 10,000. If this is the case of licensed agencies/consultancies, we can imagine the scenario of unlicensed consultancies. However, the scenario is not the same in all licensed consultancies.

There also exists compulsion for such high fees from recruitment agencies. 87 percent respondents remained silent or avoided to answer when asked about the process of licensing and time it took to be completed; though the proper channel is already mentioned on the MOIA website.

Apart from the activity of licensing procedure, when the question was asked about the functionality of a consultancy at ground level, the big picture of sub-agents popped up. However, without these sub-agents, it is actually impossible to reach remote locations unless the consultancies have a huge manpower and that too located nation-wide at grassroots level. This is something which seems impossible, explained one of the senior consultants during the field visit. It is, therefore, suggested that regularizing the channel of sub-agents would benefit the recruitment process. Nevertheless, the sub-agents should be adequately trained by the consultancies.

This initiative requires a policy intervention at the first instance. Secondly, an active government as well as non-governmental organizations' (NGOs) support will help villagers in remote areas and the prospective candidates therein to become aware about the licensed and unlicensed recruitment agencies and their pros and cons. This way they would not be lured by untrained and unauthentic sub-agents.

The overseas recruitment consultancies or recruitment agencies (licensed) try to follow rest of the steps as designed by the Ministry. Whenever they want to conduct the interview at different locations then such agencies need to take prior approval for conducting interviews for the Gulf region from the Ministry of Overseas Indian Affairs.

Also, they need to mention about the location where the interview is scheduled besides mentioning the job description of the vacancies. Further, this has to be stamped, explained Mr. Rahman (name changed), who works with a reputed recruitment agency in New Delhi for the last 10 years. During the field visit, he discussed with the researcher extensively for around 2 hours related to the whole process of recruitment for and expatriation to the UAE. The whole cost of conducting job interviews at multi-location is borne by the consultancy itself and it starts from ₹ 50,000 and can go up to ₹ 4 lakh. This expenditure includes travelling cost of consultants and clients, booking of travel cabs, venue booking, and food and lodging, depending upon the client and the level of recruitment, explained one of the consultants during the informal conversation.

When asked about how recruitment agencies get recruitment projects, one of the consultants explained that they send the company's (agency's) representative to visit the employer's place in the UAE and try to establish a networking with them. It is more or less like business development for which they need to meet personally which costs high during the initial stages. They also mentioned that there are large numbers of consultancies operating in the market that are licensed and unlicensed too. However, getting the recruitment project from a reputed client is not so easy.

It was found that 83 percent consultants opined that their recruitment agency does take job-related responsibility; and they get the employment agreement done at their office. They also make sure that the job-candidate understands all the terms and conditions of employment before signing it.

Conclusion

The varying answers of the recruitment agencies related to the amount they charge from the candidates reflect that there is no fixed criteria for it, but it is based on the ability and willingness of the candidates to pay. However, MOIA has already fixed the amount. Also, while documenting the process of expatriation, it is also found that unlicensed consultancies also operate in the market with the help of licensed consultancy's license (as licensed consultancies are not capable of fulfilling the manpower demand due to unavailability of staffs, places or contacts with sub-agents who operate in rural areas). It solicits strong implementing machinery, under the aegis of MOIA.

Efforts need to be made at the policy level to deter the exploitation of loopholes in recruitment process as well as in the issuance of license. Mere stringent rule-making will not help to curb the malpractices—the effective implementation of rules is crucial to improve the process of expatriation from India. Hence, policy intervention is the need of the hour and an active role of government as well as support from NGOs will help the aspiring candidates in remote areas to become aware about the licensed and unlicensed recruitment agencies. Pre-departure orientation programme may be beneficial for the expatriates. Recent toll free number generated by the MOIA to enquire about licensed or unlicensed consultancies may be fruitful for improving the current situation but an extensive policy research is still the requirement.

Endnotes

1. http://www.gulf-times.com/Mobile/Qatar/178/details/370704/Qatar--among--%E2%80%98top-10-countries-in-the-world-for-expat-satisfaction%E2%80%99.
2. Based on estimates made by the high level committee on the Indian diaspora, mentioned in "Return Migrant Entrepreneurs in India: Case Studies and Policy Recommendations", ILO-EU Asia Migration Project, ILO Sub-regional Office, New Delhi, 2010.
3. http://www.moneycontrol.com/news/economy/india-gets-whopping-3671bnremittances13-tops-globe_962974.html, accessed on 12th March, 2014.
4. See news item, "With Rupee Depreciating, India to Top Global Remittances Chart with $71 Billion: World Bank", *The Economic Times* (ET) Bureau, 4th October, 2013, available at: http://articles.economictimes.indiatimes.com/2013-10-04/news/42718315_1_current-account-deficit-remittances-world-bank, accessed on 21st October, 2013.
5. Mentioned in "UAE's GDP", available at: http://www.tradingeconomics.com/united-arab-emirates/gdp, accessed on 14th March, 2014.
6. Mentioned in "Country UAE", available at: http://www.globalstudyuk.com/uae-country.shtml, accessed on 14th March, 2014.
7. Mentioned by Mohammad bin Rashid Al Maktoum in his book, "My Vision: Challenges in the Race for Excellence", His highness Sheikh Mohammed bin Rashid Al Maktoum is Vice-President and Prime Minister of UAE and ruler of Dubai.

8. The word "recruitment consultancy", "recruitment agency" and "overseas recruitment consultancies" are used interchangeably in this study.

9. The word "sub-agents" are used to indicate illegal operating person or institution which are unlicensed.

10. Ibid 2.

11. "Return Migrant Entrepreneurs in India: Case Studies and Policy Recommendations", ILO-EU Asia Migration Project, ILO Sub-regional Office, New Delhi, 2010.

12. Pull factors includes demand of labour created by lots of developmental activities as a result of oil boom in the host country

13. Mentions the report titled "Beyond the Existing Structures: Revamping Overseas Recruitment System in India", by Rajan, Verghese, Jayakumar, MOIA-CDS Report, 2009, p. 6.

14. The term "licensed agents" means licenced recruitment agency or consultancy.

15. Based on field survey conducted by the researcher.

16. Toll free number awareness advertisement has been seen on Delhi Doordarshan Television Channel, on 3rd March, 2014.

17. http://www.cds.edu/download_files/MOIA-CDS per cent20Final per cent20Report per cent20June per cent202009.pdf, accessed on 18th November, 2012.

18. Statement by the Minister for Overseas Indian Affairs in the parliament and to the media on September 2007 mentions, "Dreaming Mobility and Buying Vulnerability: Overseas Recruitment Practices" by S. Irudaya Rajan, V.J. Verghese and M.S. Ayakumar.

19. See Khowla Mattar, "The Rights of Migrant Workers Ignored", *Gulfnews*, available at:
http://archive.gulfnews.com/articles/07/06/12/10131775.html.

20. The name of ICOE has been changed to India Centre for Migration (ICM).

21. Indian Council of Overseas Employment, "Impact Assessment of Global Recession on Indian Migrant Workers in Countries of the Gulf Cooperation Council and Malaysia", New Delhi: ICOE, 2009, p. 21.

22. Demand letter is an official letter of requisition for recruitment.

23. Reveals one of the selected candidates by the consultancy in skilled segment during researcher's field visit.

24. Explains one of the senior consultants, during the researcher's field visit.

References

Dito, Mohammed Ebrahim (2008), "GCC Labour Migration Governance", United Nations Expert Group Meeting on International Migration and Development in Asia and the Pacific, UNESCWA Population Division, Department of Economic and Social Affairs, Bangkok, Thailand, 20-21 September.

Jureidini, Ray (2003), "Migrant Workers and Xenophobia in the Middle East: Identities, Conflict and Cohesion", Programme Paper No. 2, United Nations Research Institute for Social Development.

Khadria, Binod (2006), "India: Skilled Migration to Developed Countries: Labour Migration to the Gulf", available at: http://meme.phpwebhosting.com/~migracion/modules/ve7/2.pdf, pp. 4-37.

Khadria, Binod (2010), "Paradigm Shifts in India's Migration Policy towards the Gulf", in *Migration and the Gulf*, Middle East Institute, Washington D.C., pp. 67-69.

Khalaf, Sulayman and Saad Alkobaisi (1999), "Migrants' Strategies of Coping and Patterns of Accommodation in the Oil-Rich Gulf Societies: Evidence from the UAE", *British Journal of Middle Eastern Studies*, Vol. 26, No. 2, pp. 271-298.

MOIA (2008), "Annual Report 2008", Ministry of Overseas Indian Affairs, Government of India.

MOIA (2009), "Annual Report 2009", Ministry of Overseas Indian Affairs, Government of India.

Rahman, A. (2010), "Migration and Human Rights in the Gulf", *Migration and the Gulf*, Middle East Institute, Washington D.C. pp. 16-18.

Sasikumar, S.K. and Zakir Hussain (2008), "Managing International Labour Migration from India: Policies and Perspectives", ILO Asia-Pacific Working Paper Series.

Wickramasekera, Piyasiri (2002), "Asian Labour Migration: Issues and Challenges in an Era of Globalization", International Migration Programme, ILO, Geneva.

"Return Migrant Entrepreneurs in India: Case Studies and Policy Recommendations", ILO-EU Asia Migration Project, ILO Sub-

regional Office, New Delhi, 2010.
"Dreaming Mobility and Buying Vulnerability: Overseas Recruitment Practices", by S. Irudaya Rajan, V.J. Verghese and M.S. Ayakumar, Routledge India, 2011.

6

Changing Geo-political Situation in WANA and Policy Implications for India

Harendra Kumar

Introduction

West Asia and North Africa region (WANA) comprises of the following: Bahrain, Kuwait, Oman, Qatar, Saudi Arabia, United Arab Emirates, Jordan, Iraq, Yemen, Lebanon, Syria, Libya, Algeria, Morocco, Egypt, South Sudan, North Sudan, and Tunisia. These countries share a common language, religion and culture i.e. Arabic and Islam. Iran and Israel are also part of WANA.

There are large disparities of income between countries in this region. The exporters of oil countries with very small population represent the region's highest per capita income and the remaining population has a very low per capita income. The most economically disadvantaged states of this region are Eritrea, Ethiopia, Somalia and Sudan. A large population is employed in agriculture which is nearly half of the total population. Economic disparities fuel migration from one country to another and from rural to urban areas within the region.

The macroeconomic and trade indicators (Tables 6.1 and 6.2) clearly show the strength and potential of the region. The average GDP growth is positive i.e. about 3.5 percent per annum which is more than the average growth of developed (1.1 percent) and transition economies (3.1 percent) but less than the developing economies. The trade export percentage in relation to total world exports was 7.18 and import percentage to the total world imports was 4.18 in 2013. The import growth rate is much higher compared to the developing economies.

Table 6.1: Macroeconomic Indicators of the WANA Region (2013)

	Population (000')	GDP (US$ mn)	GDP Growth Rate	Per Capita GDP Growth Rate	FDI (US$ mn)
World	71,62,119	5,59,96,879	2.22	1.05	2,54,64,165
Developing Economies	58,13,328	17,18,7085	4.57	3.18	84,83,009
Transition Economies	3,01,259	14,09,318	2.13	2.04	9,28,015
Developed Economies	10,47,532	37,40,0476	1.18	0.75	1,60,53,141
Northern Africa	21,00,02.4	47,41,67.3	3.10	1.38	2,41,789
Western Asia	22,01,02.2	18,65,097	3.49	1.47	6,62,803

Source: UNCTAD based on IMF, *World Economic Outlook Database*, April 2013.

Table 6.2: Trade Indicators of the WANA Region (2013)

	Exports (US$ mn)	Imports (US$ mn)	Growth Rate of Exports	Growth Rate of Imports
World	1,88,17,705	1,87,97,776	2.24	1.46
Developing Economies	84,32,934	79,81,063	2.59	3.97
Transition Economies	80,59,05.3	61,86,87.2	-2.02	0.73
Developed Economies	95,78,866	1,01,98,026	2.30	-0.37
Northern Africa	1,82,934	2,19,597	-10.64	-0.36
Western Asia	13,50,937	9,12,777	1.22	8.19

Contd...

	Trade Balance (US$ mn)	Percentage of Total World Exports	Percentage of Total World Imports
World	19,929	100	100
Developing Economies	4,51,871	44.8	42.4
Transition Economies	1,87,218	4.2	3.2
Developed Economies	-6,19,160	50.9	54.2
Northern Africa	-36,662	0.9	1.1
Western Asia	4,38,160	7.1	4.8

Source: UNCTAD based on IMF, *World Economic Outlook Database*, April 2013.

Cross-Cutting Issues in the Region and Reasons for Crisis

The current transition process in a number of WANA countries has exhibited disorderly phenomena and new variables have been added to the political situation. The crises in Iraq, Israel-Palestine, Libya and Syria have continued to challenge the traditional actors and alliances in the region. The regional power shift has caused serious disorder and the clear trend of strategic contraction of the US has caused the differentiation of geo-political forces and uncertainty in the situation. In the emerging order, there will be greater devolution of powers to the regional actors. The ongoing turmoil in this region is rooted in the Arab Uprising, which began with the most popular and widespread unrest in Tunisia in December 2010, and rapidly spread to other countries in the WANA and the Gulf region.

In the first two years, the revolts and conflicts in the region mainly led to regime changes—the fall of the regime of Ben Ali, Hosni Mubarak and Muammar Gaddafi in Tunisia, Egypt and Libya respectively. By the end of 2011, Yemeni President Ali Abdullah Saleh handed over the power; the Assad regime in Syria had poured into a deep crisis, and people started to speculate as which would be the next country.

After the first three years of the so called "Arab Spring", the over expectations of progress towards democracy have turned out to be misplaced. The initial optimism of regime change and democratization, has given way to serious concerns about the much-hyped revolutions. The revolt has impacted the Arab World in different degrees to different nations—the first group include nations which saw a series of strong and mass protests leading to regime changes such as Tunisia, Libya, Egypt and Yemen. The second group of nations saw demonstrations that were contained by the ruling regimes through targeted but limited political and economic reforms such as Kuwait, Saudi Arabia and Oman or by stern actions against protestors such as Bahrain and Jordan. The third group of nations includes Qatar and UAE, which are yet to witness any such protests and have used this as an opportunity to enhance their influence regionally.

The regional balance is in change, with Iraq supposed to have come across Iran's sway, and also there are clear divisions within the GCC, and it is evident through the withdrawal of the diplomats of Saudi Arabia, UAE and Bahrain from Qatar. A number of Arab countries are represented by Islamic political parties and Muslim brotherhood has occupied the political arena in most of the countries like Morocco, Tunisia, Egypt and Libya. In the last three years, the majority of Arab nations experienced political disorder and lost a clear line of development in the process of democratization.

In 2013, the Egyptian military overthrew the democratically elected President Morsi with the support of general public and declared state of emergency. The process causing heavy causalities—1,600 people sacrificed their lives officially but the claim it said to be more than 2,000. Following this, the Egyptian military arrested 8,000-10,000 people of Muslim Brotherhood and their supporters. The majority of Muslim Brotherhood leaders were arrested at that time. [1] Because of the severe social division, the national home security was too tense. Consequently, the Tunisian political transition also faced twists and turns and on 6th February, 2013, human rights activist Chokri Belaid was shot, causing public protest and unrest. In July 2013, the president of the People's Movement Party (the main opposition party), Mohammed Brahmi was also shot dead, causing a wave of demonstrations and retaliation across the country once again. This movement compelled the ruling and the opposition parties to come to agreement that a transitional government composed of independent persons would be established to supervise the new elections.

In many countries of West Asia and North Africa, the situation remains the same. In Yemen, the transition process is also lagging behind and the new constitution has still not been constituted and the domestic situation remains fragile. Syria is in the grip of civil war, although the chemical weapons crisis in the suburbs of the Syrian capital Damascus was ultimately eased by the Syrian government which ultimately cooperated and destroyed the chemical weapons. After the division of Sudan in north-south, the economic situation worsened and the retaliation continues, which led to an increasingly volatile situation. The elections were held in Jordan but the King did not allow the elected leader to form the cabinet as promised. Libya also went through political chaos after the violent death of the US ambassador to Libya in 2012 and on October 10, 2013, the interim prime minister was briefly kidnapped by the militants and some district of the capital Tripoli was occupied by the militants. A deep domestic crisis and other incidents show that the revolts in this region would be a long and tough process.

The changing situation in Egypt is an important indicator in the Arab region. Since the Egyptian Revolution of 2011 and 2013, people have started to talk as regards which model will emerge in Egypt—the Turkish model or the Algerian model, accompanied by the rise of political Islam represented by the Muslim Brotherhood, especially since 14th August, 2013 when the Egyptian military used force to evacuate supporters of the Muslim Brotherhood. In Algeria, the military cancelled the elections in 1991, which saw the victory of the Islamic Salvation Front. [2]

Because of the political turmoil, there is no economic development in last three years since the 2011 revolution. The Egyptian national debt has increased manifold, almost equal to the GDP. A quarter of the national revenue is to be used to pay the interest of the debts and there is also a high inflation (over 15 percent) and an unemployment rate of over 30 percent. The development of the Egyptian economy is dependent on foreign investment and tourism. The tourism is now insignificant in Egypt; many five-star hotels (more than 60) have closed nationwide and the world-famous pyramids of Giza have been deserted. The country is now in the most difficult times because of the clash between military authorities and the Muslim Brotherhood which forcefully stepped down from the peak of its power. It would be a blessing for the country and the people of Egypt if there is an end to political deadlock and social reconciliation by igniting the democratic process but situation is just the opposite.

Over and above, there is serious conflict between the moderate and radical Islam in this region. In 2013, the elected President Morsi was overthrown in Egypt and the Ennahda Movement suffered a serious setback in Tunisia. The moderate Islam and radicals have created another effect in this region. In a wider sense, different kind of "triangles" of forces have been formed like "Al-Qaeda" in Arab, "Boko Haram" in Nigeria, "Islamic Fighting Group" in Libya, etc.

In this vast region of Muslim communities, the trend since 9/11 shows that wherever the unrest appears, it appeals to the Islamic extremists and lead them to new aggregation and this can be experienced in Iraq after the 2003 war, Libya after the 2011 war and Syria that plunged into civil war in 2012. [3]

There are several possible reasons and explanation for the crisis in the region. It is a time tested truth that people cannot be suppressed or dominated by any ruler forever. After some point of time, critical threshold is reached and people become prepared for massive sacrifices that can take the face of standard models of rational choice. The democratic aspiration of the people led to mass public mobilization. No one expected and predicted that huge public discontent would force many rulers to relinquish their freedom or fight against all odds to save their rule and even they could not get time to isolate themselves from the public wrath. The youth and people of Arab world rose and hung on to their mission against the authoritarian regimes. [4] They shook the regimes in many countries in the region, successfully toppling autocrats like Hosni Mubarak, Ali Abdullah Saleh, Muammar-al-Gaddafi and Ben Ali in countries of Egypt, Yemen, Libya and Tunisia respectively. It also sparked significant regional protests in Syria, Bahrain, Saudi Arabia, Morocco and Algeria with an alacrity that took everyone by surprise.

Most of the countries in this region continue to ride on the crest of booming oil revenues—however, the recent recession has induced relative decline in the revenues. The Arab Maghreb Union states comprising of Algeria, Libya, Morocco and Tunisia had not been as rich as their counterparts in Arab region. These societies had been somewhat more open, both socially and politically, and had a history of mass activism. These rulers did manage to create their own supporters who benefited from these regimes both economically and administratively. They were the bulwark of sanity for both the masses and the rulers who had no direct means of connection. Gradually, the leaders lost their support from public in general. Globalisation had a silent impact on them. The delusion of authoritarianism could not register it. Historically, it only needed a spark to set the masses into motion. The uprising in Tunisia fuelled the inspiration and territorial borders suddenly became meaningless in the Arab world. [5]

In totality, the Arab upheaval is believed to have been inspired by discontentment with the rulers and governments, particularly by the youth. The other factors which fuelled this mass discontentment include corruption, unemployment, violations of human rights, dictatorship monarchy, increasing inflation rate and changing climate with increasing famine etc.

Another reason for the turmoil and upheaval for decades in WANA is the vested interests of Israel and Saudi Arabia along with the desire for hegemony by the US in the region. They sometimes operate along separate lines and sometimes together.

Since the creation of Israel in 1948, it is trying to exercise its dominance over the entire region to ensure its security. Israel joined hands with western countries especially with Britain and France in 1956. Further, the Israeli leaders and US adopted strategies to substantiate that the US would defend and put Israeli interests on top over anything else. The 1967 war of Israel could also be a mirrored image to unreasonable influence of US Congress and the Senate.

After Reza Pahlavi in Persia, it was thought that it happened because of the backing of the US, and this is how Israel had been involved in war. And also the war between Iran and Iraq resulted in nearly five lakh deaths.

After the Iraq-Iran War in 1988, the European powers and Israeli antagonism towards Republic of Iraq was driven by many a things. Republic of Iraq had biggest oil reserves and at the beginning years of Saddam's rule, it was presumed that a large part of this wealth would be utilized in arms and ammunition. Since the 1960s, endlessly the US began to develop a deep and intended interest among the region with the objective owing to oil. It explains why these two oil created monarchies among the region, Saudi Arabia and the Republic of Iraq, were courted. The North American country designated to invade and occupy the Republic of Iraq in 2003. [6] It had been to boot due to the need for command on oil. A recent deal between the US and Saudi Arabia has resulted in over-supply of the petroleum worldwide with low price with the objective of suppressing Russia that heavily captivated with the export of petroleum as its main earning. Many countries of the WANA region facilitate America and other western nations in many ways.

Geo-political Actors and Geo-politics in the Region

Strategic contraction of US in this region directly and indirectly affects the geo-politics. America has already been exposed in the Syrian chemical weapon crisis. Now the trend of US strategic contraction from this region is clear. The national security adviser Susan Rice for US President in 2013 re-evaluated the Middle East policy. According to the assessment report, the US will adopt a new strategy to make diplomacy the priority option and avoid military intervention in the region. Rice gave a speech on November 20, 2013, entitled "America's Future in Asia" at Georgetown University, with clear indication that "no matter how many hotspots emerge elsewhere, we will continue to deepen our enduring commitment to the Middle East". [7] The geo-political situation in the Middle East has become interlinked with the American strategic withdrawal. The American alliance on Syrian issue in the Middle East appears to have loosened. US's relations with other nations like Saudi Arabia, Israel, Turkey and Egypt are taking a different root all together.

Geographically, WANA is on collision and fusion of Eastern and Western civilizations along with the two continents of Asia and Africa. This region is a "double crossroads" in the world. Therefore, the old civilization, fusion and conflict have created a very unique geo-political situation. There are four major powers viz., Israel, Iran, Saudi Arabia and Turkey from geo-political angle and five different ethnic groups viz., Turkish, Jewish, Kurdish, Persians and Arabs. The Kurds are spread in Iran, Iraq, Syria and Turkey and in the junction territory known as Kurdistan. The issues related to Kurdish are a leading factor for instability in this region and this may become a new agenda in incoming years.

Among these all geo-political forces, the Arabs and Persians can be understood as rivals because they fought for more than a thousand of years. After the Second World War, Israel established itself as an independent state with the support of US and also fostered the Pahlavi Dynasty in Iran. So, Israel and Iran became the two pillars of US policy in the Middle East and Arabs-Israelis became the principal source of conflict in the region. The Islamic Revolution of 1979 in Iran turned Iran and the US into enemies along with Israel. The relationship has become more complex in recent years. The accession of Turkey from EU is also a cause of frustration and this factor has become more active. If the four major forces remain balanced or relatively balanced, this region will be calm and stable. When the geo-political balance is broken between these four, the whole region will be in turmoil. If any of these four forces got upper hand, the other nations would feel uncomfortable and it would in geo-political imbalance in the region.

The geo-political relationships became more complex. Since the late 1990s, Turkey's EU accession was repeatedly frustrated and Turkey returned to the Middle East. The Turkish factors in the Middle East geo-politics became more active. Historically, when all four major geo-political forces can remain balanced or relatively balanced, the Middle East will be able to maintain a relatively calm and stable situation; when the geo-political balance of power between the four is broken, the situation in the Middle East would be in turmoil. If any of the forces got an upper hand, the other nations will feel uncomfortable, and geo-political situation would start to move between turbulence and stability—it is relative. After the Islamic Revolution in Iran, there has been a domestic turmoil; US-Iran hostile relations disturbed the balance of geo-political power in the Middle East, followed by an eight year Iraq-Iran war.

The US after the Gulf War is curbing Iran and Iraq in the Middle East—while these two states constituted checks and balances on them. Additionally, US implemented, "contain Iraq in the east, and promote peace talks in the west".

The new imbalance of geo-political power appeared after 9/11; the United States of America fought two wars successively in Iraq and Afghanistan. Because of this War, the Taliban regime and the Saddam regime were destroyed and Iran gathered influence in this region. This has produced another geo-political issue. In the elections after the War, the Shiites have been in power in Iraq, which indirectly injected Iran's influence into Iraq. Iran, through its ally in the Arab world also affected the Palestinian Sunni Hamas. This "Shiite rise" in Islamic history caused panic in the Sunni Arab world and other traditional countries. Iran's dominance and this geo-political power imbalance are of course a serious threat to US interests in this region. The US maintained this regional balance of power by suppressing Iran through military threat and harsh economic sanctions. However, the attitude of America in the Egyptian military's actions to overthrow the Morsi regime and its indecisiveness in the Syrian chemical weapons crisis in 2013 has made the strategic retreat from the WANA clear now. [8]

Therefore, resumption of the situation in Egypt and the Iranian nuclear talks and the regional geo-political forces has kicked off a new round of re-differentiation. Saudi rejected the non-permanent seat at the United Nations Security Council and Turkey is ready to buy Chinese missiles HQ-9. Israel is trying to establish a fresh relationship with France and other countries of Europe. Russian Defence Minister Sergei Shoiguon on November 14, 2013 held the 2+2 talks with their Egyptian counterparts. The rapprochement of Russia and Egypt has worried the Israeli government. In fact, WANA is too important for the US that it did not really leave it. It is clear that the US has made some adjustments in its strategy and policy for this region which would lead to a strong reaction among its allies.

India's Trade with WANA

Over the last 15 years, India has created ripple growth miracle in the global economy and also its economic relations with its extended neighbourhoods. West Asian countries and GCC in particular, have also shown economic growth, backed by more oil revenues which have created great opportunities for deepening cooperation with India. The beginning of synergies—mostly from the energy-matrix in the annals of India and West Asian cooperation—primarily centre on incipient open regionalism and gradual multilateralism. Importance to such evolving regional cooperation and interdependence can be gleaned from present as well as the regional and bilateral merchandise trade in future.

The global crisis shows negligible reduction in potential growth of national income of India. Estimates suggest a reduction in the income growth in emerging economies of East Asia but marginally for India. India's growth is mostly domestic demand driven. Even fixed capital formation growth has exhibited significant acceleration in recent years.

Similarly, most of the west Asian economies during the global recession period have shown positive growth because of economic diversification and development programmes which have been running over the past couple of decades. Still these countries are heavily dependent on petroleum revenues and at the same time, economies in this region are undergoing an economic transformation by improving the non-oil sectors also. Apart from this, WANA countries have used oil and gas revenues to support industrial development, build public infrastructure and invest in programmes including education, employment and health.

The economic growth of Iran and Iraq has been badly affected due to political conflicts and economic sanctions from European countries and the US. As a result, the outlook of these countries seems to be highly uncertain. Being large producers of oil, they will continue to interact with the world—it has been visible in the last few years.

Over the years, substantial changes have been witnessed in the trade profile of India and the Gulf. India's globalization process has been followed by a more stable and transparent trade policy with a long-term vision as opposed to a short-run annual approach. Hence, the new Foreign Trade Policy takes an integrated view of the development of India's trade. The objective of the new trade policy is doubling of India's share of global merchandise trade and trade policy acts as an effective tool for economic growth with a strong emphasis on generation of employment. The policy aims at creating an environment of trust and transparency by bringing down transactions costs and identifying focus areas to nurture and develop a global hub for trade, services and manufacturing. Such positive changes have resulted in India's enhanced trade performance in the recent past.

Earlier, the petroleum exports were prominent in West Asian countries global trade profile. With the diversification of economic base, by optimizing the value chain of oil and sectors like banking, finance and tourism, imports started to take important place in global trade portfolio, thereby signifying the economic dynamism. Currently, this dynamism is gaining strength day by day.

Boosting trade cooperation requires a proper understanding of trends in bilateral trade. It is also essential to assess the relative importance of the countries of WANA as important trading partners. For this, it is important to examine the variations in the volume and composition of bilateral trade flows over a time period. An analysis of trade composition and understanding of the nature of trade to their comparative advantages is also necessary for devising a trade-augmenting bilateral policy framework. Over the last two decades, trade relations between the India and WANA have developed by leaps and bounds.

In 2010, the West Asia and North Africa (WANA) region accounted for the largest share in India's total trade. Gulf countries' contribution in India's total trade stood at 18 percent for exports and 25 percent for imports. Particularly, UAE is India's single largest trading partner followed by other countries of the region. India's trade with the West Asian countries has registered a many fold increase in volume from US$ 6.1 billion in 2000-01 to nearly US$ 200 billion in the year 2013-14.

In fact, the compounded annual average growth rate of bilateral trade between India and West Asian nations was a staggering 23 percent over the last five years. The top trading partners in the West Asia region were UAE (US$ 74.72 billion), Saudi Arabia (US$ 43.19 billion) and Iraq (US$ 21.35 billion) (Table 6.3). [9]

The structure and pattern of trade with West Asian countries shows a different picture. If you will analyze, the composition of India's exports to the West Asian countries based on comparable data from UNCTAD, suggests that five areas in HS 2-digit sectors accounted for 65 percent of exports. These are iron and steel, mineral fuels, oils, distillation products, cereals; electrical and electronic equipment and copper and articles.

Similarly, India's import composition from the same region shows that five sectors accounted for 75 percent of imports from the region. These products included mineral fuels, ores and slag, pearls and precious stones, inorganic chemicals and organic chemicals. This concludes that India's export-import basket is thinly spread and shares a wide range of sectors and is characterized by high concentration in few product categories. In other words, the trade profile is not diversified.

Policy Options for India in WANA

West Asia and North Africa is a very important region for India in many ways like homeland security, intelligence sharing, counter-terrorism, small arms trafficking, controlling money laundering and smuggling and financing of terror.

Table 6.3: Export-Import from India to West Asia and North Africa

Country	Exports 2012-13 (US$ mn)	Exports 2013-14 (US$ mn)	Imports 2012-13 (US$ mn)	Imports 2013-14 (US$ mn)	% Share 2012-13 (US$ mn)
Algeria	1,088	1,069	683	860	0.36
Bahrain	603	639	664	563	0.2
Egypt	2,897	2,562	2,553	2,388	0.96
Iran	3,351	4,971	11,594	10,307	1.12
Iraq	1,278	918	19,247	18,520	0.43
Israel	3,739	3,746	2,356	2,311	1.24
Jordan	1,000	1,595	942	610	0.33
Kuwait	1,061	1,061	16,588	17,153	0.35
Lebanon	250	293	30	37	0.08
Libya	215	287	1,834	451	0.07
Morocco	426	385	1,309	879	0.14
Oman	2,599	2,812	2,009	2,951	0.87
Qatar	687	969	15,693	15,707	0.23
Saudi Arabia	9,785	12,218	33,998	36,403	3.26
Sudan	755	863	127	436	0.25
Syria	258	234	80	76	0.09
Tunisia	298	274	215	91	0.1
UAE	36,316	30,520	39,138	29,019	12.09
Yemen	1,477.27	1,306.99	958.92	782.18	0.49

Contd...

Country	% Share 2013-14 (US$ mn)	Export Growth Rate 2012-13	Export Growth Rate 2013-14	Import Growth Rate 2012-13	Import Growth Rate 2013-14
Algeria	0.34	30.29	-1.76	-67.63	25.95
Bahrain	0.2	37.16	5.95	-26.64	-15.26
Egypt	0.81	19.63	-11.57	-14.95	-6.44
Iran	1.58	38.97	48.35	-15.92	-11.1
Iraq	0.29	67.3	-28.17	1.74	-3.77
Israel	1.19	-7.44	0.19	-10.57	-1.91
Jordan	0.51	21.86	59.5	-36.46	-35.19
Kuwait	0.34	-10.19	0.01	0.9	3.41
Lebanon	0.09	8.05	17.15	39.98	24.13
Libya	0.09	253.07	33.39	4,687.03	-75.39
Morocco	0.12	14.63	-9.6	0.29	-8.26
Oman	0.89	96.61	8.19	-39.94	46.85
Qatar	0.31	-14.95	41.02	21.5	0.1
Saudi Arabia	3.89	72.18	24.86	6.85	7.08
Sudan	0.27	5.26	14.29	-70.49	243.28
Syria	0.07	-51.76	-9.54	-54.95	-4.66
Tunisia	0.09	4.61	-8.26	30.95	-57.48
UAE	9.71	4.61	-8.26	6.48	-25.85
Yemen	0.42	102.19	-11.53	-1.22	-18.43

Source: *Export-Import Data Bank*, Ministry of Commerce and Industry, Government of India.

The effects of the so-called Arab Spring, internal violence in Syria and Iraq, have created a climate of political uncertainty in many countries in this region, and have serious regional and international repercussions, and India is not an exception to this.

Now there is a serious question on democratization process after much-hyped revolutions. The "Arab Spring" has impacted the region in different degrees—in few countries, the regime change, in other, limited to political and economic reforms and in the rest, an opportunity to enhance their regional influence.

The changing scenario in West Asia and North Africa has impelled India to rethink of its assumptions and role. India has to think and consider new options carefully while strategizing the new line of relationship. If required, India can provide political support to different nations of the region on issues of common interest in the West Asia, given her secular and non-alignment background. India can also offer capacity building assistance and institutional mechanisms.

India has a very deep rooted democracy from the beginning and we believe in "Unity in Diversity"—many a countries in the region are looking forward to this and have also expressed a desire for India to play a more active role. India is in favour of providing non-military solutions to the Syrian conflict and India attended and participated in the Geneva conference held in Montreux on 22nd January, 2014. India supported for the elimination of chemical weapons and vowed to provide technical and financial support towards the humanitarian assistance.

It would be useful to have consensus with key members of the opposition while strengthening high-level relationship with the governments. The proxy war between Saudi Arabia and Iran has potential implications for India. India should stay out of sectarian alliances and at the same time, be prepared for any extremist backlash as there is a threat of the spread of extremism in the region. We need to be very careful about such a development. Military and security cooperation on counter-terrorism, intelligence sharing, piracy, money laundering, small arms smuggling, financing terror activities etc. are the areas of concern and these should be important elements in our ties with the West Asian countries.

Instead of the regional conflict, our bilateral relations with virtually all countries of the WANA region have been progressing smoothly and India has managed to insulate its core interests from the negative fallout of regional developments. India should strengthen relations with all the regional players—ties and treaties with GCC countries in particular—to fulfil its energy requirements. Apart from this, we need continuous engagement with Iran and Israel at different levels while maintaining parallel relationship with the US, which remains important bilaterally, for regional stability. In the case of Syria and Iraq, our approach should not be misconstrued as being a partisan one.

The people of West Asia and North Africa see greater opportunities to remake their destiny. As an emerging power, India needs to take this opportunity to recreate its ties and relationships with the West Asian and North African countries. The task is unenviable. As a growing and massive energy hungry economy, India has to guarantee her oil supply from this region. But is India's concern limited merely to this commercial trigger? This question needs the attention of India's foreign policymakers at this hour. It is a question of role and not mere diplomacy.

But the political seismograph of West Asia and North Africa has become visibly unstable. India had been equivocating on Iran for a long time. India's deeply held commitment to the ideas of inviolability of borders and legal sovereignty would not allow her to join the new phase of western activism to recreate relations by military means in the interest of freedom, democracy and civilian security. Since this region increasingly looks up to New Delhi as a prospective commercial partner of tomorrow, we must rethink on our existing take on West Asia and create a new discourse in keeping with the evolving norms.

With ideological blinkers taken off for good, Indian foreign policy has become decidedly pragmatic and self-confident. India's ties with the US remain in the fulcrum of our new foreign policy. Moreover, India and the US share a whole range of interests that are structurally vital to both the states. Even in terms of norms, culture, business and demographics, the countries are remarkably convergent. India must reorient her ties with the Arab world to build an indispensable partnership. India can offset the conflict and instability by greater economic engagement with all the nations in the region. It needs to capture the untapped potential through an integrated business approach to increase trade volumes.

Endnotes

1. UK Financial Times website on November 16, 2013, "Iran will

Test Obama's Foreign Policy", the alliance between the United States and the Middle East is rapidly collapsing. The US is losing its influence on almost all its allies in the Middle East

2. Kazerooni, I. and Prince, R., October 23, 2013, "Turkey and the Middle-East Realignment: Washington has Reduced Turkey's Role in its Middle-East Supporting Cast", retrieved December 21, 2013 from http://fpif.org/turkey-middle-east-realignment.

3. Davidson, C. (2013), "After the Sheikhs: The Coming Collapse of the Gulf Monarchies", Oxford: Oxford University Press.

4. Kazerooni, I. and Prince, R., October 23, 2013, "Turkey and the Middle-East Realignment: Washington has Reduced Turkey's Role in its Middle-East Supporting Cast", retrieved December 21, 2013 from http://fpif.org/turkey-middle-east-realignment.

5. Liu, H. and Yang, G., July 2013, "On the Issue of Nigerian Boko Haram", West Asia-North Africa, No. 4.

6. Liu, Z., November 30, 2013, "The Roots and New Development of Terrorism in West Asia and North Africa", in the Thirteenth National Security Forum, Symposium on Sharing Security and Global Governance.

7. New York Times, August 5, 2013, and Pravda, November 15, 2013.

8. Xinhua News Agency, December 3, 2013 and Global Times September 25, 2013.

9. As per the Ministry of Commerce database, WANA region comprises of countries namely, Bahrain, Kuwait, Oman, Qatar, Saudi Arabia, UAE, Iran, Iraq, Egypt, Syria, Lebanon and Algeria.

References

Bozorgmehr, N. (2013), "Iran Hardliners Block Rouhani's Domestic Reforms", *Financial Times*.

Davidson, C. (2013), "After the Sheikhs: The Coming Collapse of the Gulf Monarchies", Oxford: Oxford University Press.

Kazerooni, I. and Prince, R. (2013), "Turkey and the Middle-East Realignment: Washington has Reduced Turkey's Role in its Middle-East Supporting Cast", available at: http://fpif.org/turkey-middle-east-realignment.

World Bank (2011), "Multipolarity: The New Global Economy", *Global Development Horizons 2011*, Washington D.C.

Ariff, Mohamed and Tan EuChye (1992), "ASEAN-Pacific Trade Relations", *ASEAN Economic Bulletin*, Vol. 8, No. 3, March.

Balassa, Bela (1965), "Trade Liberalization and Revealed Comparative Advantage", *The Manchester School of Economic and Social Studies*, No. 33, pp. 99-123.

Balassa, Bela (1977), "'Revealed Comparative Advantage Revisited: An Analysis of Relative Export Shares of the Industrial Countries, 1953-1971", *The Manchester School of Economic and Social Studies*, No. 45(4), pp. 327-344.

Batra, Amita and Zeba Khan (2005), "Revealed Comparative Advantage: An Analysis for India and China", Indian Council for Research on International Economic Relations (ICRIER), Working Paper No. 168, New Delhi.

Bach, Daniel C. (2012), "Patrimonialism and Neo-patrimonialism: Comparative Receptions and Transcriptions", in Daniel C. Bach and Mamoudou Gazibo (ed.), Neo-patrimonialism in Africa and Beyond, London and New York: Routledge.

Bowman, Tom (2013), "UN Report Puts Afghan Opium Poppy Cultivation at Record High", *NPR News*, 13th November, available at:
http://wap.npr. org/news/World/245057706.

Burange, L.G. and Sheetal, J. Chaddha (2008), "India's Revealed Comparative Advantage in Merchandise Trade", Department of Economics, University of Mumbai, Working Paper No. UDE, 2008.

Government of India (2009), "Foreign Trade Policy (FTP), 2009-2014".

Park, Cyn-Young, Ruperto, Majuca and Josef Yap (2010), "The 2008 Financial Crisis and Potential Output in Asia: Impact and Policy Implications", ADB Working Paper Series on Regional Economic Integration.

Pradhan, Samir Ranjan (2006), "India's Export Potential to the GCC Countries", UNESCAP Research Paper, Bangkok, Thailand.

Rao, V.L. and Das, R.U. (1996), "Comparative Advantage and Pattern of Trade in Asia-Pacific", RIS Discussion Paper, September 17-18.

7

Indian Migrant Workers in the WANA Region

Tanvi Tripathi

Introduction

The social and economic understanding of WANA (West Asia and North Africa) countries is incomplete without understanding the character and composition of migrant workforce of WANA region. The study of Indian migrant workers comprising the highest number among them is a less explored but highly fascinating tale. Consider this: Saudi Arabia, the biggest nation in the Gulf region and dominant oil and hydrocarbons producer and exporter had 1.8 million of Indian population during the year 2012 which is 20 percent of the expatriate community of Saudi Arabia (MOIA, 2012). The Indian community in the UAE, numbering 1.75 million (MOIA, 2012), constitutes 30 percent (Embassy of India, Abu Dhabi-UAE, 2014) of the total population. Yet, the Indian migrants are the unsung heroes of development story of this region even though they are one of the major contributors in the economy of the host countries and that of India.

India has one of the most diverse and complex migration histories in the world. In the modern times, political, economic and technological developments have facilitated emigration in response to demands of skill, services or labour. Thus, in the era of globalization and migration, economic trends are reinforcing mutual interdependence.

The overseas Indian community is the result of different waves of migration over hundreds of years determined by an assortment of reasons—mercantilism, colonialism and globalization. Its early experiences make up an adventure of trials, tribulations and the possible triumph of determination and diligent work. In the last three decades of the 20th century, the character of relocation started to change and 'another diaspora' headed by high talented experts moving to the western world and semi-skilled contract workers moving to the Gulf, West and South East Asia developed.

The Ministry of Overseas Indian Affairs gauges that there are approximately 6 million Indian workers living and working in West Asia, mostly in Gulf States. Of the approximately 22 million overseas Indians—which include non-resident Indians and people of Indian origin—those in the Gulf comprise the second largest expatriate Indian community in any single region in the world, with Southeast Asia accounting for the maximum (MOIA, 2012).

There has been a significant growth in the number of Indian migrants to the Gulf over the course of past four decades. In the 1970s, when Indians began moving to the Gulf in search of employment, their number was approximately 40,000. In 1980, there were 50,000 registered Indian expatriates in the Gulf States and an estimated 1 million in 1985 (Pattnayak, 2008: 64).

The number of Indian expatriates in the Gulf stood at around 3.5 million in 2011 and it was about 6 million Indian workers by 2012. The highest influx of Indians in the Gulf region is from the southern Indian states which include Andhra Pradesh, Tamil Nadu and Kerala and the rest from Gujarat, Maharashtra, Goa, Punjab, Uttar Pradesh, Bihar and Rajasthan. According to Pradhan, "The Indian expatriate community can be categorized into four broad groups:

- Unskilled workers, employed in construction companies, municipalities, agricultural farms and as domestic workers;
- Skilled and semi- skilled workers;
- Professionals such as doctors, engineers, accountants, employed in government and private sectors; and
- Businessmen" (Pradhan, 2009: 20).

The Gulf region in the past decade has experienced robust economic growth and the main force behind this growth is a strong labour force, composed mainly of migrant workers. Because of its geographical proximity, the Gulf has been a preferred destination for workers from India for many years. More recently, however, the GCC (Gulf Cooperation Council) has been attracting foreign labour from all over the world. The GCC comprises Bahrain, Kuwait, Oman, Qatar, Saudi Arabia and the United Arab Emirates (UAE). Though extraordinarily diverse, expatriate workers from around the world share one common goal: to send as much money home as possible (GCC, 2014).

The profile of Indian workers in Gulf countries has undergone a change; unlike the 1970s and 1980s, when nearly 90 percent of Indians in the Gulf were blue-collar workers, today over 35 percent of the Indian workforce comprise the white-collar professionals specializing in fast moving fields such as the service industry. Unlike in other regions, Indian expatriates in the Gulf have a higher propensity to remit back the money they earn. This is primarily because more than 65 percent of these workers are low-skilled labourers and their families back home depend solely on these remittances as a source of living (Pradhan, 2009: 24).

While importance is given to the export of services, the role and importance of private transfers or remittances to India does not gain much emphasis. Remittances offset some of the output losses that a developing country may suffer from migration of its highly skilled workers It has been known for some time now that India is among the highest remittance receiving countries in the world and that at around 4 percent of the GDP (gross domestic product) and net private transfers contribute to reining in the current account deficit on India's balance of payments (The Hindu, 2013).

India in 1991 was confronting the balance of payments crisis and migrant remittances played a noteworthy role in maintaining the foreign exchange reserves of India to run the Indian economy. In that year, foreign exchange reserves were enough only for imports for just a few weeks. Even the dollar deposits in Indian banks were withdrawn by the migrants present in other developed countries (Khadaria, 2011). This compelled India to take urgent action to avoid defaulting on its international obligations or face a collapse of its economy for want of official imports (Khadaria, 2011: 273-274). However, it was the gradual, understated and steadily growing remittances from the Indian workers in the Gulf region, which helped to save the situation for India.

According to an estimate by Reserve Bank of India (RBI), the Gulf region accounted for an average 27 percent of the total remittance inflows to India from 2006-07 to 2009-10. In the year 2008-09, when the economic crisis hit the globe, Gulf countries accounted for around 31 percent of the total remittance inflows to India (Pravasi Bharatiya, 2012).

Despite the four-year global economic slump and intermittent recessionary trends across economic sectors, overall remittances to India from around the world have increased. The depreciation of the Indian rupee has boosted remittance flows to India substantially, helping to sustain the balance of payments (Biswas, 2013).

India as per the World Bank report has consistently been the top recipient of remittances for 15 of the last 23 years including successive last five years, i.e. 2009 onwards (World Bank, 2013). India's inward remittances grew from approximately US$ 49.6 billion in 2009 to US$ 69 billion in 2012, followed by China [US$ 60 billion], the Philippines [US$ 24 billion] and Mexico [US$ 23 billion], (World Bank Report, 2012). Further, it is observed that nearly half of over US$ 61 billion sent by expatriates in the Gulf countries in 2012 went to India. A total of US$ 29.69 billion was sent as remittances by Indian expatriates living in Bahrain, Kuwait, Oman, Qatar, Saudi Arabia and the UAE (World Bank, 2013). This is more than 40 percent of the total remittances India received globally. Since the remittance India receives from around the globe is 4 percent of GDP, thus it can be deduced that remittances from Gulf region represents around 2 percent of the Indian GDP.

Although the economic contribution to India by these migrants is a widely acknowledged fact but what remains widely ignored is the harsh realities of their lives. In the remaining of this paper, we will analyze their social and working conditions focusing on the problems faced by these migrants.

Profile of Indian Migrants in the WANA Region

Before outlining their socio-economic conditions, it is important to understand the profile of these workers and underscore their contribution to the host country. The following section describes the profile of only those countries in the WANA region that have a significant Indian population.

Bahrain: The influx of immigrants due to the discovery of oil in 1934-45, led to expansion of the Bahrain's economy. Indians started migrating to Bahrain to work as managers, salesman, assistants and workers or start business. With a population of 350,000, Indians constituted the largest expatriate community in Bahrain (MOIA, 2012).

Indians are present in significant number as doctors, engineers, chartered accountants, bankers, managers and other professionals and play a vital role in Bahrain's economic development. Around 70 percent of the Indian workforce is employed in the construction, contracting and maintenance and service sectors. Others work in retail and other business activities like hardware, jewellery, electronics and also as storekeepers, chemists, carpenters, barbers etc. (Embassy of India-Kingdom of Bahrain, 2014).

Today, in most of the established Bahraini business organizations, Indians employees hold important positions in their operations. The top Bahraini business houses such as Zayanis, AlMoayyads, Fakhroo, Kanoo, Ahmed Mansour Al Ali, Abdullah Nass, Mohammed Jalal, as well as companies like Bahrain Aluminium, banks, petrochemical and ship repairing industries, etc. all have Indians in their senior or middle management positions (World Factbook/Bahrain, 2014).

Kuwait: The population of Indian expatriates in Kuwait is about 0.75 million, which is the largest expatriate community (MOIA, 2012). Indian migrants are present as highly qualified experts in technology areas, especially in the software and financial sectors. In the field of health, Indians are present as top specialists along with paramedical staff. Indian expatriates include professionals like engineers, doctors, software professionals, and semi-skilled workers. A large proportion of the Indian expatriates are also unskilled and semi-skilled workers. There are approximately 0.27 million Indians employed in the domestic sector whereas about 0.36 million are deployed in the private sector (Pradhan, 2009: 22).

Oman: Indians in Oman constitute the largest expatriate community in the country which is around 0.7 million Indians (MOIA, 2012). They include skilled workers and technicians and professionals such as doctors, engineers, bankers, finance experts, managers, etc., with many holding high positions in the corporate sector. Several Indians also hold official positions in Omani government departments and public undertakings. Many unskilled workers are employed in construction also (World Factbook/Oman, 2014).

The contribution of Indians to the development of Oman, particularly in the fields of commerce, healthcare, education, horticulture, finance, construction and communication is widely acknowledged. According to Pradhan, a number of persons of Indian origin (PIO) have been granted Omani nationality, some of them being recipients of high awards of the Omani government (Pradhan, 2009: 22).

Qatar: Presently, Qatar has a huge Indian population, which is around 0.5 million (MOIA, 2012), thus being the largest among the expatriate population in the country.

Indians are involved in different fields and on various levels in public or private sector. A huge number of Indians are engaged in unskilled and semi-skilled work. The service industry is manned mainly by Indian manpower that is multi-talented, skilled and cheaper. Thus, Indian professionals constitute a small but significant component of their community in Qatar. The Institution of Engineers, Indian Medical Association and the Institute of Chartered Accountants of India keep up dynamic sections in Qatar, with an extending enrolment and on-going exercises. In addition, specialists working in other fields like management, education, pharmacies, computers, etc. are present too (World Factbook/Qatar, 2014).

While migration is essentially male-dominated but there are proportionally larger number of females in the Indian population in Qatar unlike in most other Gulf countries. Nurses and housemaids also constitute the workforce (World Factbook/Qatar, 2014). Indians at Qatar send a huge amount of remittances to India. Interestingly, it is said that the average annual remittance to India by the Indians at Qatar equals or exceeds Qatar's net export earnings from the Gulf (MOIA, 2014).

Saudi Arabia: Before the oil boom, the Saudi economy was under-developed and most of its people had a marginal existence but the visits of Indian affluent pilgrims from India used to be a source of excitement among the native people (World Factbook/Saudi Arabia, 2014).

Due to the oil boom, there was a steady increase in the employment of Indian nationals in Saudi Arabia. Hence, by 1983, the number of Indian workers in Saudi Arabia had increased to 0.27 million from a mere 15,000 in 1975 and to 0.65 million by 1990. After the Gulf crisis in 1990-91, there has been a regular increase in the number of Indian migrants, taking the total number to 1.5 million by the end of the 20th century. By the year 2005, the Indian community in Saudi Arabia was 1.43 million, the largest Indian passport holding community abroad, constituting 20 percent of the expatriate community of Saudi Arabia, which was somewhere around 7 million (World Factbook/Saudi Arabia). In the year 2012, the Indian population increased to 1.8 million (MOIA, 2012).

The Indian diaspora in Saudi Arabia may be seen involved in various work categories. There are professionals like doctors, engineers, charted accountants, scientists, technocrats and managers working for both the government and the private sectors constituting around 10 percent of the Indian community. Then there are workers in white-collar jobs such as clerks, secretaries, accountants, storekeepers, etc. constituting around 10 percent of the workers. The majority, which is around 80 percent, consists of organized labour and technicians working on project sites and industrial establishments along with operations and maintenance jobs. Besides, it also includes a large number of unorganized labourers, working as shepherds, agricultural farm labourers, housemaids, house-drivers etc. Indians are the preferred community in Saudi Arabia for their high quality of technical expertise and discipline and the capacity to adjust well with the Saudi social life. They have the reputation of being peaceful and not involved in illegal activities (Pradhan, 2009: 21).

UAE: The Indian community in the UAE, numbering 1.75 million (MOIA, 2012), constitutes 30 percent (Embassy of India, Abu Dhabi-UAE, 2014) of the total population. It is the largest expatriate community in the country. It extraordinarily gives an expansiveness in terms of categories of workers employed, which distinguishes it from every other expatriate community in the UAE. The profile of the Indian workers has changed with the evolving needs of the country. Back in the 1970s and 1980s, when the key requirement was for blue-collar workers; around 85-90 percent of the Indian community was blue-collared with a negligible percentage of professionals. In the 1990s, with the rising need for professionals in the expanding service sector, the profile of the Indians changed and today, 15 to 20 percent of the Indian community is made up of professionally qualified personnel (World Factbook/UAE, 2014).

The UAE population, which is estimated to be around 7.8 million, has two-thirds of its population as immigrants, including India (UN, 2013). Around 65 percent Indians belong to the blue-collar category in which most of them are employed in construction companies, municipalities and agricultural farms. 20 percent of them belong to the white-collar non-professionals which include clerical staff, shop assistants, sales men, accountants, etc. and 15 percent are professionals and businessmen and their family members (World Factbook/UAE, 2014).

The Indian community has been a major player in the economic growth of the UAE in the last 35 years (World Economic Forum, 2007). They are respected for their technical competence, sense of discipline and minimal involvement with criminal activity compared to other expatriate communities. However, the main point in their favour is the non-involvement in local and regional political issues. In view of these qualities, Indian expatriates enjoy an advantage over other nationalities like Chinese, Koreans, Filipino, Pakistani, Bangladeshi or Arab expatriates (World Factbook/UAE, 2014).

Israel: There are about 80,000 Jews of Indian-origin in Israel, most of which are Israeli passport holders. The main waves of immigration into Israel from India took place in the 1950s and 1960s. There are about 10,000 Indian citizens in Israel in which around 8,000 are caregivers. Their involvement can be seen as diamond traders, information technology professionals, students and unskilled workers (Embassy of India, Tel Aviv-Israel, 2014).

Other nations of WANA region like Algeria, Egypt, Iran, Iraq, Jordan, Lebanon, Libya, Morocco, Palestine, Syria, Tunisia and Yemen hold negligible proportion of Indian population.

Problems and Challenges Faced by Indian Migrants

Apart from the socio-economic factors, this section engages with the political events in the WANA region that have had an impact on the lives of Indian migrant workers.

Socio-economic Problems:

A. Social Division of Labour: Immigrants usually face multiple social and cultural challenges when adjusting in the environment of a new country. Among the Asians, Indians are placed slightly higher than the others (Malecki and Ewers, 2007: 467-484).

Expatriates from different nations are extended different social treatment and Asian expatriates do not enjoy the same social status as their counterparts from western world do. The social interactions of most of the expatriates in GCC with the local population are primarily limited to professional reasons.

B. Salary Gap within Different Expatriate Communities: Despite having similar educational qualifications, work experience and job responsibilities, expatriates from western nations are paid higher salary in the Gulf region in comparison to other expatriates from Asian countries. Differences in salary lead to different categories of expatriates. One is the preferred category from the western nations and the second is the general category of Asian expatriates (Naithani and Jha, 2010: 101).

C. Work Permit and Visa: The majority of migrants in the Gulf nations cannot attain citizenship (Sater, 2013: 292-302). Migrants here work on temporary permits. Work visa are generally issued until the age of 60 years and needs to be renewed after every 2 years which creates a sense of uncertainty and job insecurity in the minds of migrants as the labour laws are heavily skewed in the favour of the employers and the work contracts can be terminated at any time by them (Al-Ali, 2008: 365-379.). For example, Qatar does not give citizenship to the expatriates, which make all the Indians remain Indian citizens. This gives a lot of scope for exploitation of the foreign workers. The Indians have registered a number of cases of exploitation by the employers.

Another major threat and problem for the Indians is the recruitment agencies which are known to be unscrupulous. There are many cases of fraud and extortion by the recruitment agencies. There is a need to have a check on the recruitment agencies. Even immigrants get duped and exploited by the employers because of the present system of recruitment.

Also, *Nitaqat* law as enforced in Saudi Arabia, in its quest for Saudization makes it mandatory for local companies to hire one Saudi national for every 10 migrant workers. Those employing under-10 workers are exempt but those with up to 49 workers have to have 10 percent Saudis. Bigger workforces have to include higher number of Saudis. Depending on their level of compliance, the enterprises are being categorized into four; those that totally fail to comply will be in the 'red' zone. Those complying with the *Nitaqat* norms would be rewarded with incentives while those failing would have to fold as the work permits of their expatriate workers would not be renewed. There had been a widespread perception that the policy would lead to denial of job opportunities for a large number of Indian migrants working there which is the biggest expatriate community. Since the work permit is mandatory for getting the residential permit (*iqama*), the expatriate workers would become illegal residents when denied the work permit renewal and thus would be forced to leave the kingdom (The Hindu, 2013).

D. Weak Labour Laws: Labour laws in Gulf nations are weak. Under the *kafala* system, which is a sponsorship system that regulates residency and employment of the workers, thus making the visa status tied to the sponsor, is widespread in the Gulf nations (Bajracharya, 2012) and for which migrant workers must obtain an exit permit from their employer to return to their home country. Many workers find that they have been deceived on work conditions and want to return but their employer can hold them back by refusing the exit permit. It also entails working under the same employer for the period of migration and in most cases; the employer confiscates the passport and other documents of the migrant workers thus easily exposing the migrant workers to exploitation. One big reason that *kafala* system has not been abolished is because the migrant-sending countries have been unable to exert sufficient pressure. It is also feared that if they try to set minimum standards for their nationals in Gulf countries, employment opportunities will diminish (Migration News, 2012). Even the trade union activity is effectively banned in UAE, Saudi

Arabia and Oman and in other Gulf nations; the rights of the unions are very limited (World Socialist Web Site, 2014).

E. Work Conditions: There have been a number of cases in these Gulf countries regarding non-payment of salaries, absence of proper basic amenities, non-renewal of labour card and visa, non-payment of gratuity on termination of job, employer's refusal to give permission to travel to India (Sahai and Chand, 2004: 58-93). For example, in Kuwait, the Indian workforce is known for its work ethics, commitment, and law abiding nature but there have been cases of mistreatment and exploitation regarding withholding/non-payment/delayed payment of salary, long working hours, retention of passports, refusal of emergency leave and non-payment of overtime allowance etc. along with difficult working and living conditions in Kuwait specially in summer months (Embassy of India, Kuwait, 2014).

F. Impact on the Families: Millions of workers along with their nuclear families migrate to the Gulf region in search of better jobs and salaries. The dividing line between single migrants and migrant families is almost entirely attributed to their economic class, for the Gulf States require minimum incomes for family visas. These state-mandated minimums, however, often prove insufficient, for the costs of living, and particularly the costs of educating children in private schools required for transnational life, push the real cost of maintaining a family in the Gulf much higher than the state-mandated minimums (Gardner, 2011: 17).

G. Right to Own property: Foreign nationals and migrants are not allowed to buy properties and even own businesses in the Gulf countries. This makes the migrants prone to exploitation as it is required that the local citizens should have major stakes in their ventures even though they may be sleeping or not very active partners (Khadria, 2008: 91).

H. Religious Freedom: Bahrain shows a flexible and liberal attitude towards the expatriate community in contrast to others, regionally. This is reflected in the fact that the Indian community has 30 registered and 15 unregistered socio-cultural organizations in addition to 5 schools. It is notable that Bahrain permits religious freedom, which is not generally the case elsewhere in the region (World Factbook/Bahrain, 2014).

Other example is of Qatar, where, various socio-cultural and professional associations, schools, restaurants, clubs and other organizations representing Indian community are present but with strict restrictions. The country is said to follow zero tolerance policy especially regarding religious expression (Kanchana, 2012).

Political Problems:

A. War and Terrorism: The WANA region, especially the Middle East has been prone to war for a very long time. Ever since the eruption of the regional street revolution, these forces have been extending their spheres of influence and trying to enter into the national politics of the relevant countries.

Recently developed terrorist network, ISIS (the Islamic State of Iraq And Syria) is a serious threat and can have spills in the Arabian Peninsula. A group of 46 Indian nurses working in Iraq were kidnapped by ISIS militants in July 2014 who were later released (Deccan Chronicle, 2014). Scores of other Indians working in Iraq too returned to India. However, the issue of war and terrorism does not make this region any less attractive to the Indian migrants and the Arabian Peninsula has not seen a spillover effect of terrorism in the region.

B. Arab Uprisings: Since the end of 2010, series of street revolutions characterized with anti-government demonstrations swept across and drove many governments into political crisis in the WANA region. The evolving political turmoil was ignited by some accidental events in Tunisia, where the situation went beyond control and into chaos. It ultimately sweeps the entire region but the impact on the migrants has not been worrisome.

Indian Migrant Women Workers

Of late, Gulf region and North America have been

prominent destinations for migrants from South Asia and there has been an increase in the number of female international migrants. Women constitute half of the international migrants, thus the term 'feminization of migration' as propounded by Thimothy and Sasikumarcan be used to capture the varying pattern of female migration patterns (Thimothy and Sasikumar, 2012).

It is a common notion that migration is mainly a male movement; with women as either being left behind or joining men as dependents even though almost equal number of women and men are engaged in migration. But the irony remains that even though women are equally involved in productive work after migration, they still are seen as secondary earners and dependents in the process of migration (Thapan, 2005: 9-22).

Since, majority of male migrants are engaged in technical, production and construction sector, females are largely involved in the service and entertainment services. This pattern can be clearly seen in the Gulf region. Their working conditions are likely to be precarious in the above sectors but are determined mainly by the labour market structure of receiving countries and their social and cultural practices. A majority of female migrant workers are engaged as domestic workers in the Gulf region. The largest groups of migrant female domestic workers are in Saudi Arabia and Kuwait (Thimothy and Sasikumar, 2012).

Several reasons can be factored in, which have influenced the demand for female caregivers and domestic workers in the Gulf. The improvement in the economic conditions paved way for the hiring of the domestic workers. At the same time, the shortage of local labour, which was also more expensive, has led to increased number of migrant female workers from India. Currently, Indian female migrant workers in Gulf as percentage of all international migrants' workers, account for 48.7 percent of such workers (Thimothy and Sasikumar, 2012).

However, there are significant problems faced by migrant women workers beginning with the exploitation from the recruitment agencies. The existing visa system of the Gulf countries further adds to their agony. According to Timothy and Sasikumar, "lack of adequate social protection for the women migrants and gender insensitive immigration policies are major factors perpetuating their insecurities. Working under the *kafala* system aggravates the situation for the migrant domestic worker. Deaths of migrant workers under suspicious circumstances or reports of rape are merely filed as complaints and their perpetrators rarely brought to justice in many instances. Foreign workers in the Gulf countries are completely out of the country's labour laws that renders their situation very vulnerable" (Thimothy and Sasikumar, 2012). Female migrant domestic workers thus are subjected to long or undefined working hours, low salaries and late payment of salaries and poor and repressive living conditions. Lack of contractual clarity often ends up making them carry out multiple forms of work: as babysitters, kitchen helpers, cleaners, working for the families and their relatives homes too (CEDAW, 2008).

A substantial number of Asian female migrants in Gulf are engaged as domestic workers which highlights the fact that professional expatriate women have limited opportunities and social and cultural factors are responsible for lack of work opportunities for single women as some of the Gulf countries do not easily allow work permits for single females or married females unaccompanied by husbands. Thus, the majority of professional female workers are the ones who have accompanied working spouse or parents on a family visa and have later managed to attain a job opportunity (Malecki and Ewers, 2007).

Even though, the gender specific challenges have not been addressed, in the recent past, Indian government has put in some efforts to provide migrant workers better protection. For example, a compulsory insurance scheme has been introduced where Indian migrant workers are given insurance, which is valid as long as their job-contract lasts. Smart cards are being issued to first time migrants, which would have details of their passport, work contract data and insurance among others. All these measures along with pre-departure training is given which familiarizes the migrants with problems they could encounter in the receiving country and how to deal with them (Thimothy and Sasikumar, 2012).

Conclusion

In the WANA region, it is in the Gulf countries where one sees the highest influx of Indian migrants. Lack of job opportunities back home due to the ever-rising population, and the shortage of labour in Gulf countries both in skilled or unskilled sectors, have led to this exodus from India to the Gulf region.

Outward migration eases the pressure from labour markets at home, leading to higher wages and lower unemployment rates in India.

Around 6 million Indian workers find employment in these countries comprising a large percentage of the workforce (a scarce resource for Gulf nations) while sending more than USD 30 billion back home in remittances (2 percent of India's GDP). Indian workers can be seen in prominent positions in both public and private sectors in Gulf countries.

However, these migrants are often exploited by recruitment agents and also employers, an aspect generally overlooked and their problems largely ignored by both the host and Indian governments. The visa rules should be simplified so as to eliminate the role of middlemen such as recruitment agents who generally benefit at the expense of unsuspecting low and unskilled migrant workers. A human element has to be injected in the visa and work system so as to make the lives of these workers better than getting treatment as mere economic entities. Also a change in the mindset and policies of Gulf governments is necessary which, besides acknowledging the economic benefits of the migrant labourers, also recognizes and enforces the rights of these workers. Strengthening and making the labour laws more stringent and abolishing the *kafala* system could be effective ways of redressing the exploitation and abuse experienced by the migrant male and female workers, especially the semi-skilled and unskilled, so that the Gulf region can remain as an attractive work destination. Also, special steps should be taken to enforce better laws for the safety of female workers along with an environment where females do not suffer from work related biases.

Any policy to protect the interests of the migrants would be effective only when the employers take a lead since non-adherence of labour laws by the employers is one of the major weaknesses in work environments. Thus, the need of the hour is that the governments in Gulf region need to ensure that the employers play a more effective role toward expatriates.

References

Al-Ali, J. (2008), "Emiratisation: Drawing UAE nationals into their Surging Economy", *International Journal of Sociology and Social Policy,* Vol. 28, No. 9-10.

Biswas, Soutik (2013), "Why India Remains Top of Remittances League", available at:
http://www.bbc.co.uk/news/world-asia-india-21570622, accessed on 20th August, 2014.

CEDAW (2008), "The Situation of Women Migrant Domestic Workers in Bahrain", submitted to the 42nd session of the CEDAW Committee.

Deccan Chronicle (2014), "Iraq Crisis: 46 Indian Nurses Freed by ISIS Militants to Reach Kochi Tomorrow", available at:
http://www.deccanchronicle.com, accessed on 21st August, 2014.

Embassy of India, Abu Dhabi- UAE, available at:
http://indembassyuae.org, accessed on 18th August, 2014.

Embassy of India, Kingdom of Bahrain, available at:
www.indianembassybahrain.com/living_working_conditions.html, accessed on 16th August, 2014.

Embassy of India, Kuwait, available at:
   http://www.indembkwt.org, accessed on 11th August, 2014.
Embassy of India, Tel Aviv, Israel, available at:
   http://www.indembassy.co.il, accessed on 21st August, 2014.
Gardner, A.M. (2011), "Gulf Migration and the Family", *Journal of Arabian Studies*.
Gulf Cooperation Council, available at:
   www.gcc-sg.org, accessed on 12th August, 2014.
Kanchana, Radhika (2012), "Qatar's White-collar Indians", in Prakash C. Jain, Kundan Kumar (ed.), Indian Trade Diaspora in the Arabian Peninsula, New Academic Publishers, New Delhi.
Khadria, Binod (2008), "India: Skilled Migration to Developed Countries, Labour Migration to the Gulf", in Stephen Castles and Raúl Delgado Wise (ed.), Migration and Development: Perspectives from the South, International Organization for Migration.
Khadria, Binod (2011), "Bridging the Binaries of Skilled and Unskilled Migration from India", in Irudaya Rajan and Marie Percot (ed.), Dynamics of Indian Migration: Historical and Current Perspectives, Routledge, New Delhi.
Malecki, E. J. and Ewers M. C. (2007), "Labour Migration to World Cities: With a Research Agenda for the Arab Gulf", *Progress in Human Geography,* Vol. 31, No. 4.
Migration News (January 2012), Vol. 19, No. 1, available at:
   http://migration.ucdavis.edu/mn/more.php, accessed on 12th July, 2014.
Migration News (January 2012), Vol. 19, No. 1, available at:
   http://migration.ucdavis.edu/mn/more.php, accessed on 28th July, 2014.
MOIA (2012), Ministry of Overseas Indian Affairs, available at:
   www.moia.gov.in, accessed on 3rd August, 2014.
MOIA (2014), Ministry of Overseas Indian Affairs, available at:
   http://moia.gov.in/pdf/qatar.pdf, accessed on 8th August, 2014.
Naithani, Pranav and Jha, A.N. (2010), "Challenges Faced by Expatriate Workers in Gulf Cooperation Council Countries", *International Journal of Business and Management,* Vol. 5, No. 10.
Pattnayak, Satyanarayan (2008), "The Indian Diaspora in Persian Gulf: An Analysis", *Think India Quarterly,* Vol. 14, No. 2.
Pradhan, Samir (2009), "India's Economic and Political Presence in the Gulf: A Gulf Perspective", in India's Growing Role in the

Gulf: Implications for the Region and the United States, Dubai, Gulf Research Centre.

Pravasi Bharatiya, (2012), Vol. 5, Issue 7.

Sahai, P.S. and Chand K. (2004), "India: Migrant Workers Awaiting Recognition and Protection", in Pong-Sul Ahn (ed.), Migrant Workers and Human Rights: Out-Migration from South Asia, International Labour Organization, available at: http://www.ilo.org, accessed on 30th July, 2014.

Sater, J. (2013), "Citizenship and Migration in Arab Gulf Monarchies", *Citizenship Studies,* Vol. 18, Issues 3-4, available at: www.tandfonline.com, accessed on 21st August, 2014.

Thapan, Meenakshi (2005), "Series Introduction", in Meenakshi Thapan (ed.), Transnational Migration and Politics of Identity, Sage Publications: New Delhi.

The Hindu, March 27, 2013, available at: www.thehindu.com/news/national/kerala/saudi-malayalis-jittery-as-nitaqat-deadline-ends-today, accessed on 28th July, 2014.

The Hindu, September 23, 2012, available at: www.thehindu.com/opinion/columns/Chandrasekhar/the-source-of-remittances, accessed on 13th July, 2014.

The World Factbook: Oman", Central Intelligence Agency, available at: cia.gov/cia/publications/factbook, accessed on 12th August, 2014.

The World Factbook: Qatar", Central Intelligence Agency, available at: cia.gov/cia/publications/factbook, accessed on 14th August, 2014.

The World Factbook: Saudi Arabia", Central Intelligence Agency, available at: cia.gov/cia/publications/factbook, accessed on 14th August, 2014.

The World Factbook: UAE", Central Intelligence Agency, available at: cia.gov/cia/publications/factbook, accessed on 15th August, 2014.

Timothy, Rakkee and Sasikumar, S.K. (2012), "Migration of Women Workers from South Asia to the Gulf", V.V. Giri National Labour Institute, New Delhi.

United Nations (2013), Department of Economic and Social Affairs, Population Division, International Migration, available at: http://esa.un.org, accessed on 19th July, 2014.

World Bank Report (2012), "Migration and Remittances Flows: Recent Trends and Outlook, 2013-16".

World Bank (2013), "Migration and Development Brief 20", Washington D.C., Migration and Remittances Unit, Development Prospects Group, available at:

http://siteresources.worldbank.INTPROSPECTS/Resources, accessed on 8th August, 2014.

World Economic Forum (2007), "The UAE and The World: Scenarios to 2025", in World Scenario Series, available at: http://www.weforum.org, accessed on 30th July, 2014.

8

Deterrence in Israeli Counter-Terrorism

Jaikhlong Basumatary

Deterrence and related strategies were predicated on specific but typically implicit expectations of opponent decision-making and behaviour. These expectations followed from the application of a narrowly defined "rational actor" model to the question of how opponents should be expected to make decisions and behave in response to a particular State's deterrence strategies. At the most basic level, deterrence is convincing a person, group or State that the reaction to a contemplated course of action would result in a degree of pain or punishment that would exceed the expected benefit of such action. [1] Further, deterrence is a form of strategic coercion, which is related to offence and defence in terms of a State's security goals. [2] Therefore, to achieve deterrence, an actor can shape the adversary's perception of the costs or benefits of a particular course of action. [3]

Our understanding of deterrence in the present context is rooted in how to deter the phenomenon of terrorism. Originally, however, deterrence is very much a Cold War concept and a key pillar of US strategy against the Soviet Union, while deterrence in the context of terrorism is but only one element of a broader counter-terrorism strategy of any given State dealing with the scourge of terrorism. Analysts have argued that deterrence is a necessary component of an effective counter-terrorism strategy and directly contributes to a comprehensive counter-terrorism strategy of offensive operations to attack and disrupt terrorist networks, defences to protect the State, and efforts to counter ideological support for terrorism. [4]

The face of terrorism is changing rapidly. Terrorist events force us to adjust to a violent reality, one which because of 24/7 media coverage, the line between victim and spectator is often blurred. The primary target of terror strikes is not those actually killed or injured in the attacks, but those made to witness it. It is indeed the second hand experience of the spectator that has made terrorism such a potent force in the present times. Terrorism commonly evokes images of maximum violence against innocent victims carried out in the name of higher cause.

Throughout its existence as a state, Israel has had to cope with intense terrorism—within its territory, across the borders, and abroad. Terrorism against Israel has been considered as a major political and psychological factor in Israel's reality and the need to cope with it has forced the Israeli public and its government to deal with the scourge of terrorism, sometime unacceptable to various quarters. Since the establishment of the state of Israel, its leaders felt that their country faced an existential threat from the Arab state's desire to eradicate the Jewish state. As such, for Israel, terrorism is an extension of war, and counter-terrorism is often and naturally discussed as a part of a "war paradigm". [5] It is in this context, that this paper will analyse deterrence in Israeli counter-terrorism.

Since its creation, the state of Israel has had to deal with waves of terrorist activities at its borders, in the occupied territories, and inside Israel itself. Palestinians and other Arab *fidayeen* elements were intent on carrying out small-scale cross-border terror raids into Israel. Such attacks were initially targeted against property; subsequently, however, they quickly escalated into murder of civilians. [6]

Such cross-border terror operations were carried out with an intention to cajole the Israeli Defence Force (IDF) into retaliating, which in turn would escalate tensions between Israel and its terrorist hosting Arab neighbours to the point of bringing about a full-scale war.

Israel initially attempted to impede such terror raids

through diplomatic channels, using force solely to fend off attacks within its territory. Yet, when such actions proved unfruitful; then Ben-Gurion government authorised in 1953, reprisal raids, which has been argued to be appropriate to deal with insurgency, border strife, cease-fire violations and armistice. [7] Such reprisal raids were often carried out into neighbouring states with a rationale of deterring the Arab states' governments from aiding and hosting any terrorist groups bent on attacking Israeli civilians and civilian installations. According to Moshe Dayan, the then IDF Chief of Staff, *"Israel cannot guard every pipeline from explosion and every tree from uprooting. Israel cannot prevent the murder of a worker in an orchard or a family in their beds. But it is in our power to set a high price on our blood, a price too high for the Arab community, the Arab army or the Arab government to think worth paying"*. [8]

This sort of opinion by a high ranking official dealing with terrorism at that point in time in a way summed up the beginning of deterrence strategy in Israeli counter-terrorism. In this context, it is important to note that from its inception, Israeli counter-terrorism policy aimed at lowering the effects of terror to a tolerable level whereby Israeli civil society could function normally despite the grave risks it faced from the scourge of terrorism. Most importantly, deterrence by punishment was the Israeli counter-terrorism strategy adopted during the early years of its fight against terrorism. At the same time, it has been observed that not all terrorist attacks on Israel provoked a response as much of Israel's counter-terrorism activities, aimed at pre-emption, prevention and disruption rather than simply retaliating.

Israel's strategic thinking during the Cold War period revolved around building a militarily strong country, which David Ben-Gurion, Israel's first Prime Minister felt was extremely important to survive in West Asia. Furthermore, he felt that allies cannot be totally relied upon, which led to a great emphasis on self-reliance. In other words, Israel emphasised upon the freedom to act when challenged and the military ability to do so effectively. Although cognisant of the limitations inherent in a small state predicament, Israel hoped to achieve a capacity to respond unilaterally to any emerging security challenges and to establish a deterrent power. [9]

In the post-Cold War period, with global realignment, West Asian peace process, as well as changes within Israel, there had been an emergence of a new strategic thinking. Its present prevalence is linked to Labour's return to power and to the dominance of its dovish thinking. The collapse of the Soviet Empire was seen by the Israeli leadership as creating a new international atmosphere and is often credited for opening the door to West Asian peacemaking. Israel's adversaries lost their Soviet umbrella, a politico-military relationship that was an important factor in the Arab ability to confront Israel. However, with the dwindling threat emanating from the Arab states in the post-Cold War period, Israel faced a new security challenge with the rise of Palestinian terrorism, which challenged the state of Israel.

Subsequently, Islamic fundamentalists declared Jihad against Israel, which is held culpable for the reprehensible policies against the Palestinians. [10] Israel became an experimental ground for new terrorist techniques and had to counter a wide rage of foe, hell bent on wiping out Israel from the face of the earth. It has been argued that Israel has faced every type of foe in the terrorist pantheon. Some of the attackers have been tightly disciplined, others loosely organised. Some were state-backed, others independent. Some operated through small revolutionary cells, others as part of mass movements. While the state of Israel encountered the challenges of terrorism early on in its existence, it responded to such acts of terrorism by enacting the Prevention of Terrorism Ordinance (PTO) in 1948, which was amended in 1980, 1986, and again in 1993. Acts of terror, most frequently committed by Palestinian extremist groups against Israeli citizens, have caused Israel to be constantly on the defence.

Recognising the threat to its national security, the government of Israel made a "commitment to combat terrorism in all its aspects". [11]

Israel's Arab policy is based on self-survival and defence. Its response to terrorism has been founded on the principles of deterrence, pre-emption, prevention, and reprisals. [12] In strictly military terms, Israel has won every conventional war it fought against its larger Arab neighbours, defeating them time and again, and seizing additional territory until most of its adversaries more or less gave up the struggle and some concluded peace. However, in spite of all the successes against the conventional forces, Israel has been bogged down by endless Palestinian terrorism against them. [13]

Historically, the Yishuv, as the Jewish community in Palestine was known, faced a recurrent threat of Arab violence as it strove to create a Jewish state in Palestine. The violence of the Yishuv's in early years would continue to plague the new state of Israel in years to come. Therefore, it has been argued that though the threat remains to the present day, it has changed as the ideologies, societies, and politics of the Arab world fluctuated in the decades after Israel's creation. As the threat changed, so did Israeli counter-terrorism. One of the most important aspects of how Israel fights terrorism is deterrence.

In other words, the belief that Israel's enemies would remain hostile but that the threat of or demonstrative use of force would stop them from engaging in attacks. [14] When Popular Front for Liberation of Palestine (PFLP) sought to use spectacular acts of terrorism to draw attention to the Palestinian issue, which they subsequently did, Israel responded through swift and severe response to any deliberate abetting of anti-Jewish violence. [15] Israeli authorities imposed curfews to punish villages and towns that allowed militants to take shelter. The IDF also destroyed the homes of those who sheltered attackers and at times those who gave them food or information. In Gaza, Israel responded harshly to the violence there and made few efforts to win over the locals unlike in West Bank where Shin Bet, the Israeli domestic intelligence agency worked with petty criminals offering them pardon in exchange for information. The IDF arrested thousands in Gaza and destroyed the homes of suspected militants and their supporters. Israeli authorities placed Gaza under curfew, deported suspected troublemakers, and used roadblocks to hinder the flow of goods and people.

With the culmination of Operation Wrath of God following the release of terrorist involved in the Munich massacre of 1972, marked a return to the offensive in Israeli counter-terrorism. Through this operation, Israel would hunt down terrorists around the world. It is important to note here that retaliation went beyond punishing the Munich attackers. Israel conducted high-profile raids in Lebanon and staged a dramatic and heroic hostage rescue mission in Uganda. In other words, Israel responded to terrorism aggressively justifying that the strikes were ways to deter future attacks and disrupt existing groups. With a great many variations, the essence of Israel's counter-terrorism strategy has been always "to go outside the fence and make the terrorist feel the same fear as they make the citizens of Israel feel, and if necessary meet terror with terror". [16]

Israel has used a variety of methods to kill. Helicopters fired Hellfire missiles at the cars and homes of suspected terrorists, and the air force used F-16s and more powerful platforms when it wanted to deliver bigger bombs. Overtime drone aircraft grew more important than aircraft. When the Israelis found that the Hellfire caused too much collateral damage, Israel invested in technology to build smaller warheads, enabling them to take out a terrorist or two in a crowded area without killing nearby civilians. Further, Israel regularly uses snipers, though they receive less publicity. Israeli intelligence also bobby-traps cars, places bombs in place of bricks in walls that terrorists pass by, and in one case put a bomb in a tiny model of the al-Aqsa Mosque. [17]

Sealing the border became an increasingly important Israeli counter-terrorism toll after groups like Hamas and Islamic Jihad intensified suicide attacks against Israel. Since 1967 War, Palestinians living in the West Bank and Gaza has been allowed to travel into Israel as well as back and forth. During the First Intifada, which began in December 1987, Israel began to issue identity cards for Gazans and during the first Gulf War in 1991, Israel changed the rules and denied Palestinians the right to go to Israel freely. [18] All these changed after the Oslo Peace Process (1993), when rules became tighter and closures occurred after terrorist attacks.

The outbreak of Al-Aqsa Intifada prompted Israel to respond to Palestinian attacks with several large-scale military operations designed to destroy homes and places of business. Part of those operations included incursions into the Gaza Strip and West Bank to destroy homes of families of suicide bombers. Such strategies also included imposing closures and curfews as well as random checkpoints in Palestinian-controlled areas. In other words, the Israeli military endeavoured to demolish terrorist infrastructures in the West Bank and Southern end of the Gaza Strip. [19] Further, Israel also used a tactic of "collective punishment" in order to retaliate against Palestinian terrorists. For instance, in response to a terrorist attack during the Israel Passover holiday in 2002, the IDF launched a 'collective punishment' code named Operation Defensive Shield. This particular Operation involved the mass arrest of suspected terrorists from West Bank towns of Bethlehem, Jenin, Nablus and Ramallah. Many of the suspects were then held in military prison camps or detainment facilities without trial.

Israel also adopted the strategy of border control to counter terrorism against Israel. The Israeli border control includes inspectors, agents and their ability to manage the movement of individuals, conveyances and vehicles inside their territory. One border control mechanism of Israel that has been implemented as a result of Al-Aqsa Intifada is the construction of a wall along the Green Line that separates the West Bank from the rest of Israel. First proposed in June 2002, the Wall was designed to curtail the ability of suicide bombers to come into Israel from the West Bank. It was also designed to help the Israelis find a way to "keep Jewish majority within its borders". [20]

The border mechanism includes a combination of fences, walls, ditches, patrol roads and electronic surveillance devices. Additionally, border control mechanism includes a policy of restricted zones. For instance, in March 2002, following an escalation of Palestinian violence, the IDF turned many West Bank towns into restricted military zones with residents under sustained curfew for days at a time. In other words, all non-humanitarian goods had to be off-loaded from incoming trucks and re-loaded onto local trucks at various checkpoints near major West Bank cities. The restrictions also applied more rigorously to manufacturers and traders attempting to move goods out of Palestinian cities than to those bringing goods from Israel. The checkpoints restricted the freedom of movement from homes to places of work, and forced the Palestinians to rely upon the Israeli security guards for passage into other areas.

Israel's counter-terrorism strategy is aimed at depriving Palestinian terrorists of natural solidarity and support of the local population for the Palestinian struggle against Israel. [21] It is important to note here that Israel's policy has tried to balance between fighting the terrorists and not wishing to stir up the population or create a natural incubator from which new terrorists can be drafted. A major focus of Israeli counter-terrorism operations is to prevent the Palestinian terrorists from the West Bank from infiltrating into Israel to stage attacks. Since suicide bombers are difficult to identify and intercept, Israel has sought to prevent suicide attacks by disrupting them at the organisational, training, and planning stages before the suicide bomber is on their way to the target. IDF operations to eliminate terrorist infrastructure are directed against the activists who recruit and train the suicide bombers, manufacture the explosive belts, gather operational intelligence, drive the suicide bomber to the target, and otherwise whoever provides logistical and moral support. [22] Since terror organisations continually recruit new operatives and require a large network of supports; aggressive counter-terrorism campaign weakens the morale of the terrorists, hamper enlistment efforts, and deter collaborators.

It has long been Israel's policy to respond forcefully to terrorist attacks and threats against its citizens. Israel's counterforce, impeding, and punishment operations have been targeted both at terrorist leaders and rank and file. Over the years, numerous air, naval, and ground force strikes have been mounted against suspected terrorists and terrorist sites outside Israel and a variety of clandestine attacks have been conducted against individual terrorists. [23] When Hezbollah abducted two Israeli soldiers on the Israeli-Lebanese border in July 2006, [24] the situation quickly spiralled into a war that lasted for 34 days. Evaluating the conduct and results of the war, Israel's own Winograd Report [25] concluded that Israel initiated a long war, which ended without its clear military victory. A semi-military organisation of a few thousand men resisted, for a few weeks, the strong Israeli army, which enjoyed full air superiority and size and technology advantages.

While analysing Israel's military strategy when it went to war against Hezbollah and Lebanon in 2006, it has been argued that Israel's decision to go to war was not based on a thorough in-depth analysis of the specific situation at hand, rather rooted in its strategic outlook cultivated in the decades preceding the events on 12th July, 2006. The thinking has largely focused on the concept of deterrence, and should deterrence fail, to militarily compel the adversary in such a forceful manner that it would restore deterrence and ensure that the opponent would refrain from similar actions in the future. [26] Additionally, Israel's more overarching and strategic approach to the war appears to stem from a culture which to a large degree allows, or even demands, a forceful military response.

At the heart of Israel's collective perception is a sense of struggle against hostile environment. When it finds itself with no other choice but to fight wars, Israel seeks clear and rapid victory in blitzkrieg operations that transfer hostilities to enemy territory. The desire to avoid such wars, however, has brought military planners to place great emphasis on deterrence. [27] In the long-term, Israel aims for "cumulative deterrence" to persuade Arab states that they cannot defeat Israel and thus must recognise it and make peace; in the short-term, it tends to undertake "deterrence by punishment". Should adversaries harm Israelis, harsh reprisals are adopted to send out a clear signal that Israel does not surrender to violence. [28] Whether confronting a threat from states, non-state actors, or states that host such non-state actors, Israel has typically invoked the same deterrent strategy—threats and retaliation designed to force the adversary to change its calculations of the costs and benefits of defiance. Besides sending out a very loud message and clear signal to its adversaries, Israel has periodically chosen to speak using a big "stick". [29]

Israel's strategic landscape during the 1990s and 2000s had witnessed a gradual shift from threats originating in the conventional military might of states to challenges from armed non-state organisations. The upheavals in the Arab world since 2010 created an atmosphere wherein such non-state organisations could proliferate, as Arab states lose control over their territories and national arsenals. Moreover, the ascendance of political Islam in the Arab world buttresses the ideological opposition to Israel of such non-state groups. In contrast to the Arab states, organisations such as Hamas, Islamic Jihad or Hezbollah cling to a radical Islamist ideology, denying Israel's the right to exist. [30] For these organisations, the strategic goal is to demonstrate continuous violent resistance and keep the historic struggle against the Zionist entity alive at a time when the Arab states seem to have given up on the goal of destroying the Jewish state. Moreover, they believe that time is on their side as Israel will eventually disappear as a result of the protracted struggle. [31]

Under such circumstances, Israel's perspective in the statist dimension of the Arab-Israeli conflict was projected on the new reality. Israel perceives that these non-state organisations are implacable enemies, who want to destroy the Jewish state and there is very little Israel can do on the political front to mitigate this risk. While there is a hope that these non-state organisations will evolve along the Palestinian Liberation Organisation (PLO) trajectory that shifted from armed struggle to the political arena, allowing for a political engagement. Israel realises that it cannot affect the motivation of these organisations to fight the Jewish state in the short run, at the same time realising there are problems in producing deterrence against these organisations. Yet, Israel justifies its use of force hoping to deter these organisations, thereby greatly reducing the military capabilities of these non-state actors in order to lower the damage caused to Israel.

In the present environment, where terrorism has become a global phenomenon, Israel is not aiming for victory or for ending the conflict. [32] Scholars have argued that Israel realises the impossibility of defeating the radical ideologies on the battlefield. In contrast, Israel has refrained from winning the hearts and minds of the Arab insurgents. As a result, Israel prefers to respond to advances aiming to hurt Israel made by these non-state actors in a way that these actors are unable to bear the cost. In Israel's thinking, the concept of deterrence is not understood as 'absolute deterrence' but rather as 'cumulative deterrence'. [33] Cumulative deterrence aims to postpone each round of violence as much as possible. Destruction and denial of capabilities serves to strengthen deterrence. [34] However, there are complexities when it comes to deterrence in asymmetrical wars especially when non-state actors take over territory and act as de facto governments. Hezbollah and Hamas, after taking control of Lebanon in 2005 and Gaza in 2007 respectively are case in point. As such, some Israeli strategies have suggested that in the face of growing capabilities there might be a need for stronger retaliatory measures to deter these organisations.

An important component of deterrence against terrorism is the perception by the terrorist organisations that the deterring state enjoys intelligence dominance. Israel has enjoyed an image of an intelligence superpower with the ability to target terrorist leaders at will. This image has been reinforced by successes in targeted killings of senior terrorist leaders, and even the narrow escapes of other terrorist leaders when such attempts failed has not severely impaired it. The theories of deterrence tend to focus on the relationships between states and on the unspeakable damage that can be inflicted at the high end of potential conflict, either between conventional armies or in a nuclear conflict. However, Israel has succeeded in maintaining strategic deterrence vis-à-vis actual and potential adversaries through high-end conventional capabilities on the ground and in the air and through declared or assumed non-conventional capability. [35]

While it is true that the individual suicide bomber cannot be deterred but when it comes to deterrence toward terrorist organisations, Israel has achieved temporary and fragile deterrence vis-à-vis Hezbollah and the Palestinian terrorists over the years. It has been argued that the occasional tactical deterrence has been achieved not by the threat of force or by an image of Israel's capabilities, but by actual application of force and by inducing the fear that the force would be reapplied and even increased.

Deterrence against non-state groups and without the use of nuclear weapons is far more complex. The level of punishment dispensed by conventional weapons is less apocalyptic than that from nuclear arsenal. Additionally, non-state groups are less responsible to their populations and tend to be less pragmatic. Despite these problems, Israel has regularly tried to deter Hamas, Hezbollah, and other terrorist groups. The record has been mixed. [36] It has been found, that fearing the Israeli response, these groups have at times limited attacks or refrained from them altogether. But both the sides (these groups and Israel) have resumed violence when their internal politics changed or because they believed the other side was behaving too provocatively.

In addition to their use of terrorism, these groups also have mini-armies, run political parties, and operate schools and hospitals, making them more like quasi-states than a group like Al-Qaeda which has no territory, is ideologically extreme, and has fewer constituents to lose. Israel and Hezbollah clashed in Lebanon in 1993 and 1996, and then again more massively in 2006, with Israel hitting infrastructure and displacing hundreds of thousands of civilians while attacking Hezbollah's fighting wing. In Gaza, it has been argued that Israel has little choice but to rely on deterrence. Israel tried ruling Gaza from 1967 until 2005, when it withdrew in the face of Hamas-led attacks. Ruling Gaza would require Israel to take formal responsibility for caring for Gaza while waging a low-level counter-insurgency against an entrenched and motivated Hamas.

In Israel's efforts to achieve deterrence, the country has suffered from constant criticism for the harshness of its methods. In the aftermath of the response to the rocked attacks in 2014, the United Nations' High Commissioner for Human Rights, NaviPillay, condemned Israel's military actions in Gaza citing strong possibility of violating the international law amounting to war crimes. Additionally, referring to the Gazan children killed playing in the beach in 16 July 2014, Pillay held Israel responsible for blatant disregard for international humanitarian law.

While Israel is trying to preserve an image adhering to Western principles of justice and proportionality, [37] yet despite Israel's efforts, it has been found that Israel is facing difficulties in harmonising proportionality and deterrence. Additionally, since Israel is arguably the most casualty-sensitive country in the world, deterrence is considered even harder to achieve. Taking into consideration the fundamental factors of a recurring conflict between the Israelis and the Palestinians, it is doubtful whether the Israeli deterrence capabilities are at all effective. Interactions with counter-terrorism experts in Israel have resulted in diverse opinions. For some, Israeli deterrence strategies have been effective while others opine that had Israeli deterrence strategies been effective, there would be no recurring rocket attacks from Gaza.

To conclude, it is worth noting that the purpose of Israeli deterrence is to prevent its enemies from initiating existential threats against it, and if need be, to defeat those enemies, expending the lowest human and economic price possible. An inherent difficulty facing the Israeli deterrence capability is that the IDF cannot win wars in the Clausewiczian manner—i.e. by imposing for example, the end of the conflict upon its enemies or to bring about the suspension of hostility against it. In any case, the IDF proved its ability to deter the Arabs from waging frequent wars or intolerable violent actions.

Endnotes

1. Edward Ifft (2008), "Understanding Deterrence", *Nuclear Doctrine and Strategies,* 44(1): 17(16-24).
2. For details, see "Deterrence and Complacence" by Professor Bratislava L. Slantchev, available at: http://slantchev.ucsd.edu/courses/ps12/08-deterrence-and-compellence.pdf.
3. For example, during the Cold War, the United States attempted to deter Moscow from invading Western Europe by threatening to respond with a massive nuclear attack.
4. Deterrence approaches are only one of several classes of strategies for countering terrorism. Other strategies include persuasion (winning "hearts and minds"), economic aid and democratisation, appeasement, and military force. The definition of deterrence subsumes what Glenn Snyder has called "deterrence by punishment" and deterrence by denial". The logic upon which deterrence theory rests is on persuading a target that

the costs of taking an action outweigh the possible benefits the action might provide. During the Cold War and in inter-state relations more generally, deterrence was most actively associated with the threat of retaliation.

5. Ian O. Lesser, Bruce Hoffman et al. (1999), "Countering the New Terrorism", California: Rand Corporation, p. 120.

6. Sergio Catignani (2005), "The Security Imperative in Countertenor Operations: The Israeli Fight Against Suicidal Terror", *Terrorism and Political Violence*, 17(1-2): 248.

7. Michael Walzer (2006), "Just and Unjust Wars: A Moral Argument with Historical Illustrations", New York: Basic Books, p. 216.

8. Gunther E. Rothernberg, "Israeli Defence Forces and Low-Intensity Operation", in David Charters and Maurice Tugwell (eds.) (1989), Armies in Low-Intensity Conflict: A Comparative Analysis, London: Brassey's Defence Publishers, p. 56.

9. EfraimInbar (2008), "Israeli National Security: Issues and Challenges since the Yom Kippur War", New York: Routledge, p. 86.

10. N.S. Jamwal (2003), "Counter-Terrorism Strategy", *Strategic Analysis*, 27(1), p. 6.

11. Israel have developed an extensive network of government authorities, a body of domestic legislation, a range of practical policies and an intense commitment to combat terrorism in all its aspects. For details, see Israel Ministry of Foreign Affairs (2001), "Israeli Response to the UN Committee on Counterterrorism", 27th December 2001, available at: http://mfa.gove.il/MFA/MFA-Archive/2001/Pages/Israel%20Report20to%20the%20UN%20Committee%20on%20Counterro.aspx, accessed on 7th January 2015.

12. Jamwal (2003), p. 7.

13. Martin Van Creveld (2004), "Defending Israel: A Strategic Plan for Peace and Security", New York: St. Martin's Press, p. 2.

14. For details, see Yoav Ben Horin and Barry Posen (1981), "Israel's Strategic Doctrine", California: Rand Corporation.

15. Benny Morris (1993), "Israel's Border Wars: 1949-1956", New York: Oxford University Press, p. 149.

16. Quoted in Thomas L. Friedman, "Israel Turns Terror Back on the Terrorist, But Finds no Political Solution", *The New York*

Times, 4th December 1984.

17. For details, see Daniel Byman (2011), "A High Price: The Triumphs and Failures of Israeli Counter-terrorism", New York: Oxford University Press.

18. For details, see Amira Hass (2002), "Israel's Closure Policy: An Ineffective Strategy of Containment and Repression", *Journal of Palestine Studies*, 31(3): 5-20.

19. During the operations, the IDF destroyed hundreds of homes, businesses, agricultural lands and roads. For details, see Human Rights Watch (2004), "Razing Rafah: Mass Home Demolitions in the Gaza Strip", available at: http://hrw.org/reports/2004/rafah1004/rafah1004text.pdf, accessed on 7th January 2014.

20. David Makovsky (2004), "How to Build a Fence", *Foreign Affairs*, 83(2), p. 50.

21. Gazit, "Israel" in Yonah Alexander (ed.) (2006), Counterterrorism Strategies: Success and Failures of Six Nations, Virginia: Potomac Books, Inc., p. 234.

22. Boaz Ganor, "Suicide Attacks in Israel", in The International Policy Institute for Counter-Terrorism (ed.) (2001), Countering Suicide Terrorism: An International Conference, Herzilya: International Policy Institute for Counter-Terrorism, pp. 142-143.

23. For details, see Stephen T. Hosmer (2001), "Operations Against Enemy Leaders", California: Rand Corporation.

24. On 12 July 2006, a patrol of two Hummers with seven IDF soldiers were attacked by Hezbollah on the Israeli-Lebanese border. Two IDF soldiers, Udi Goldwasser and Eldad Regev were abducted by Hezbollah, while three other soldiers were killed during the abduction. Two soldiers were wounded during the attack, but managed to escape. For details, see Avi Issacharoff (2008), 34 Days: Israel and the War in Lebanon, New York: Palgrave Macmillan.

25. After the war, the Israeli government appointed a commission to investigate and draw lessons from the Israel-Hezbollah War— "The Commission of Inquiry into the Events of Military Engagement in Lebanon 2006". The Commission was chaired by retired judge Eliyahu Winograd, and has since often been referred to as the 'Winograd Commission'. The final conclusions of the 'Winograd Report' were put forward in

January 2008.

26. Dag Henriksen (2012), "Deterrence by Default? Israel's Military Strategy in the 2006 War against Hezbollah", *The Journal of Strategic Studies,* 35(1): 96.

27. Boaz Atzili and Wendy Perlman (2012), "Triadic Deterrence: Coercing Strength, Beaten by Weakness", *Security Studies,* 21, p. 309.

28. For details, see Martin Van Creveld (1998), "The Sword and the Olive: A Critical History of the Israeli Defence Forces", New York: Public Affairs.

29. Shmuel Bar (2008), "Deterring Terrorists: What Israel has Learned?", *Policy Review,* 149, p. 42.

30. They adhere to a doctrine of resistance, "Muqawama" that assures its adherents that the long, historic, currently difficult struggle against Israel will eventually end in a victory, despite temporary setbacks. For details, see EfraimInbar and Eitan Shamir (2014), "Mowing the Grass: Israel's Strategy for Protracted Intractable Conflict", *The Journal of Strategic Studies,* 37(1): 65-90.

31. Inbar and Shamir (2014), p. 70.

32. Ibid, p. 71.

33. Israel Tal (1996), "National Security: The Few Against the Many", Tel Aviv: Dvir, pp. 61-88.

34. For details, see Robert Pape (1996), "Bombing to Win: Airpower and Coercion in War", New York: Cornell.

35. Bar (2008), p. 41.

36. Byman (2014), "An Eye for a Tooth: Israel's Problem with Deterrence", available at:
http://foreignpolicy.com/2014/07/24/an-eye-for-a-tooth,
accessed on 8th January, 2015.

37. Israel drops leaflets and sends warnings via SMS to notify Gaza's that it will soon bomb a building or area here they live and uses small munitions to "knock on the roof" to scare inhabitants into fleeing before a large bomb levels a target.

References

Alexander, Yonah (ed.) (2006), "Counter-terrorism Strategies: Success and Failures of Six Nations", Virginia: Potomac Books Inc.

Atzili, Boaz and Perlman, Wendy (2012), "Triadic Deterrence:

Coercing Strength, Beaten by Weakness", *Security Studies*, 21: 301-335.

Bar, Shamuel (2008), "Deterring Terrorists: What Israel has Learned?", *Policy Review*, 149: 29-42.

Black, Ian and Morris, Benny (1991), "Israel's Secret Wars: A History of Israel's Intelligence Services", New York: Grove Weindenfield.

Byman, Daniel (2011), "A High Price: The Triumphs and Failures of Israeli Counter-terrorism", New York: Oxford University Press.

Catignani, Sergio (2005), "The Security Imperative in Counter-terror Operations: The Israeli Fight against Suicidal Terror", *Terrorism and Political Violence*, 17(1-2): 245-264.

Charters, David and Tugwell, Maurice (eds.) (1989), "Armies in Low-Intensity Conflict: A Comparative Analysis", London: Brassey's Defence Publishers.

Creveld, Martin Van (1998), "The Sword and the Olive: A Critical History of the Israeli Defence Forces", New York: Public Affairs.

——(2004), "Defending Israel: A Strategic Plan for Peace and Security", New York: St. Martin's Press.

Friedman, Thomas L. (1984), "Israel Turns Terror Back on the Terrorist, But Finds no Political Solution", The New York Times, 4th December.

Hass, Amira (2002), "Israel's Closure Policy: An Ineffective Strategy of Containment and Repression", *Journal of Palestine Studies*, 31(3): 5-20.

Henriksen, Dag (2012), "Deterrence by Default? Israel's Military Strategy in the 2006 War against Hezbollah", *The Journal of Strategic Studies*, 35(1): 95-120.

Horin, Yoav Ben and Posen, Barry (1981), "Israel's Strategic Doctrine", California: Rand Corporation.

Hosmer, Stephen T. (2001), "Operations against Enemy Leaders", California: Rand Corporation.

Ifft, Edward (2008), "Understanding Deterrence", *Nuclear Doctrine and Strategies*, 44(1): 16-24.

Inbar, Efraim (2008), "Israeli National Security: Issues and Challenges since the Yom Kippur War", New York: Routledge.

——and Shamir, Eitan (2014), "Mowing the Grass: Israel's Strategy for Protracted Intractable Conflict", *The Journal of Strategic Studies*, 37(1): 65-90.

Israel Ministry of Foreign Affairs (2001), "Israeli Response to the UN Committee on Counterterrorism: 27th December 2001", available at:
http://mfa.gove.il/MFA/MFA-Archive/2001/Pages/Israel%20Report20to%20the%20UN%20Committee%20on%20Counterro.aspx, accessed on 7th January, 2015.

Jamwal, N.S. (2003), "Counter-Terrorism Strategy", *Strategic Analysis*, 27(1): 56-78.

Lesser, Ian O., Hoffman, Bruce et al. (1999), "Countering the New Terrorism", California: Rand Corporation.

Makovsky, David (2004), "How to Build a Fence?", *Foreign Affairs*, 83(2), pp. 50-64.

Miller, Martin A. (2013), "The Foundations of Modern Terrorism: State, Society and Dynamics of Political Violence", Cambridge: Cambridge University Press.

Morris, Benny (1993), "Israel's Border Wars: 1949-1956", New York: Oxford University Press.

Nasr, Kameel B. (1997), "Arab and Israeli Terrorism", North Carolina: McFarland and Company, Inc.

Natanyahu, Benjamin (2001), "Fighting Terrorism: How Democracies Can Defeat the International Terrorist Network?", New York: Farrar, Straus and Giroux.

Pape, Robert (1996), "Bombing to Win: Airpower and Coercion in War", New York: Cornell.

Tal, Israel (1996), "National Security: The Few against the Many", Tel Aviv: Dvir, pp. 61-88.

"The International Policy Institute for Counter-Terrorism" (ed.) (2001), Countering Suicide Terrorism: An International Conference, Herzilya, International Policy Institute for Counter-Terrorism.

Trager, Robert F. and Zagorcheva, Dessislava P. (2005/06), "Deterring Terrorism: It Can be Done", *International Security*, 30(3): 87-123.

Walzer, Michael (2006), "Just and Unjust Wars: A Moral Argument with Historical Illustrations", New York: Basic Books.

9

India-Senegal Trade Relations

Paramjit, Suresh Kumar and Vibha Gupta

Introduction

The Republic of Senegal got independence from French Colonialism on 20th June, 1960. The post-Independence Senegal government initiated the reforms in the financial sector and nationalized banks on the one hand and opened new state banks and non-bank financial institutions, having fixed interest rates for savings and lending on the other hand.

Table 9.1 explains the limited external capital transactions to increase savings in the banks that could strengthen the areas of high economic and social priority. The World Bank and other international financial institutions supported these affirmative steps of the Senegalese government. Financial sector reforms introduced in the 1990s tried to correct these problems.

Table 9.1: Inflation, Interest Rate Spreads and Real Interest Rates in Senegal, 1980-97 (in percent)

	Inflation			Interest Rate Spread Lending Rate Minus Deposit Rate			Real Interest Rate
Country	1980	1990	1997	1980	1990	1997	1997
Senegal	8.7	0.3	1.8	8.3	9	----	-----

Source: World Bank, 1999.
http://www.tradingeconomics.com/senegal/interest-rate-spread-lending-rate-minus-deposit-rate-percent-wb-data.html,
accessed on April 2, 2015.

While the scope and pace of reforms differed across African countries, they were based on two pillars:

liberalization and balance sheet restructuring. 'Most reforms liberalized interest rates and removed ceilings and other controls on credit allocation. Though the details varied, the outcomes were similar' (Soyibo, 1997: 40).

There were complex issues at the time of Independence in Senegal including employment and wage issues. "In two areas, however, political commitment remained severely lacking— fighting HIV/AIDS and reducing fertility. Not all African leaders were convinced of the seriousness of the HIV/AIDS epidemic, nor did they realize the potential impact it will have on their countries.

Because of this, not all made HIV/AIDS, a high priority. Strong political commitment to fighting AIDS was crucial—to provide the resources, leadership, and enabling environment needed to control the epidemic's spread and care for the nation. Accurate and relevant data is a powerful tool for convincing leaders to increase their commitment in confronting HIV/AIDS.

Where there is political commitment, AIDS can be met head on—as in Senegal, where high infection rates have been brought down" (Can Africa Claim the 21st Century?, 2000: 117).

In addition to this, "Unlike those in many African countries, Senegal's leaders chose not to deny the existence of the HIV/AIDS epidemic, but to face the challenges from the start. Enlisting all key actors as allies in a timely and aggressive prevention campaign helped the country maintain one of the lowest HIV infection rates in Africa (1.8 percent). The small number of HIV positive individuals allowed the government to consider using treatment schedules that otherwise would not have been affordable" (World Bank, 2009b: 117).

The human development in Africa in general and Senegal in particular needs political assurance. "What is needed for effective investment in human development is sustained and specific political commitment. This involves focus, sustained resources and active involvement. Focus can come from a commitment towards the poor, especially poor children. Poor children require political commitment because they are voiceless in society, even though those under 15 typically account for 45 percent of African population—a portion unlike anywhere else in the world. Children represent these societies' futures as well as half their present.

A commitment to poor children is also a commitment to equity. Closing urban-rural and male-female gaps is a central challenge for human development" (Alan H. Gelb, 2000: 124).

Senegal is equally concerned about the education and provided special provisions in the Constitution under the rights of children.

Article 21 says, 'the State and the public collectivities create the preliminary conditions and the public institutions which guarantee the education of children'; Article 22 highlights that 'the State has the duty and the responsibility [charge] of the education and of the instruction of youth through public schools. All children, boys and girls, in all places of the national territory, have the right of acceding to school.

The institutions and the religious or non-religious communities are equally recognized as means of education. All the national institutions, public or private, have the duty to make their members literate and to participate in the national effort of literacy in one of the national languages'; and Article 23 refers that 'private schools may be opened with the authorization and under the control of the State' (Senegal Constitution, 2009:8).

The country's Social Fund has enabled communities to mitigate the consequences of drought and economic stagnation and even helped empower communities further. Community schools are also growing rapidly along with the government schools.

Aloysius Ajab Amin and Tharcisse Ntilivamunda stated, 'The study shows that the adult literacy rate, per capita GDP, the growth rate of GDP, education expenditure as a ratio of GDP, and educational expenditure as a ratio of total public budget all tend to have a positive impact on the gross enrolment rate, while an increase in unit cost per pupil tends to reduce primary school enrolment.

In 1970, the Senegalese government spent 20.8 percent and in 2007 it spent 34.3 percent of its total budget on education; it has increased to 40 percent' (Aloysius Ajab Amin, September 2009: 3). The health sector is another area of concern for the Senegalese government.

"Policy makers have become more keen in the composition of public expenditures; as it has been known that proper spending on education and health do promote equity, reduce poverty and increase growth" (Gupta et al., 2002: 717-737).

Post-1990 period is known for foreign direct investment (FDI) flows, which have grown rapidly all over the world and particularly in Africa. 'This is because many developing countries see FDI as an important element in their strategy for economic development' (Ayanwale, 2007: 165).

This has led to many countries improving their business climate to attract more FDI. In fact, 'one of the pillars for launching the New Partnership for Africa's Development (NEPAD) was to accelerate FDI inflows to the region' (Funke and Nsouli, 2003: 336).

Today, the FDI is needed to boost the growth in their economy. It is claimed that FDI can create employment generation, increase technological development in the host country and improve the economic condition of the country in general.

Essentially, it is a summary of the key deliberations at six workshops organized by the Multilateral Investment Guarantee Agency (MIGA) and the Foreign Investment Advisory Service (FIAS) on "Implementing Deregulation and Promoting Foreign Direct Investment in Africa" (Backmann, 1996: 54). The workshops were organized consecutively in six countries: Zimbabwe, Tanzania, Uganda (in 1993) and Senegal, Côte d'Ivoire and Benin (in 1994). Among the participants were high-ranking civil servants and key private sector stakeholders. A few officials from some of the developing countries who have been successful in attracting FDI (Indonesia, Mauritius, Morocco, Pakistan, Tunisia and Turkey) were invited to the workshop to share their countries' experiences.

Senegal as one of the representative country is affirmatively looking for an increasing FDI in the country and in the region being a member of Community of Sahel-Saharan States (CENSAD), Economic Community of West African States (ECOWAS) and African Union (AU).

Recent developments in the sub-region suggest that the future performance of Western Africa as far as FDI inflows is concerned need a change like Senegal with successful democratic transition.

Today, Senegal is a multiparty democracy; a country spanning over an area of about 200,000 square kilometres and a population of 12.17 million, which sends a good signal to foreign investors and other governments in the sub-region.

Real GDP growth in Africa is projected to accelerate further to 6.5 percent in 2014, supported not only by the growth in exports and commodity prices, but also by robust domestic demand.

Several resource rich neighbouring countries of Senegal such as Botswana, Algeria, Chad, Gabon and Nigeria used additional government revenues from natural resources to finance government spending on infrastructure investment and public consumption.

Similarly, Senegal's domestic demand is expected to drive growth to a large extent (Table 9.2). In resource-rich countries, the mining sector has again become the main driver of growth, and in some countries new oil fields are coming on stream.

Average growth rates among Sub-Saharan economies are projected to be higher over the next two years, compared with 2012, supported by sizeable governmental infrastructure investment. Robust private and public consumption underpin this strength, as many countries use macro-economic policies to help speed the recovery from the crisis-induced slowdown.

Table 9.2: Real GDP Growth and Consumer Price Inflation in Senegal

Region/ Country	Real GDP Growth (percent)				Consumer Prices (percent)			
	2012	2013	2014	2015	2012	2013	2014	2015
Senegal	3.5	4.0	4.6	4.7	1.4	1.2	1.6	1.7

Source: IMF, WEO, October 2013 (e-estimates).

Senegal, an agriculture based country, is having principal resource accounting for almost 50 percent of the country's total exports from land. Fishing is a significant sector of the economy along with the agriculture.

It has huge potential for fresh vegetables, flowers, fish, exotic fruits and seafood, which have been identified as potential new sources of foreign exchange earnings. A survey of African investment promotion agencies undertaken by UNCTAD suggests that these are already host sectors and that more FDI is anticipated (UNCTAD, 1999a: 430-433).

Peanuts is the main commodity produced in the country, but attempts have been made to diversify into others, particularly cotton, the second largest export commodity and millet, sugarcane, fruits and vegetables.

Phosphate is the most important mineral resource, although there are also significant iron ore deposits as well as oil. India-Senegal relations are working within the framework of Forum Summit of 2008 and aim at transfer of technology and mutual partnership in different developmental sectors. The attraction of trade and investment opportunities in Senegal is as follows:

- Senegal is 5th top reformer globally and first African in the World Bank's 2009 'Doing Business Report' and the second best business destination in the 2011 'WAEMU Report'.
- Senegal is signatory to international conventions

protecting the environment, human rights, trade, copyright and employment law.

- Extensive privatization has profoundly transformed broad sectors of Senegal's economy.
- Senegal has been extensively upgrading its key infrastructure in a consistent pattern based on public-private-partnership.
- Public investment is focused on key sectors like health, education, water, social housing, energy and agriculture.
- Good education provides pool of skilled manpower in different fields having proficiency in English, Spanish, Arabic and Italian along with French language.
- Ambitious reforms of tax code, legislations and custom procedures provide clear incentives to invest. Double taxation relief agreements provide investors tax status transparency.
- Recent reforms involve land ownership, building permit formalities, labour legislations, taxes and migrating import/export procedures online.
- Senegal enjoys preferential access to European markets through ACP-EU agreements and to the US through AGOA.
- Senegal is a member of WAEMU of eight countries having 70 million consumers and ECOWAS, a market of 200 million consumers.
- Senegal shares a single currency, the CFA Franc with 7 other WAEMU States in West Africa.

India's Approach of Mutual Partnership in Africa

In recent years, besides being major recipients of global foreign direct investment (FDI) inflows, India is emerging as an important global investor with increasing overseas investments in target markets.

Though India had business interest and investment in Africa since very long, these were largely driven by small and medium enterprises and traders. But the recent wave of FDI from India to Africa is driven by the bigger Indian companies. Most of these companies have made significant investments in the extraction sector of different African countries (Table 9.3).

The continuous increase in commodity prices along with an increasing demand for energy and raw materials in the domestic economy seems to be the major driving force for these companies.

Table 9.3: India's Approved Overseas Direct Investment in the African Region (US$ mn)

Country	April 96 to March 08	2008-09	2009-10	2010-11
Senegal	23.3	---	---	---
Total in Africa	6,865.7	2,827.9	2,521.9	13,346.7
India's Total	54,345.1	17,147.4	17,987.2	43,929.0
% share in India's Total	112.6	16.5	14.0	30.4

Contd...

Country	2011-12	2012-13	Total (April 96-March 13)
Senegal	---	---	1.1-- 24.3
Total in Africa	7510.0	4,717.5	7,789.8
India's Total	30,862.9	26,872.4	1,144.1
% share in India's Total	24.3	17.6	19.8

Note: '---' not available

Sources: Ministry of Finance, Government of India and Reserve Bank of India, 2013.

Exim Bank: A Partner in Africa's Development

Exim Bank of India has one of the representative offices in Senegal, which plays a key role in facilitating economic cooperation with it and is closely associated with several of the Bank's initiatives.

This representative office interfaces with multilateral institutions such as African Development Bank, Afreximbank, regional financial institutions such as Development Bank (PTA Bank) and West African Development Bank (BOAD) along with the developmental financial institutions as well as Indian Missions in the region.

To enhance bilateral trade and investment relations through

FDI, Exim Bank of India has in place several lines of credit (LoCs) extended to a number of institutions/agencies in Africa. These LoCs supplement the "Focus Africa" program of the Government of India and are extended especially to priority sectors, identified by the Government of India for mutual cooperation and benefit.

Besides these operating LoC extended at the behest of Government of India, Exim Bank extends its own commercial lines of credits to various financial institutions and other entities in Africa, such as PTA Bank, Banque Ouest Africaine De Development (West African Development Bank, covering 8 countries in the west African region) and Afreximbank.

These LoCs facilitate import of project-related equipments and services from India on deferred credit terms. At the same time, many of these LoCs are earmarked for infrastructure and related projects. Currently, 101 LoCs are in operation amounting to around US$ 4 billion covering more than 48 countries in the African region.

Exim Bank of India plays a pivotal role in promoting and financing Indian companies in execution of projects. Towards this end, the Bank extends funded and non-funded facilities for overseas industrial turnkey projects, civil construction contracts, supplies as well as technical and consultancy service contracts.

In the African region, Indian companies have implemented numerous projects, spanning across various sectors, with support from Exim Bank of India. These projects, in turn, facilitate and support infrastructure development in host countries, thereby contributing to the overall development process in the region. Such projects include transmission projects in Senegal also.

Background of India-Senegal Relations

India-Senegal relations are working within the framework of Forum Summit of 2008 and 2011 aimed at transfer of technology and mutual partnership in different developmental sectors. The introduction of scientific agriculture implements, irrigation facility and environment friendly fertilizer and seeds is aimed at strengthening this sector on the one hand and generating skill-based employment opportunities, infrastructure development on the other hand and thereby strengthening the stability of the government.

The investment in horticulture and floriculture is encouraged and the government is looking for the public-private-partnership in these sectors.

80 Indian agricultural companies invested £ 1.5 billion in Ethiopia, Kenya, Madagascar, Senegal and Mozambique and £ 500 million was loaned by the Indian government to these companies. US$ 2.5 billion has already been invested by Indian companies in Africa's agricultural sector alone, which has also enhanced the public-private-partnership between the Government and Indian agro companies.

For commercial farming, Indian companies in Africa have collectively invested US$ 2.3 billion including Senegal. 'In Senegal, a joint public-private Indian group has invested US$ 250 million for a stake in a colonial era enterprise, *Industries Chimiques du Senegal*, which owns rock phosphate mines and plants to produce phosphoric acid used in agriculture' (Karl P. Sauvant, 2010: 265). Indian oil companies are also venturing into Senegal. There have been significant investments in other raw materials sector also.

Pan-Africa network has already covered 43 countries in Africa including Senegal. Underdeveloped ICT is often attributed to a lack of understanding about it. 'Rapid changes in this technology require constant awareness not only of new developments but also of what has been done in other countries.

Many African countries have already developed a wealth of best practices that could be shared. Several countries have substantially privatized telecommunications. All these efforts offer lessons for other countries.

Thus, there is a need to develop awareness-raising

programs to improve government and public understanding of information technology applications as they are being used elsewhere.

There is a need for establishment of 'centres of specialization' that train policymakers and government and private users and provide opportunities for advanced training at existing regional centres of excellence. Offering training that uses distance learning technology to introduce users and policymakers to the creative use of existing infrastructure would prove beneficial' (Alan H. Gelb, 2000: 158).

One of India's leading IT services firm with a presence in nine African nations—South Africa, Nigeria, Senegal, Ghana, Botswana, Senegal, Libya, Sudan and Zimbabwe—has been rewarding meritorious students in Africa by providing scholarships. In fact, its IT scholarship test in Nigeria in 2010 attracted more than 2,00,000 students. The firm has focused on developing Africa's skilled ICT manpower for more than a decade and has trained thousands of students.

Over the past few years, India and Africa have initiated several collaborations to give impetus to the African health care industry. Within telemedicine domain, India, in a joint venture with the AU, has initiated the Pan-African E-network Project, wherein African medical personnel can seek medical consultation from Indian medical specialists in various disciplines.

The second phase of this project was initiated in August 2010, wherein telemedicine consultations are regularly being conducted from super-specialty hospitals in India to African countries. Furthermore, 11 Indian super-specialty hospitals have initiated regular continued medical education (CME) sessions since April 2009, and till 2013, around 654 CME sessions have been conducted through this network (Pan-African E-network, 2013).

The company is mainly active in Nigeria and Cameroon, with its Côte d'Ivoire office catering to other West African countries such as Benin, Togo, Burkina, Mali, Niger and

Ghana. In January 2008, the company established a new representative office in Senegal to further develop its business in West African countries such as Guinea, Gambia and Mauritania.

India-Senegal Mutual Partnership

Agriculture Partnership: Agriculture sector employs 70 percent of the Senegalese population and is central to the country's development. India has put at disposal, 510 tractors, equipment for tilling, carts, drilling machines, pumps, trucks and maize processing and enriching equipment under the Indo-Senegalese Cooperation arrangement. Senegal government and Indian Farmers Fertilizer Co-operative Limited (IFFCO) signed an agreement of about US$ 240 million.

There are tremendous export opportunities in the agri-business sector, including floriculture, fruit cultivation and market gardening, cashewnut plantation and industrial processing of groundnut.

India has supported Senegal's agriculture sector on lines of credit (LoC) by facilitating US$ 15 million for acquisition of agricultural material and the creation of rural enterprises and US$ 27 million for irrigation projects with a view to achieve self sufficiency in rice production. 'Within eight weeks of receiving the LoC, 1,600 pumps bound for Senegal left the Indian shores.

As one knows that Senegal is dependent on imported rice, the infrastructural improvements increased its rice production and the country achieved self-sufficiency in rice production by 2012-13. More than 85,000 hectare of land was under irrigation which produced 460,000 tons of rice in 2008-09' (Senegal Story, 2011; Kirloskar, 2008: 3).

Today, the Senegal government offers investment opportunities in this sector particularly in Senegal River Valley region. Senegal has become a leading exporter of cherry tomatoes, fine green beans, basil, green asparagus, onions, potatoes and aborigines. Approximately 80 Indian companies have collectively invested US$ 2.3 billion in Ethiopia, Kenya, Madagascar, Senegal and Mozambique.

Fishing is a significant sector of the economy along with agriculture. Peanuts is the main commodity produced in the country, but attempts have been made to diversify into others, particularly cotton, the second largest export commodity and millet, sugarcane, fruit and vegetables. Table 9.4 refers to the agricultural projects of India in Senegal that explains the nature of investments.

The agro-industry in Senegal needs farm mechanization that will facilitate increase in productivity. The production boost in agriculture is the only way to initiate the agro-industry in Africa.

It should be remembered that once there will be surplus production of food in Africa, the agro-industry will get the input of raw materials to produce different food products and cater to the needs of urban as well as rural areas.

Table 9.4: India's Projects in Pipeline in Africa

Country	Project	Executing Agency	Project Cost (US$ million)	Funding Agency
Senegal	Minor Irrigation project	Ministry of Agriculture	26.4	African Development Bank

Sources: India-Africa Project Partnership, March 2005, AfDB; Exim Bank, India; Ministry of Commerce and Industry, India; Ministry of External Affairs, India.

Some African countries are offering land on lease for 99 years to overseas farmers, and several farmers from India have already migrated to these countries and begun farming (*The Economic Times,* 28th January, 2011). Close to 70 Indian companies are working in the farming sector in this region. Such investments will generate local employment as well as create opportunities for local skill development.

Indian companies can explore the possibilities of

investment through joint ventures or contract farming, setting up of agro processing firms and investments in key stages of value chains.

India's investment in Senegal could result in improving the agricultural sector of the host country through skill development, job creation, and technological upgradation, supply of quality inputs like seeds, better supply chain management and biotechnology. India's transfer of technology could help Senegal to deal with the problem of food crisis. Indian scientific and agricultural research institutions have assisted many entrepreneurs for developing their business ideas in countries of Africa including Senegal. Indian investors could also focus on providing quality infrastructure to enhance the farm productivity in Senegal.

The LoCs extended by the Exim Bank of India to Senegal is earmarked for agriculture, irrigation and related projects, which would also serve to contribute towards development of the agricultural and related sectors in the region (Table 9.5). The production of rice in the Kolda region of Senegal aims to increase sustainable production and farm incomes through the development of valleys and lowlands, improving the rate of land development, increasing crop yields and diversification of crops and livestock development while preserving the natural resources.

The horticulture project explains about the creation of 100-150 clustering projects (farms) targeting streams of horticulture (fruit and vegetables) and livestock (dairy and poultry). The development of agriculture storehouses-cum-grain corridors would help in strengthening grain producing irrigated agricultural basins of millet/rice/maize.

Similarly, the LoC is provided to install hand pumps and submersible pumps, pump sets and irrigation equipment and export of tractors from India to Senegal. With these LoCs in place, increased exports of agro-related machinery and equipment to the Senegal by Indian entrepreneurs/exporters would serve to enhance bilateral cooperation in the agricultural sector further.

Table 9.5: LoC in Agriculture Sector in Senegal

Project Description	Total Value (US$ mn)	Contact Details
Production of Rice in the Kolda region, Senegal	54	sodagri@orange.sn demcspc@gmail.com
Clustering Projects focused on Horticulture	17.8	asano@apix.sn mountaga.sy@apix.sn
Development of Agriculture Storehouses	620	asano@apix.sn mountaga.sy@apix.sn

Source: 10th CII-Exim Bank Conclave on India-Africa Project Partnership, 2014, Government of India, pp. 132-137.

India's foreign investments in agriculture cultivation would lead to possible benefits for rural poor, including the creation of a potentially significant number of farm and off-farm jobs, development of rural infrastructure, and social improvements, leading to poverty reduction in Senegal.

Moreover, the Senegal Government with a view to addressing the serious issue of food shortage should frame policies towards attracting investors in the agricultural sector to tackle food, employment and sustainability crises.

Energy, Power and Infrastructure Partnership: Development of these sectors in African countries is very important for the development and growth of the region. The dependence of many countries of Africa on primary commodity exports, combined with reliance on manufactured imports has negatively affected the growth of the region. Also the recent global economic crisis has reduced development assistance and private capital flows to the region. Hence, development of a strong infrastructure is necessary.

The entire installed generation capacity of Sub-Saharan African countries excluding South Africa is only 28 giga watts, and 25 percent of that capacity is unavailable because of aging plants and poor maintenance. Only about 29 percent of the

Sub-Saharan Africa's population has access to electricity, as compared to about half in South Asia and more than 80 percent in Latin America and the Middle East and Northern Africa.

Also, African manufacturing enterprises experience power outages on an average of 56 days per year. Many African countries are seeking support and technical assistance for development of petroleum pipelines, petroleum exploration and production in the region.

There is an immense potential for investment and cooperation in Senegal, particularly in the electricity generation and power transmission areas. Energy deficit is expected to continue, posing a serious challenge for the overall development of Senegal and the West African region. Insufficient investment in the energy sector, leading to underdeveloped infrastructure including electricity transmission and distribution networks, have exacerbated the energy problem in the region.

Despite the potential for energy generation, insufficient use of existing energy systems has resulted in generation of electricity which is less than the installed capacity due to drought, lack of maintenance and rehabilitation and also general system losses of electricity which includes transmission and distribution. In light of these, development of the energy infrastructure is a priority area for the Senegalese government.

The Line of Credit (LoC) extended by the Exim Bank of India to countries in Africa, which are earmarked for power generation and transmission projects, would also serve to contribute towards development of the energy sector and power generation and transmission. Table 9.6 shares the number of projects in energy and power sectors in different African countries including Senegal. It depicts six different sectors in twelve African countries worth US$ 7936.57 million.

An important area of bilateral cooperation could be infrastructure development in African countries. Investment in infrastructure development, due to an increasing need for better infrastructural facilities, coupled with the endeavour of Senegal for rapid economic growth, could prove to be a mutually rewarding area of bilateral cooperation. Lack of forward and backward linkages among different modes of transportation, declining air connectivity, poorly equipped ports, and inadequate access to all-season roads are key challenges facing the Senegalese economy. Areas that hold immense investment opportunities include development of highways and roadways, development of railway networks and power systems, which would also help in regional integration to a great extent. Large Indian construction companies could explore opportunities to meet the infrastructural requirements in African countries, also contributing largely to economic development in the host countries.

Table 9.6: Energy and Power Sectors in Africa

Sector	Sub-sector	Number of Projects	Total Value (US$ mn)	Country
Power and Energy	- Thermal, coal - Dams, oil and gas, petroleum products, renewable energy, etc.	28	7936.57	- Benin, Burkina Faso - Cameroon, Congo - Gabon, Malawi - Mozambique, Namibia - Senegal, Togo - Zambia, Zimbabwe

Source: Project Opportunities, 2011, India-Africa Project Partnership, EXIM Bank, CII and Government of India.

The system of roads in Senegal is relatively well developed with an approximate road network of 14,500 km., responsible for 90 percent of the movement of people and goods. The Senegal River is also used for the transport of goods within Senegal and for transit to Mauritania. Dakar Port is the largest in West Africa and extends over 3,260,000 square meters. The railway network stretches to 1,057 km. with a main axis from Dakar to Mali. Senegal has three international airports; the Dakar Airport being a major hub in Economic Community of West African States (ECOWAS), with a flow of 1.2 million per year.

The Indian Railways (IR), the Indian state-owned railway enterprise, has one of the world's largest and most profitable networks in the world. The IR has already stepped into Africa by supplying locomotives to Senegal. Furthermore, the IR can share its low-cost models with Senegal with fewer financial resources to develop railway infrastructure economically. The infrastructure projects are operative in Senegal through EXIM Bank. The tourism infrastructure development of Senegal is growing and attracting the Indian investors.

Since infrastructure investments offer a high stimulus multiple in terms of economic growth, Senegal has announced such similar programs, though on a much smaller scale. This remarkable growth has clearly occurred in a limited set of countries and sectors. India has strong resources to assist Senegal in developing railway network.

The Indian Railways (IR) has already stepped into Senegal by supplying locomotives and coaches. Furthermore, the IR can share its low-cost model with Senegal with fewer financial resources to develop railway infrastructure economically. Recent examples of large Indian companies leveraging opportunities in Africa's infrastructure sector are highlighted in Table 9.7.

The development of a 12 hectare site at Platform Millennium at Daimniadio in Dakar region for a knowledge city as per international standards, will develop products useful in home automation, energy saving and environment. The project deals with the construction of a new track with a standard gap between Dakar and the Blaise Diange

International Airport Diass (ABID) which is around 50 km.

Table 9.7: Project Opportunities in Different Sectors of Senegal

Project	Sub-Sector	Value (US$ mn)
Development of a 12 hectare knowledge city as per international standards	Infrastructure	200
Dakar-AIBD Railway	Infrastructure	209.032
DAKAR Campus International	Infrastructure	164.535
Touristic development of the Joal-Finio island called the seashells island which is 800 metres long	Infrastructure	16
Touristic development of the Mbodiene area over a total area of 504 hectares	Infrastructure	406
Touristic development of Pointe Sarene over an area of 110 hectares	Infrastructure	282
Rehabilitation of the A. Le Dantec hospital in Dakar	Infrastructure	92
Construction of the plant for desalinization of sea water into fresh water	Infrastructure	493.568
10 years programs of building 10,000 social housing per year	Infrastructure	459.869
Tramway project in Dakar	Infrastructure	767.041
Development of various universities in Dakat, Saint Louis, Diourbel, Thies, Ziguinchor, Kaolack etc.	Infrastructure	290.541
Construct ion of an ore port	Mining	736
Business city and regional vocation centre	Infrastructure	564.972
Construction of a dry port at Kaolack	Infrastructure	60

Source: Exim Bank, Developing Initiatives and Enhancing Relations, Project Opportunities, 9th-11th March 2014.

The Mbodiene tourist place needs four large hotel units

ranging in size from 50 ha to 80 ha with a capacity of 6,000 rooms with ancillary facilities. Moreover, two shopping malls, 18-hole golf courses, a thematic amusement park, corridors of public access to the lagoon and the beach and three pedestrian bridges overlooking the lagoon and giving access to the public beaches are also on the anvil.

The development of Pointe Sarene aims at construction of five hotels with an area ranging from 5 ha to 10 ha and having a capacity of 1,600 rooms with auxiliary facilities.

Others projects which are underway include construction of 120 upscale villas offering panoramic views to the sea, construction of a shopping centre with a mini auditorium, water-sports and a marina, construction of corridors of public access to the beach and development of beaches and dunes on a stretch more than 8 km. long.

There is also a proposal for construction of a plant for desalinization of sea water into fresh water (drinkable and to be used for irrigation) that will separate the salt and will be equipped with desalination systems based on distillation or condensation principles.

The 10-year programme of building 10,000 social housing units per year will provide land servicing, road and sewage networks and construction of social community facilities in Dakar with a particular focus on the triangle, Diass-Diamniadio pout. The tramway project in Dakar highlights the establishment of a comprehensive system of tramway having a length of 35 km., including setting up of equipment and rolling materials (railways, trains, electrical sub-stations), construction of platforms, stations, signals and staff training and building and equipment of a maintenance centre having command and supervision position.

The business city and regional vocation centre at a cost of US$ of 546.9 $ million highlights a readymade office park and premium infrastructure for the establishment of large multinational headquarters and regional vocation companies. The city plans also includes establishment of a residential area of 220 ha having 50 headquarters and 3,000 residential homes near the Leopold Sedar Senghor airport, Pink Lake and Lecterc military camp. Lastly, the construction of a dry port at Kaolack with an area of 70 ha for the port and 40 ha for secondary activities consists of components including storage areas and related facilities.

Additional infrastructure facilities would include handling, unloading, packaging, port facilities and infrastructure for cereal products, handling platform, connected railway and truck parking.

Overall, Indian investors are attracted towards Senegal as Senegal free zone is exempt from all taxes and duties for acquisition of goods, equipments, raw materials, reduced system tax concerning the corporate income tax; a lump sum tax equal to 2 percent of the total turnover, exemption from the specific tax on salaries, capital gains taxes, business license tax, land taxes, registration fees and exemption from payment of withholding taxes from dividends arising out of the free zone investments.

Senegal will arise from dependence to self-sufficiency in food security by this relationship that works continuously as a part of the South-South Cooperation.

India's Role in Strengthening Senegal Education: The country-wise implementation status of tele-education refers to 43 countries that include Senegal as well. The AU has shown interest in 5 broad areas of education. Along with it, the educational programmes offer various courses in different universities as mentioned in Table 9.8.

The Dakar campus needs to build up its higher education for international recognition, especially through the establishment of partnerships with leading international academic institutions. The integrated campus will come up in the same area with services necessary for the development of a high quality education.

Overall, the feedback from the participating nations about this education network relates to 4,000 students who have registered for various courses so far.

**Table 9.8 Educational Programmes Offered in
Different Universities**

S. No.	Different Courses	University
Post-Graduate Programs (4/5 semesters)		
1.	MBA (HR/Marketing) (English)	IGNOU
2.	MBA–International Business	AMITY
3.	M.Sc. –IT	Madras University
4.	Master of Tourism Management	IGNOU
5.	Master of Finance and Control	AMITY
6.	MBA (HR, Marketing–French)	AMITY
Under-Graduate Programs (3 years/6 semesters)		
1.	BBA (in English)	Madras University
2.	BBA (in French)	AMITY
3.	B.Sc. –IT,	AMITY
4.	Bachelor of Finance & Investment Analysis	AMITY
5.	Bachelor of Tourism Studies	IGNOU
Diploma Programs (1 year)		
1.	French Language	AMITY
2.	PG Diploma–IT	AMITY
3.	Business Management	AMITY
4.	Tourism Studies	IGNOU
5.	Early childcare and Education	IGNOU
Certificate Programs (6 months, 1 year)		
1.	Database and Information System (1year)	BITS
2.	Networking and Operating System (1 year	BITS
3.	Electronics and Instrumentation (1 year)	BITS
4.	English Language	Delhi University
5.	Accountancy	Delhi University
6.	German Language	Madras University
7.	Arabic Language	Madras University
8.	Tourism Studies	IGNOU
9.	Nutrition and Childcare	IGNOU
10.	Environmental Studies	IGNOU
Medical Disciplines Offered		
General (Internal) Medicine, Radiology, Adult Cardiology, Paediatric, Cardiology, Neurology, Dermatology, Endocrinology, Infectious Diseases/ HIV-AIDS, Gastroenterology, Nephrology, Pathology, Psychiatry, Paediatrics, Medical Oncology, Urology, Genetics, Gynaecology and Ophthalmology.		

Source: ITEC, 2013, www.tcil.com.

Under this endeavour, Senegal has experienced patients
saving time and money through the extension of tele-education
and tele-medicine in rural areas through public private

partnership (PPP) model. Along with it, the government has strengthened environmental protection, science and technology and information and communication technology (ICT) areas to integrate locals with the international community.

The use of ICT provides opportunity to skilled persons to obtain employment in the country and abroad accordingly. It also helps the business community in introducing their agro and other products and diversifying their export basket while supplying the processed goods as per the demand.

Along with it, the Indian Technical and Economic Cooperation (ITEC) programme in 2008 has helped transform capacity, building and skills transfer to hundreds of thousands of students, professionals, and mid-career diplomats in 160 countries across continents, including Africa, Asia, Latin America and East and Central Europe including Senegal.

The success of the solar engineering training would ensure that it becomes a regular feature of the ITEC. Over the next three years, more than 150 women would be trained to spread the light in their homeland.

On an average, India spends about ₹ 500 million (US$ 10.8 million) on varied ITEC activities. Since 1964, India has provided nearly US$ 2.5 billion worth of technical assistance to developing countries, including the neighbouring countries. Over the years, India has spent around US$ 1 billion over ITEC-related activities involving the African countries (ITEC, 2013).

Against the backdrop of the burgeoning popularity of the ITEC programme in African countries, India's Prime Minister Manmohan Singh, announced 20,000 slots for African students at the maiden India-Africa Forum Summit held in Addis Ababa in May 2011. "We will enhance opportunities for African students to pursue higher studies in India.

As an immediate measure we propose to double our long-term scholarships for undergraduates, post-graduates and higher courses and increase the number of training slots under our technical assistance programmes every year. Both India and Africa are blessed with young populations. It is only by investing in the creative energies of our youth that the potential of our partnership will be fulfilled", he said in the presence of African leaders (India Africa, 2011).

Similarly, NIIT has training and educational centres in Senegal. NIIT, the leading global talent development corporation, ventured into the Africa over a decade ago by setting up its first IT education centre in Botswana in 1997. For more than a decade now, NIIT has been involved in creation of skilled ICT manpower in the continent and has trained nearly 150,000 students till date.

The talent development company is touching over 20,000 learners every year, through three dozen learning centres in 8 African countries including Senegal.

Similarly, the DNIIT program is the most popular IT training program in many African countries. NIIT has enabled thousands of young people in these countries to join the global IT workforce, many of whom are working in large IT and non-IT organizations such as Debswana, Government of Botswana, Zenith International Bank, Shell Corporation, Total, Dunlop, Chevron Texaco, Tower Aluminium, Unilever, Mobitel, Grant Thorton, Barclays, Standard Bank, Multilink, Shell, Afribank International, Unilever, First bank, Union Bank, Zenith Intl Bank, UBA, Linkserve, KPMG, Ericsson etc.

NIIT is active since 2007, having one centre in Dakar with 500 students pursuing career as well as non-career courses. The medium of instruction is the French language.

Opportunities in Health Sector: Senegal offers interesting investment opportunities in health sector, particularly in medical clinics and specialized services. The government has established a comprehensive program prioritizing epidemiological surveillance, reproductive health, STD/AIDS and endemic diseases control (mainly malaria, bilharzias, onchocerciasis or river blindness and tuberculosis). The emergence of several advanced health services such as MRI, laser treatment of eye disease and refractive laser surgery aims to establish Dakar as a sub-regional medical hub, attracting and retaining patients from all West Africa sub-regions.

There are efforts to rejuvenate the A. Le Dantec hospital of Dakar, which has the greatest potential of human resources in the health sector throughout West Africa and Central Africa.

Senegal offers attractive investment opportunities throughout the value chain, from R&D to generics and phyto-pharmaceuticals. The following opportunities have been identified:

- Cardiology and cardiac surgery.
- Neurology.
- Nephrology and the treatment of kidney diseases.
- Laser surgery.
- Ophthalmology.
- Radiology and medical imaging.
- Rheumatology.
- Urology.

Challenges for Inclusive Development and Conclusion

Senegal needs to strengthen the continuation of participatory people's democracy, multiparty system and a decentralized approach of governance. The recognition of the constitution and its practice gets respect here. The experience of India's democracy may work to strengthen the Senegal's democratic institution.

The democratic governance allows in analysing the global policies for people's development, which will further show the way towards economic growth. Good governance should be viewed not as a mere function of the multiplicity of political parties, but in terms of the real empowerment of the people in all their diversity.

The right kind of people-oriented policies having elements of balanced privatization may enrich the real democracy, which is a necessity for propelling Senegal's economic growth and global participation. Diversification will require the development of the necessary economic infrastructure, better labour skills, improving status of women and making both women and civil society partners in the development process. Mass participation will check the ongoing practice of 'when you do not know what you want, you accept anything that is given to you'.

The globalised economy in Senegal and India need to build culture of hard work, honesty, productivity, transparency and quality management, amongst many other ethical and managerial norms and values.

The African Union needs political renaissance to obtain maximum benefits from the globalization process, so as to contribute to greater economic growth in terms of increased inter-state and intra-state trade, capture a greater share of foreign capital and, consequently, produce higher per capita incomes.

Regional cooperation of Senegal will intensify possibilities for diversifying exports to less developing regions to take the utmost benefit of South-South cooperation. It will strengthen both the countries in the collective bargaining power besides the developed markets and move from being dependant to self-sufficiency in food security.

References

Adedoyin Soyibo (1997), "The Informal Financial Sector in Nigeria: Characteristics and Relationship with the Formal Sector", *Development Policy Review*.

"Africa Oil", available at: http://www.iimcal.ac.in/research/download/OFDI_Partha-pal.pdf, accessed on 9th March, 2011.

Alan H. Gelb (2000), "Can Africa Claim the 21st Century?" The International Bank for Reconstruction and Development, The World Bank, Washington D.C.

Aloysius Ajab Amin and Tharcisse Ntilivamunda (2009), "Education Expenditure and Outcome in Senegal", GDN Working Paper Series Working Paper No. 16, Global Development Network (GDN) 1999-2009, New Delhi.

A.B. Ayanwale (2007), "FDI and Economic Growth: Evidence from

Nigeria", AERC Research Paper 165, African Economic Research Consortium, Nairobi, available at: http://opendocs.ids.ac.uk/opendocs/bitstream/item/2943/RP%20 165.pdf?sequence=1, accessed on 2nd April, 2015.

Heinz Backmann (1996), "Implementing Deregulation and Promoting Foreign Direct Investment in Africa", World Bank/IFC/MIGA, Washington D.C.

"India-Africa 2nd Forum Summit, 2011", Address by Dr. Manmohan Singh, Prime Minister of India, 20-22 May, Addis Ababa. Ethiopia.

"ITEC, 2013", available at: http://2billiondreams.in/index.php?param=chapterdetails/10, accessed on 5th August, 2013.

Karl P. Sauvant and Jaya Prakash Pradhan (2010), "The Rise of Indian Multinationals: Perspectives on Indian Outward Foreign Direct Investment", Palgrave Macmillan.

Kirloskar (2008), "Food Security in Africa through Water Management", Kirloskar Brothers Ltd., Delhi.

N. Funke and S.M. Nsouli (2003), "The New Partnership for Africa's Development (NEPAD): Opportunities and Challenges", IMF Working Paper No. 03/69, International Monetary Fund, Washington, D.C.

"Pan-African E-network for Education and Health Care", October 11, 2009, *The Hindu,* accessed on 4th January, 2013.

Sanjeev Gupta, Marjin Verhoeven and Erwin Tiongson (2002), "The Effectiveness of Government Spending on Education and Health Care in Developing and Transition Economies", *European Journal of Political Economy,* Vol. 18, No. 4, Thomson Scientific.

"Senegal Constitution of 2001 with Amendments through 2009", 2012, William S. Hein & Co., Inc., translated by Jefri J. Ruchti, available at: https://s3.amazonaws.com/landesa_production/resource/2782/Se negal_Constitution_2009.pdf?AWSAccessKeyId=AKIAICR3IC C22CMP7DPA&Expires=1428151112&Signature=scYIyeIuZ7 Eusb3AAp9nFByJiUA%3D, accessed on 4th April, 2015.

Suresh Kumar (2008), "Nurturing the Tilling Fields of Africa", *Africa Quarterly,* Vol. 48, No. 3, Delhi.

UNCTAD (1999a), "Foreign Direct Investment and Development", World Investment Report, 1999, United Nations, New York and

Geneva.
World Bank (2009b), "World Development Report 1999/2000: Entering the 21st Century", Oxford University Press, New York.

10

Outward FDI from India to WANA Region

Rachna Madaan, Jitender Bhandari and P.S. Bisht

Introduction

Although developed countries remain the leading source of outward foreign direct investment (FDI), developing and transition economies have emerged as an important source of outward FDI since the 1990s. Traditionally, developing nations have played the role of host countries, attracting FDI from industrialized economies and leveraging it to the alleviation of poverty, unemployment and accelerating economic development domestically. Eminent theorists and researchers have given various theories ranging from market imperfection (Hymer, 1960) to ownership, location and internalization (OLI) (Dunning, 1977, 1981) paradigm to explain this phenomenon of FDI emanating from a developed nation to a developing one.

But during the last couple of decades, a new phenomenon has surfaced, wherein the traditional host countries are increasingly acting as source countries for outward FDI. Various firms from developing countries especially those from the Asian region have remarkably registered their arrival at an international level in a shorter span of time vis-à-vis their competitors from the industrialized world.

Review of Literature

The systematic work on the theory of MNCs was first developed by Hymer (1960) who explained that the imperfect markets across different countries marks the decision for relocation of production facilities leading to what is called "traffic jumping". As a result, FDI is carried out to replace excessive transaction costs involved in trade. The theory of

MNCs was further developed by Rugman (1986), who gave the internalization theory illustrating FDI as a means to replace markets by internalizing the operations, especially in intermediate product markets across affiliates in various host countries. This kind of FDI was proposed as "efficiency seeking". However, the above theories were insufficient in explaining as to why FDI inclined to develop pertinent assets in a few countries. Against this backdrop, OLI model of Dunning (1993) specifically combined the locational factors with firm-specific advantages and transaction costs elements for explaining international production. Amongst the accessible theories that explicate the happening of FDI, "eclectic theory" of Dunning on international production emerged as the most comprehensive approach.

The above mentioned theories have focused mainly on FDI from developed countries, examining why FDI occurs from a developed country to another developed country, or from a developed country to less developed countries (LDCs) or newly industrialized economies (NIEs). These theories could not explain the rise of MNCs from developing regions like Asia-Pacific, as firms from these regions emerged despite not possessing firm-specific advantages unlike the firms from the developed countries. In the light of changing global scenario, other studies (Dunning and Narula, 1996; Cantwell and Mudambi, 2001; Rasiah, 2000 and Gammeltoft, 2006) were carried out to incorporate the emergence of MNCs from developing countries.

Further, this new phenomena of late comer firms rapidly catching up with incumbent global players, was explained by Mathews (2006) who proposed an alternative framework to OLI, which he terms as 'linkages, leverage and learning (LLL)' framework. Mathews (2006), argues that it is the changes in the character of the world economy and innovative features that these MNEs share, such as their accelerated internationalization, strategic innovation and organizational innovation, that fit particularly well with the characteristics of the emergent global economy.

Motives and Types of FDI: Theoretical Background

The internalization theory of FDI (Buckley et al., 1976; Hennart, 1991) argued that organizations extend their movement to remote areas and being proficiency seekers, need to diminish the transaction costs of cross fringe exercises. This thought of transaction costs is further connected by the OLI hypothesis of John Dunning (1981, 1988). The OLI basically holds that FDI is an after-effect of firms having in possession, particular ownership advantages (O) that they need to endeavour in outside locations (L), which they accomplish through internalization (I). In spite of the fact that these theories of FDI were generally created in light of the encounters of developed nations, however it can well clarify the motivational components behind the transborder extension of developing nations firms' (Dunning 1981; Lall 1983).

Concerning location preferences (L), MNCs will, as an outcome of their particular (O) advantages, have a tendency to centre their exercises in nations at the same or lower phases of economic development (Dunning et al., 1986). Regarding internalization factors (I), MNCs will have a tendency to choose joint ventures to get to nearby market learning, innovation and capital and in this way, adjusting for their inborn asset constraints (Lecraw, 1981). Taking into consideration the types of O-FDI, four main types of investments are notable: horizontal FDI, vertical FDI, planned asset-seeking FDI, as well as resource seeking FDI (UNCTAD, 2006). Horizontal or market-seeking FDI is goaded by the need to get hold of market access and evade trade resistance in the host countries. It is directed by the proximity-absorption trade-off in which nearness to the host market evades trade costs.

FDI of this type happens when firms make a decision to serve foreign market all the way through local production than through exports. It happens when a firm remains its production process internationally, placing every phase of production in the nation where it can be completed at the lowest cost. The third vital cause for outward FDI from developing nations is the planned asset-seeking motive. Strategic asset-seeking FDI occurs when investors try to gain entrance to globally recognized brand names and local supply networks in order to toughen their worldwide competitive position. Strategic asset-seeking FDI too happens in the shape of technology-sourcing FDI while firms try to gain entry to foreign technology by also purchasing foreign firms or launching R&D facilities in overseas centres of excellence. Lastly, the resource seeking FDI takes place when firms recognize explicit host country locations as a striking cause of natural assets at the minimum cost. Such FDI is often linked with export of resource-based products from the host nation (Herzer, 2011).

Outward Direct Investments (ODI): Global Trends

Global ODI has witnessed an upsurge during the last decade with FDI outflows increasing from US$ 748 billion in 2001, to a peak of US$ 2,198 billion in 2007, before moderating to US$ 1,451 billion in 2010, and then bouncing back in 2011, to register a 16.7 percent increase to aggregate to US$ 1,694 billion. A discernible trend in the world FDI outflows has been the emergence of developing economies as key contributors to these flows. The share of developing economies (including transition economies) in world FDI outflows rose two and a half times over the last decade—from 11 percent in 2001 to 27 percent in 2011. Within the developing countries, it was the Asian region which accounted for the bulk of the outward FDI stock—62.6 percent in 2011, marginally higher than 62.3 percent in 2001. Among the Asian economies, Hong Kong was the predominant source of outward FDI stock, although its share in Asia declined from 59.5 percent in 2001 to 40.7 percent in 2011. As against this, the shares of China and India recorded significant increases, from 5.8 percent to 14.2 percent, and from 0.4 percent to 4.3 percent, respectively.

Evolution of Outward Foreign Investment Policy in India

Change in policy environment across the economies has greatly influenced the outward investment pattern in the global economy. Nonetheless, recognizing the concerns of capital outflows, governments in different countries, particularly emerging and developing economies, have been relatively more circumspect on undertaking policy liberalization of outward investment. Therefore, it is important to highlight how the Indian policy in this regard has evolved over time.

In the Indian context, overseas investments in joint ventures (JV) and wholly owned subsidiaries (WOS) have been recognized as important channels for promoting global business by the Indian entrepreneurs. The broad approach has been to facilitate outward foreign direct investment through joint ventures and wholly owned subsidiaries and provision of financial support to promote exports including project exports from India. With a steady rise in capital inflows, particularly in the second half of 2000s, the overall foreign exchange reserve position provided comfort to progressive relaxation of the capital controls and simplification of the procedures for outbound investments from India. Three distinct overlapping phases as under can be discerned in the evolution of the Indian outward FDI policies.

Phase I (1992 to 1995): Period of Liberalization of Indian economy: Guidelines on outward FDI were in place before the process of liberalization and globalization of Indian economy in 1991-92. Policy changes since 1992 were undertaken keeping in view the changing needs of a growing economy. Understandably, the rules were quite restrictive and subject to conditions of no cash remittance and mandatory repatriation of dividend from the profits from the overseas projects. During 1992, the 'automatic route' used for foreign investments was initiated plus cash remittances were permitted for the first time. Nonetheless, the entire value was limited to US$ 2 million with a cash component not beyond US$ 0.5 million in a slab of 3 years.

Phase II (1995 to 2000): Creation of a Fast Track Route: In 1995, a comprehensive policy framework was laid down and the work relating to approvals for overseas investment was transferred from Ministry of Commerce to the Reserve Bank of India to provide a single window clearance mechanism. The policy framework articulated a cohesive approach that was flexible enough to respond to likely future trends. It reflected the need for transparency, recognition of global developments, capturing of Indian realities and learning of lessons from the past. The basic objectives of the policy, *inter alia*, was to ensure that such outflows, were determined by commercial interests but were also consistent with the macroeconomic and balance of payment compulsions of the country, particularly in terms of the magnitude of the capital flows.

In terms of the overseas investment policy, a fast track route was adopted where the limits were raised from US$ 2 million to US$ 4 million and linked to average export earnings of the preceding three years. Cash remittance continued to be restricted to US$ 0.5 million. Beyond US$ 4 million, approvals were considered under the 'Normal Route' approved by a Special Committee comprising of the senior representatives of the Reserve Bank of India (Chairman) and the Ministries of Finance, External Affairs and Commerce (members). Investment proposals in excess of US$ 15 million were considered by the Ministry of Finance with the recommendations of the Special Committee and were generally approved if the required resources were raised through the global depository receipt (GDR) route.

Phase III (2000 till date): Liberalized framework under FEMA: In 2002, the per annum upper limit for automatic approval was raised to US$ 100 million. Such upper limit was, however, discontinued when the automatic route for outward FDI was further liberalized in March 2003 to enable Indian parties to invest to the extent of 100 percent of their net worth. Since then, the limit of outward FDI has been gradually increased to 400 percent. The ceiling of 400 percent of net worth, however, is not applicable for:

- Investments made out of balances held in the exchange earners' foreign currency (EEFC) account of the Indian party or out of funds raised abroad through ADRs/GDRs.
- Indian companies betrothed in the power and natural resources region, for example, oil, gas, coal along with mineral ores, although they would call for prior sanction of the Reserve Bank of India.

At present, any Indian party can make overseas direct investment in any *bonafide* activity except certain real estate activities [i.e. buying and selling of real estate or trading in transferable development rights (TDRs)] and banking business (which are considered by an inter-Ministerial group) that are specifically prohibited. For undertaking activities in the financial services sector, certain conditions as specified by the Reserve Bank, however, need to be adhered to. Access to international financial markets was also progressively liberalized for the Indian corporate sector and they were allowed to use special purpose vehicles (SPVs) in international capital markets to finance their cross-border acquisitions. The impact of policy liberalization is now reflected in cross-border acquisitions by Indian corporate, growing at an accelerated pace.

Ever since 2000, India has observed the maximum boost in outward FDI, together with provisions of FDI accumulation as a percentage of GDP as well as FDI flow as a proportion of gross fixed capital formation.

India's Outward FDI: Trend Analysis

Even though policy changes undertaken in respect of overseas investment have facilitated the growing cross-border acquisitions by the Indian corporate sector, other structural reforms undertaken since 1992, such as, industrial deregulation, trade liberalization and relaxation of regulations governing inward FDI, led to major restructuring in the Indian industry. In fact, many of the leading companies owe their competitiveness to the reforms process. Greater exposure to internal as well external competition proved to be instrumental in building confidence among the Indian companies to compete with foreign competitors in world market. Apart from liberalized policy environment for overseas investment, India has gained ground as an important investor on the back of: (a) rapid economic growth, (b) easy access to financial resources and (c) strong motivation to acquire resources and strategic assets abroad.

There has been an enormous rise in O-FDI from India within the last 15 years. In line with the data published by the Ministry of Finance, Government of India, O-FDI as of India improved from US$ 0.1 billion in 1990-91 to US$ 16.8 billion in 2010-11 (Table 10.1).

Table 10.1: Overall Outward FDI from India along with India's Portion in Developing Economies' Entire Outflow

Year	Outward FDI from India (US$ bn)	Total FDI in Developing Economies (US$ bn)	Portion of India in Developing Economies (in percent)
1990-91	0.1	11.9	1.0
1995-96	0.5	55.2	0.9
2000-01	1.7	134.2	1.3
2001-02	2.5	82.5	3.1
2002-03	2.4	49.7	4.8
2004-05	2.2	121.4	1.8
2005-06	2.5	122.1	2.0
2006-07	9.7	226.7	4.3
2007-08	14.6	294.2	4.9
2008-09	19.4	308.9	6.3
2009-10	14.8	270.7	5.5
2010-11	16.8	327.6	5.1

Source: Calculated by author; *World Investment Report* (various issues), UNCTAD.

As apparent from Table 10.1, the amount of FDI outflow

from India is rising at a pace of 42.8 percent per annum which is statistically important at 5 percent level of significance. The outline also indicates the continuous boost in the Indian FDI share to the whole outflow of developing economies.

A trend analysis shows that the level of outward FDI from India has increased manifold since 1999-2000. The level of net outward FDI flows (on balance of payment basis), however, recorded a sharp uptrend at US$ 74.3 billion during the second half of 2000s (2005-06 to 2009-10) as compared to US$ 8.2 billion in the first half of 2000s (2000-01 to 2004-05). Even though the trend in India's outward FDI was moderately affected during the crisis year of 2009-10, a sharp rebound was seen in 2010-11 (Table 10.2).

Table 10.2: Year-wise Position of Actual Outflows in Respect of Outward FDI and Guarantees Issued (US$ million)

Period	Equity	Loan	Guarantee Invoked	Total	Guarantee Issued
2000-01	602.12	70.58	4.97	677.67	112.55
2001-02	878.83	120.82	0.42	1,000.07	155.86
2002-03	1,746.28	102.10	0.00	1,848.38	139.63
2003-04	1,250.01	316.57	0.00	1,566.58	440.53
2004-05	1,481.97	513.19	0.00	1,995.16	315.96
2005-06	6,657.82	1,195.33	3.34	7,856.49	546.78
2006-07	12,062.92	1,246.98	0.00	13,309.90	2,260.96
2007-08	15,431.51	3,074.97	0.00	18,506.48	6,553.47
2008-09	12,477.14	6,101.56	0.00	18,578.70	3,322.45
2009-10	9,392.98	4,296.91	24.18	13,714.07	7,603.04
2010-11	9,234.58	7,556.30	52.49	16,843.37	27,059.02
2011-12*	4,031.45	4,830.01	0.00	8,861.46	14,993.80
Total	75,247.61	29,425.32	85.40	104758.30	63,504.05
* April 2011 to February 22, 2012					

Source: Reserve Bank of India (RBI) Report, 2013.

In recent years, outward FDI continued to be mainly financed through equity and loans. Although guarantees issued have been rising, their invocation has been negligible during 2009-10 and 2010-11. It has been observed that the number of outward FDI proposals under the automatic route during 2000s has also been on the rise (Table 10.3), indicating the growing appetite of the Indian corporates to establish their footprints abroad and the liberal regulatory regime.

Table 10.3: Number of Proposals under Approval and Automatic Route

Period	Approval Route	Automatic Route	Total
2008-09	6	974	980
2009-10	4	690	694
2010-11	19	1187	1206
2011-12*	10	1123	1133
* April 2011 to February 22, 2012			

Source: RBI Report, 2013.

FDI Inflows to Africa

MNCs of India might invest in African economies since the firm specific advantages also produce superior revenues and/or lesser costs that can compensate the costs of operating at a remote foreign site. As regards the location or nation specific advantages of O-FDI, it is particular to a foreign country so as to distinguish between economic advantages (such as factors of production, market size, transportation and other infrastructure overheads), political advantages (for instance political stability, FDI policies) and social-cultural advantages (for example cultural similarity, language, along with outlook towards foreigners). With regard to internalization advantages, the MNCs have diverse choices on entry modes displaying from arm's length transactions within the market to setting up a wholly owned subsidiary.

In conditions where markets perform poorly with soaring transaction costs, internalization is the favoured choice to take advantage of ownership-specific as well as location-specific advantages equally. Additionally, internalization of production assures product quality and guards property rights. This is verified by cross-border acquisitions and the big number of greenfield investments by Indian corporations in diverse African countries.

Inflow of FDI to Africa grew for the second year successively by 5 percent to US$ 50 billion, causing it one of not many regions that recorded an annual growth in 2012. FDI outflows from Africa nearly tripled in 2012, to US$ 14 billion. Transnational corporations from the South are progressively more vigorous in Africa, building on a drift in recent years as regards the top share of FDI flows to the region from upcoming emerging markets. Regarding FDI stock, Malaysia, South Africa, China and India (in that order) are the major developing nation investors in Africa. Transnational corporations (TNCs) from developing nations are progressively more dynamic in Africa, building on a drift in current years accounting for a major share of FDI flows approaching from rising markets. Malaysia, South Africa, China and India are the chief developing-country sources of FDI in Africa.

Africa is one of the few regions to enjoy year on year growth in FDI inflows since 2010. Investment in exploration and exploitation of natural resources, and high flows from China, both contributed to the current level of inward flows. More generally, the continent's good economic performance—GDP grew at an estimated 5 percent in 2012—underpinned the rise in investments, including manufacturing and services. Investor confidence appears to have gone back to North Africa, since FDI flows increased by 35 percent to US$ 11.5 billion in 2012. A great part of the development was due to an increase in investment in Egypt. While the country experienced a net divestment of US$ 0.5 billion in 2011, it attracted net investment inflows of US$ 2.8 billion in 2012. Across the sub-region, FDI flows also increased to Morocco and Tunisia, but decreased in Algeria and Sudan. In contrast, there was a 5 percent decrease in FDI flows to West Africa, to US$ 16.8 billion, due to an expansive degree owing to decreasing flows to Nigeria. Weighed down by political insecurity and the weak global economy, the country saw FDI inflows falling from US$ 8.9 billion in 2011 to US$ 7.0 billion in 2012.

India's relations with African nations are time-tested and historical. While the Indian Ocean separates the Horn of Africa and the Indian subcontinent, it is not out of place to visualize the same waters lapping and linking the two shores. Indeed, geographic proximity has played an important role in developing the relationship since ancient times. Between 2003 and 2012, India accounted for 6.4 percent of FDI flows into Africa, especially in sectors such as telecom, energy and mining.

The volume of India's FDI in Africa, amounting to US$ 14 billion, particularly in landlocked developing countries (LLDCs) in Africa, are on the rise. In terms of geographical distribution, the largest consumer markets in Africa also count among the continent's main FDI destinations for consumer oriented FDI in manufacturing and services. However, foreign investors are not limiting themselves to consumers in these markets only. For instance, telecommunications companies such as South Africa-based MTN and India-based Bharti Airtel are both present in at least 15 African countries.

Opportunities for Indian Companies in Africa

India can plan a four-fold increase in its revenue from the African region by 2025 to USD 160 billion by mounting its presence in regions where India has an exclusive value proposal and African nations have soaring needs, for instance, IT services, infrastructure, agriculture, pharmaceuticals plus consumer goods. India can aspire to capture almost 7 percent of the IT services market, 5 percent of the FMCG space, 10 percent of the power sector, and 2 to 5 percent of the agri-allied services.

Africa has more cities (more than 50) whose population exceeds 1 million compared to India, and this number is expected to double by 2025. In fact, Africa and China share similar levels of urbanization. By 2025, Africa is expected to be 47 percent urbanized as compared to 40 percent in 2013. Consumer spending is expected to increase to US$ 2.2 trillion by 2025 driven by an 80 percent increase in middle class households to around 190 million.

Africa has a significant and under-explored share of global mineral reserves, e.g., platinum group metals such as diamonds, bauxite, phosphate, etc., which will feed future global demand and hence would be a key growth driver. Africa would also continue to benefit from oil and gas including development of major new finds on the east and west coasts.

Almost 60 percent of the world's uncultivated arable cropland is in Africa, attracting significant FDI. Simultaneously, there exists a huge potential of at least 30 to 50 percent upside across Africa by improving yields. India's development cooperation with Africa has significantly expanded since 2005, when India became a full member of the Africa Capacity Building Foundation, and was granted observer status at Common Market for Eastern and Southern Africa (COMESA), South African Development Community (SADC) and Economic Community of Western African States (ECOWAS). IT benefits, shopper merchandise, pharmaceuticals, auto, horticulture and infrastructure are areas where African countries' chance can be supplemented by the Indian business' quality.

Opportunities and Potential in Lead Sectors

An entrepreneurial mindset, engineering talent and the proven track record in the Indian market can help Indian companies participate in building Africa's infrastructure sector. India's expertise in manufacturing and robust distribution networks in agrochemicals, fertilizers, farm equipment, etc. can allow Indian companies to support the aspirations of African agriculture.

Africa's consumer goods market would more than double to around US$ 1.2 trillion by 2025; 30 cities spread across Africa will witness consumption growth of more than US$ 2 billion in the next 5 years. Indian companies such as Dabur, Godrej, Marico and Emami currently have limited presence in Africa's consumer goods landscape following their recent entry. Africa's IT spends is expected to triple itself to US$ 80 to 95 billion by 2025. India can offer African nations a comprehensive, integrated package to help strengthen their IT sector. India's technical expertise in verticals such as banking platforms, mobile applications, etc., the ability to develop local talent, as well as the capabilities to set up low cost IT parks can help Indian companies make inroads in various countries and boost the sector. The ability to train people and formulate innovative delivery models can allow India to boost Africa's IT services sector and create jobs at large scale.

Africa's aspired "green revolution" could raise its agricultural output from US$ 280 billion in 2010, to around US$ 880 billion by 2030 through the cultivation of new land, yield improvement and shift to high-value crops. Indian companies can help African nations make the "New Rice for Africa Initiative" a success, by sharing learning from the green revolution. They can further enable low cost mechanization of the farms to improve utilization of inputs and enhance yield per acre, e.g., low-cost tractors, drillers, irrigation solutions, etc., and help develop local talent and companies to make the model self-sustainable.

India and Africa have enjoyed a healthy and mutually beneficial relationship since times immemorial. In the context of a changing world, it is time to reinvent and strengthen that relationship. The Indian industry could take the lead to jointly continue to enhance the well-being of two ancient civilizations.

FDI Inflows in West Asia

FDI to the United Arab Emirates—West Asia's third largest recipient country—increased by 25 percent to US$ 10 billion, continuing the recovery initiated in 2010 but remaining below the US$ 14 billion reached in 2007. High public spending by Abu Dhabi and strong performance in Dubai's non-hydrocarbon division has facilitated rebuilding of foreign desire for direct investment in the region. United Arab Emirates and Saudi Arabia intended for 83 percent of FDI inflows to the GCC economies. FDI to Kuwait more than doubled, reaching US$ 2 billion, boosted by Qatar Telecom's acquisition of additional shares in Kuwait's second mobile operator Wataniya, which raised its stake to 92 percent. FDI inflows also increased in Bahrain, Oman and Qatar.

FDI inflows in West Asia have failed once again to recover. FDI to West Asia in 2012 registered its fourth consecutive year of decline, although at a slower rate, decreasing by 4 percent to US$ 47 billion, half of the 2008 level. Growing political uncertainty at the regional level and subdued economic prospects at the global level are holding back foreign investors' propensity and capacity to invest in the region. Significant diminution in FDI inflows was registered in the two main recipient countries—Turkey (-23 percent to US$ 12.4 billion) and Saudi Arabia (-25 percent to US$ 12.2 billion)—that accounted for 52 percent of the region's overall inflows. For the first time since 2006, Saudi Arabia ceded its position as the region's largest recipient country to Turkey.

Conclusion

When considering the opportunities and challenges in WANA region, it is important to remember: WANA region falls into two continents. There are 19 countries at different stages of development with different agendas. However, the majority of these belong to regional groupings, which implies different cross-border arrangements between states, depending on membership of these groups. WANA region offers great opportunity for Indian companies. Recently, there is a lot of economic activity happening between India and WANA region and the scope is still there for much larger cooperation. The

Indian government and the corporate sector should work together and focus on this important region of the world for mutual growth and development.

References

Buckley, P.J. and Casson, M.C. (1976), "The Future of the Multinational Enterprise", London, Holmes and Meier.

Cantwell, J. and Mudambi, R. (2001), "MNE Competence Creating Subsidiary Mandates: An Empirical Investigation", International Investment and Management, Discussion Paper No. 285, Reading University, Reading.

Dunning, J.H. (1977), "Trade, Location of Economic Activity and the MNE: A Search for an Eclectic Approach", in B. Ohlin, P.O. Hesselborn and P.M. Wijkmon (eds.) The International Location of Economic Activity, London: Macmillan, pp. 395-418.

Dunning, J.H. (1981), "Explaining Outward Direct Investment of Developing countries: In support of the Eclectic Theory of International Production", in Kumar and McLeod (eds.), Multinationals from Developing Countries, Lexington, Massachusetts: Lexington Books.

Dunning, J.H. (1988), "The Eclectic Paradigm of International Production: A Restatement and Some Possible Extensions", *Journal of International Business Studies*, Vol. 19, No .1, pp. 1-31.

Dunning, J.H. and Narula, R. (1996), "The Investment Development Path Revisited: Some Emerging Issues", in Dunning, J. and Narula, R. (eds.), Foreign Direct Investment and Government: Catalysts for Economic Restructuring, Routledge, London.

Gammeltoft, P. (2006), "Internationalisation of R&D: Trends, Drivers and Managerial Challenges", *International Journal of Technology and Globalisation*, Vol. 2, No. 1/2, pp. 177-199.

Hennart, J.F. (1991), "The Transaction Cost Theory of the Multinational Enterprise", in Pitelis and Sudgen (eds.), The Nature of the Transnational Firm, London: Routledge.

Herzer, D. (2011), "The Long-run Relationship between Outward Foreign Direct Investment and Total Factor Productivity", Evidence for Developing Countries, *Journal of Development Studies*, Vol. 47, No. 5, pp. 767-785.

Hymer, S.H. (1960), "The International Operations of National Firms: A Study of Direct Investment", Ph.D. Thesis,

Massachusetts Institute of Technology, Cambridge, MA., Published in 1976 by MIT Press: Cambridge, MA.

Lall (1983), "The New Multinationals: The Spread of Third World Enterprises", New York: John Wiley & Sons and Wells, L.T. (1983), "Third World Multinationals: The Rise of Foreign Investment from Developing Countries", Cambridge, MA: The MIT Press.

Lecraw (1981), "Internationalization of Firms from LDCs: Evidence from the ASEAN Region", in Kumar and McLeod (eds.) Multinationals from Developing Countries, Lexington, MA: Lexington Books.

Mathews, J.A. (2006), "Response to Professors Dunning and Narula", *Asia Pacific Journal of Management*, Vol. 23, No. 2, pp. 153-155.

"Outward Indian FDI: Recent Trends and Emerging Issues", Address delivered by Shri. Harun R Khan, Deputy Governor, Reserve Bank of India at the Bombay Chamber of Commerce & Industry, Mumbai on March 2, 2012, Mckinsey Asia Centre Report, March 2014.

Rasiah, R. (2000), "Globalization and International Private Capital Movements", *Third World Quarterly*, Vol. 21, No. 6, pp. 917-929.

Rugman, Alan M. (1986), "New Theories of the Multinational Enterprise: An Assessment of International Theory", *Journal of Economic Research*, Vol. 38, pp. 101-118.

Subramanian, Ravi, Sachdeva, Charu and Morris, Sebastian (2010), "FDI Outflows from India: An Examination of the Underlying Economics, Policies and their Impacts", *Working Paper, Indian Institute of Management*, Ahmedabad, No. 2010-03-01, March 2010.

UNCTAD (2006), "World Investment Report 2006: FDI from Developing and Transition Economies: Implications for Development", United Nations, New York.

UNCTAD (2011), "World Investment Report: Non-Equity Modes of International Production and Development", New York: United Nations.

Yang Yongzheng and Gupta, Santee (2005), "Regional Trade Arrangements in Africa: Past Performance and the Way Forward", *African Development Review*, Vol. 9, No. 3.

11

South Sudan and the
East African Community (EAC) [1]

Christopher Zambakari

Introduction

South Sudan celebrated its second anniversary of Independence on July 9, 2013. The emergence of a new state in Africa with the secession of South Sudan from Sudan marked the most important development in the post-colonial period since South Africa transitioned to a democracy in 1994. The Sudanese civil war, [2] one of Africa's longest and most intractable conflicts has produced the largest number of casualties and the forceful displacement of millions of civilians than any other African civil war over the last century. South Sudan is attempting to build a state from the bottom up. This study seeks to make a contribution to the ongoing debate on nation and state building, economic development and the East African Community's attempt to build a monetary union followed by a political federation.

Violence and State Formation in South Sudan

The history of state formation around the world is replete with violence. The process of constructing a democratic polity, building a nation out of diverse nationalities, is a contested field. The challenge for the state in South Sudan is how to "bring together diverse people with a history of hostility into a framework of one state". At its root is a crisis of citizenship and the modern African state's attempts to build a unified nation. When the Comprehensive Peace Agreement (CPA) was signed in 2005, it was done with the hope that the civil war in Sudan, namely the war between the National Congress Party (NCP) in the North and the Sudan People's Liberation Movement/Army (SPLM/A) in the south would come to an end.

Whereas the violence between the NCP and SPLA/M was brought to an end, the issues driving violence in the north and south were left unresolved. The result is that the post-CPA period has seen a proliferation of arms and violence throughout South Sudan to the North. Sudan continues to experience violence in the east (Kassala, Red Sea, and Gedarif), west (Darfur), and in the border states (Abyei, Blue Nile, and Southern Kordofan). The spreading of political violence in particular, raises the question of whether the new Republic of South Sudan will be able to build a nation and a viable state, in a region plagued by conflicts and instability.

The political crisis that engulfed South Sudan in mid-December 2013, sending the country into another civil war, has exacerbated a delicate balance in the country, delayed the process of reconciliation, and cast a shadow over South Sudan's viability as a state. Since December 15, thousands of civilians have been killed; more than 908,000 people have been displaced by violence, of which 705,800 within South Sudan and 202,500 have sought refuge in neighbouring countries. An exchange between soldiers in the military barracks in Juba, the capital city of South Sudan, disintegrated into crisis that has since engulfed most States in South Sudan. The government claimed that there was an "attempted coup" instigated by leading figures within the SPLA/M and proceeded to detain without due process of law, 11 senior SPLA/M members. [3]

South Sudan's Development Challenges

The challenge of building a nation out of diverse nationalities poses significant hurdles for the nascent state. Violence and lack of economic development, two sides of the same coin, presents the new country with its ultimate test of building a modern democratic state in East Africa. The biggest political challenge facing South Sudan in the post-referendum period is the political violence and the task of nation-building. The second big question for the South Sudan government is how to build a developmental state that is equipped to spearhead economic development. Amidst the many outstanding challenges facing the new country, is a campaign to include South Sudan into the East African Community (EAC). [4] South Sudan seeks to build a state that accommodates diversity, it faces the same question faced by many African countries, namely how to build a nation that embraces diversity within the country and move beyond the urban-rural divide and the ethnic divisions that threaten to undermine the process of nation-building.

Any meaningful discussion about South Sudan must begin by addressing what it is instead of what it is not. South Sudan is a landlocked country lacking a major port that could connect it to the outside world. Infrastructure is very limited and underdeveloped. By the beginning of 2013, the country had only 110 kilometres of tarmac roads in the capital. Development experts, familiar with the predicament of South Sudan, its young institutions, underdeveloped infrastructure, and underdeveloped sectors, recognize the need to focus on human capital development and investment in basic social services. The religious preoccupation with oil is inconsistent with the reality of South Sudan and what it must do to achieve self-sufficiency. Resource allocation toward social services, education, healthcare, and infrastructure has been limited despite the fact that that responsibly lies with the government. Instead the government has delegated its fundamental responsibility to international non-governmental organizations (INGOs).

The consequences of political instability, conflicts, lack of basic infrastructure and rule of law, skilled labour, and utter failure of leadership to stir the country in the right direction, makes South Sudan the most vulnerable entity in east Africa compared to its more established neighbours. In addition to these challenges, comes the problem of land tenure. Here, South Sudan is like most countries in East Africa, where countries have failed to reform a colonially-imposed land tenure system and citizenship laws. The result has been a heavily contested citizenship and land rights, leading to mass violence. The East African countries face the challenge of reconciling between claims based on ethnicity and those based on residence. The former claim finds its genesis in the colonial period, and the latter is rooted in the post-colonial nation-state, which provides for equal rights to all citizens.

East African Community (EAC)

The predecessor of the current EAC was established in 1967 which collapsed in 1977 and was revived in 2000. The causes of the collapse have not been resolved, yet a new community has been launched. It is illuminating to study the reasons for the failure if there is any chance that the current community will be given a fair chance to succeed. There are many unanswered questions about the EAC that deserves sustained debate about its prospects and challenges. Will the integration of markets in East Africa proceed from a political federation? What is to be the basis of the new citizenship—ethnic or territorial? Will the monetary union lead to a political union or should the political infrastructure be laid before the monetary union?

The need for a healthy public discourse on important matters, national agreements and policies in South Sudan has been covered elsewhere. Without such open discussion, decisions will be uniformed by a broad base, be made undemocratic, and enjoy no public support from the population. The lack of a genuine democratic debate about important decisions before they are taken has plagued the East African countries for decades. South Sudan should learn the lessons before it begins the journey on a well-travelled path. Mamdani noted the failure of the predecessor or today's EAC in his keynote address to the East African Legislative

Assembly Symposium. To limit the discussion, as it is at the moment, to State Ministers and Heads of State is to miss the internal failures that led to the collapse of the first community. According to the keynote address:

"If we limit the discussion on the old community to external rivalries that imploded the old Community from within, then we will inevitably conclude that there is little we can do about forces we do not control. But if we can expand the discussion to look at our own failure to develop a public discourse on East African issues, then we can move a step forward. The discussion needs to involve broad sectors of East African society. By not leaving the initiative to the political class, we can contribute to exploring different options and rallying new forces.

The issue at stake for the state of South Sudan is sovereignty. It is the issue at stake for all members. Losing sovereignty to the federation could mean a loss of control of currency, fiscal and monetary policies. When national governments lose sovereignty over their 'national currency, the policy-making power over monetary aspects', the outcome can be serious for citizens who have to live with the consequences of decisions made by an undemocratic bureaucracy that does not consult with those governed". [5] A look at East Africa shows that genuine democracy has been elusive. In the absence of a democratic decision-making process or public discourse over national policies, decision tends to be delegated to a body that is politically unaccountable. Without resolving the underlining issues that led to the failure of the old community, the EAC is setting up to create what the European Union created in Europe—market fundamentalism.

Some of the problems that led to the collapse of the first union have already started to surface. The monetary union calls for the removal of trade barriers, movement of goods, labour, services and capital. While this sounds promising on paper, the reality is different. According to the Economist Intelligence Unit, the "implementation of this legislation has been lacklustre at its best".

The debate about the EAC in member states has been absent and acceptance varies from country to country, with strong opposition in Kenya and Tanzania, greater acceptance in Rwanda and Burundi, to lack of debate about the EAC in South Sudan (which has submitted its application for membership in the EAC). The competition between member states and lack of proper coordination of economic activities that led to the demise of the old community has surfaced again. Kenya is the biggest economy in East Africa. Its strength has been received with mixed reactions. In some cases, fear of Kenya has led to tariff being levied on Kenyan goods. Without the easing of anxiety among member states, accommodation of weaker economies, and engaging the general public about the community, the EAC will face an uphill battle on its way to forming a political federation, if that ever happens at all.

Despite the enthusiasm for a federation of East African countries, the loss of sovereignty that will be required to sustain a fiscal union is not something that most countries are willing to do in the near future. The Economist Intelligence Unit noted that "without the necessary supporting economic framework in place, it would surely not be long before the EAC breaks up, once more". The framework is political in nature. Without proper infrastructure and reassurance for weaker economies, the challenges ahead with the federation are daunting. In the absence of the necessary political and economic framework required to enable a monetary union and a political union, the EAC will stand on shallow ground, making its ambitious project untenable.

The infrastructure of the EAC does not have a clear program for the weaker economies. South Sudan, which is set to be admitted once the Council of Ministers reach a verdict, will join the EAC, not as the biggest and strongest economies, but one of the weakest. Unlike other members of the community, South Sudan's key institutions are either still in the formative stage or have to be completely built from a scratch. What provisions, programs, initiatives currently exist to manage the weaknesses without turning the market in South Sudan into the dumping ground of goods and services from neighbouring economies is a big question? What EAC provision is there to assist South Sudan to develop the productive powers of its infant industries? Have South Sudanese been consulted about membership? What is the popular sentiment in South Sudan about membership in the EAC? Has there been a sustained debate about the inclusion of South Sudan into the EAC? Without a democratic process, the outcome will inevitably be undemocratic and society will be sacrificed in order to achieve narrow political and economic aims for a minority interest.

East African countries are not equal by any measure, politically, economically or socially. On the path of economic development, each country is at a different stage. Some countries are more established and have been running the race with other nation-states longer than others. While they are all developing countries, some are less developed than others. Hence, one finds some better off than the rest. The fault line in East Africa, according to Mamdani, is no different from the one that has emerged in Europe; one that divides countries into rich and poor, the Germany and Greece of the world. The question that arises immediately is who is to protect the weaker countries from being dominated by the stronger and more established market players? Historically, the safety mechanism against market forces has been political democracy. In the absence of a political democracy, nothing stands between the teeth of market forces and the population.

If the law of the market is might is right, then the basis of citizenship is political equality. If the market stands for rights, then citizenship stands for justice. In a democracy, the poor and the weak look to political power to give them minimum protection against those who rule the marketplace.

One of the biggest challenges before South Sudan and the other EAC member states is how they can form a monetary union without sacrificing political union that protects social democracy in the process. In the absence of a political union, monetary unions have a tendency to turn into market fundamentalism. The EAC must thus balance "rights with that of social justice and market fundamentalism with that of social equity?" At the root of the debate is a distinction between competing forms of democracy—economic, political and social. The second challenge that remains unresolved within the infrastructure of the EAC is that of land tenure.

Conclusion and Way Forward

One of the biggest challenges that the government of the Republic of South Sudan is facing is how to build a developmental state that is equipped to spearhead economic development. The task is complicated by the fact that South Sudan is emerging from decades of war. The campaign to include South Sudan into the East African Community is part of this larger project to help and foster economic development in the country. When violence erupts in a country, it signals that the centre can no longer hold. This calls for a reordering of society and a new dispensation. South Sudan's descent into a civil war in mid-December is a signal that unless a new political dispensation that is inclusive of the diverse nationalities in the country is put forth, the foundation of the state will remain unstable. For the leaders in South Sudan, this will require addressing the root causes of the conflict both historical and contemporary by democratizing the political party, opening up the political space, completing the ongoing disarmament, demobilization, and reintegration of rebel groups, reforming the security sector, and initiate a deep national reconciliation process throughout the country.

On its development priorities, South Sudan should focus on developing its domestic institutions first, before turning to oil exploration and extraction. The sequencing is important. If oil exploration goes ahead in the absence of strong institutions, it is likely to be captured by strong groups, and multinational corporations, and other sustainable industries will be neglected as is the case in most resource-rich countries in Africa. The tentative recommendations for South Sudan have also been summarized by Laura N. Beny and Matthew Snyder in their study prepared for the Ministry of Commerce, Industry and Investment. Without a manufacturing base, industries of its own, a skilled labour force, a good starting point is what South Sudan actually has—abundant natural resources, arable land, forest, and a willing labour force. This fact is supported by Beny and Snyder who also recommend that South Sudan diversify its economy by "revitalizing its agricultural industry, diversifying its exports and developing its non-oil industries, and making trade within the region easier and more efficient".

The immediate task for leaders of the EAC is how to balance rights with that of social justice and market fundamentalism with social equity? In a region where there are multiple claims to land, the EAC has to address the land tenure system in East Africa by reconciling between various claims to land and citizenship, one ethnic and the second based on residence. Contested citizenship and competing rights to land are two unresolved problems that have led to mass violence throughout East Africa. South Sudan and the EAC member states will have to reconcile between private, public, state ownership of land (freehold/leasehold land tenure) and communal land ownership within the framework of an inclusive citizenship.

For South Sudan the fulfilment of its national aspirations, contained in 'The South Sudan Vision 2040' [6] cannot be achieved without a significant investment in human resources, institutions of governance and physical infrastructure. Peasants find a defence against market forces by calling on customary law. Migrants, immigrants, and internally displaced groups call on the right of citizenship granted by the state. Unless South Sudan begins by reconciling between the two demands for citizenship, ethnic and residence-based, it will not resolve the crisis of citizenship.

At the regional level, unless the EAC reforms the infrastructure laid in the colonial period, inherited by all countries in East Africa except Tanzania (which successfully reformed the colonial regime), the infrastructure of the EAC will remain weak and fragmented, containing within itself the seeds of its future unravelling. These regional challenges raise questions of how to form a monetary union without sacrificing political union that protects social democracy in the process. The immediate task for leaders of the EAC is how to balance rights with that of social justice, market fundamentalism with social equity? In a region where there are multiple claims to land, the EAC has to address the land tenure system in East Africa by reconciling between various claims to land and citizenship, one ethnic and the second based on residence.

Acknowledgements

The author would like to thank Jackline Aridi, MDG Centre, East and Southern Africa, Columbia Global Centre, Nairobi and Journalist Nel Hodge, United Kingdom, for their insightful comments and constructive feedback on the earlier draft of this paper.

Endnotes

1. A shorter version of this article was published by the Harvard Africa Policy Journal. Parts of that article have been incorporated into this manuscript.
2. I am indebted to Dr. Richard Lobban, the Sudan Studies Association Executive Director based in the Department of Anthropology, at Rhode Island College, for pointing out to me that when it comes to conflicts on the African continent, the period one is interested in as well as one's definition of "state-to-state wars; wars of resistance; continuous wars; counter-insurgency wars, historical wars, ancient wars and so forth" matters.
3. This list of detainees included Deng Alor (former minister of cabinet affairs), Pagan Amum (former secretary general of SPLM), Cirino Iteng (former minister of culture), Madut Biar Yel (former minister for telecommunication and postal services), Oyai Deng Ajak (former minister for national security in the office of the president), Majak D' Agoot (former deputy minister

of defence), Chol Tong Magay (former governor of Lakes state), Ezekiel Gatkuoth Lul, former GoSS ambassador to the United States), John Luk Jok, former justice minister), Kosti Manibe (former minister of finance), Gier Chuang Aluong (former minister of roads and bridges).

4. The East African Community consists of Uganda, Tanzania, Rwanda, Kenya, and Burundi.

5. Something Greece and the weaker economies in European are painfully finding out. The social democratic rights of countries with weaker economies have been subordinated and their sovereignties. have come under assault by the more powerful European States seeking to impose austerity measures from above without putting into place democratic mechanisms for accountability.

6. Government of The Republic of South Sudan 2011. "South Sudan Development Plan 2011-2013: Realising Freedom, Equality, Justice, Peace and Prosperity for All". Juba, South Sudan, Ministry of Finance and Economic Planning, South Sudan, available at:
http://www.jdt-juba.org/wp-content/uploads/2012/02/South-Sudan-Development-Plan-2011-13.pdf.

Index

Index